THE PEOPLE
OF SOUTH A

THE PEOPLES AND POLICIES
OF SOUTH AFRICA

LEO MARQUARD

Fourth Edition

OXFORD UNIVERSITY PRESS
LONDON   OXFORD   NEW YORK
1969

OXFORD UNIVERSITY PRESS

LONDON OXFORD NEW YORK

GLASGOW TORONTO MELBOURNE WELLINGTON

CAPE TOWN SALISBURY IBAᴵ AN NAIROBI LUSAKA ADDIS ABABA

BOMBAY CALCUTTA MADRAS KARACHI LAHORE DACCA

KUALA LUMPUR SINGAPORE HONG KONG TOKYO

First published by Oxford University Press, London, 1952

Second edition, 1960

Revised (third) edition first published as an Oxford University Press paperback, 1962

Fourth edition, 1969

Printed in Great Britain
By Hazell Watson & Viney Ltd, Aylesbury, Bucks

TO THE MEMORY OF FOUR GALLANT
SOUTH AFRICANS WHO FOUGHT AND
DIED FOR THEIR COUNTRY

JOHN, CHRIS, IAN, AND GERHARD

PREFACE

THE purpose of this book, when it was first published in 1952, was to provide a current account of South Africa and such history as might be necessary to illuminate the present. This remains the purpose, but 'the present' is now almost two decades later than it was in 1952. Events that appeared important then have been overshadowed, and what once seemed of minor importance has assumed greater significance. If a revised edition is to retain the original purpose such new perspectives must be shown even if this entails omitting some of the less important events of the last twenty years. I have some sympathy with a reviewer of the second edition who hoped that, next time, I would leave the original untouched and simply add the changes. It has proved impossible to do this without making the book intolerably long and complicated. Any reader who is anxious to compare 1968 with 1962, 1958, and 1952 will, I am afraid, be compelled to consult the previous editions.

Two changes from previous editions must be noted. South Africa adopted a decimal coinage in 1961 and it seems sensible to give all money figures, both before and after 1961, in rands and cents (R. and C.). At the time of conversion R2 was equal to £1, but devaluation of the pound in 1967 altered the ratio.

The second change concerns South-West Africa and the former High Commission Territories of Basutoland, Swaziland, and Bechuanaland. These were described in Chapter 10 of previous editions as the Union's 'Colonies', a term intended to indicate the nature of their relationship with South Africa. Since the three territories became independent the term 'colony' is clearly unsuitable and South Africa's relations with them have become a matter of foreign policy. I have therefore changed the heading of this chapter to 'The Republic's Neighbours', a term that includes South-West Africa.

The writer of contemporary history must distinguish between the basic facts on which the society he is describing rests, and the more fluid conditions that will, in the long run, alter that society. Generally speaking, I have used the past tense to describe the basic facts, and have reserved the present tense for those conditions that seem likely to continue as long as the ruling white class in South Africa is able to maintain its monopoly of power. This may sometimes give the appearance of an arbitrary alternation between the tenses.

My thanks are due to those readers who took the trouble to write encouraging letters about the first three editions, and to point out errors and criticize statements. The errors have, I hope, been removed, and the criticisms have all been carefully weighed.

Finally, I am deeply indebted to my wife for her constant encouragement, careful criticism, and abiding patience.

Claremont
Cape June 1968   L. M.

NOTE

I T is necessary to remark on the use of terms to denote the various population groups of South Africa. It is, of course, unscientific to speak about the European or the non-European 'race', though the terms are convenient and are generally understood in South Africa. I have come to prefer the terms white and non-white to distinguish broadly between, on the one hand, South Africans who are classified as 'white' and, on the other, Coloured, Asian, and 'black' South Africans.

Coloured, Asian, and white are self-explanatory, but it is not helpful to describe as 'black' a South African who is brown-skinned and whose mother-tongue is one of the Bantu languages. He used to be called a 'kaffir', a word now only used in public by cruder politicians. Since 1910, legislation refers to 'native', and it gradually became customary to give the word an initial capital. Somewhere between 1910 and 1940 the word Bantu came to be used by those white people who felt that 'Native' was derogatory, and in 1958 it was given legislative sanction when the Department of Native Affairs was changed to the Department of Bantu Administration and Development.

In the meantime, the word 'African' had come to be used by a number of white people and by Africans themselves whose leaders had never really accepted any other designation; as early as 1912 the South African Native National Congress was established, and by the 1920's it was commonly known as the A.N.C. or African National Congress. Since the growth of African nationalism everywhere in Africa, the use of the term has become widespread. There are linguistic, ethnographic, and political arguments for and against the use of Bantu and of African, and much energy is expended on proving that one or other term is 'correct'. It is reasonably clear, however, that the leaders of roughly two-thirds of the population of South Africa wish to call themselves Africans, and no anount of legislation will change that. In this book, therefore, the word African is used except where reference is made to official and other documents or where its use would be confusing.

CONTENTS

1

HISTORICAL BACKGROUND

IN the mid-seventeenth century the elements of what were to become a complicated human society began to assemble in South Africa. At that time England was colonizing North America, Holland was a thriving commercial and trading state, and France and Holland and England were competing for the trade of the East. In southern Africa Hottentots and Bushmen roamed at will, hunting game and fighting each other; and African tribes from central and eastern Africa were migrating southwards and settling in parts of what were later to become the Transvaal, the Orange Free State, Natal, the Cape Province, South-West Africa, Lesotho (formerly Basutoland), Swaziland, and Botswana (formerly Bechuanaland.) Then, in 1652, European civilization came to southern Africa when a trading station was established at the Cape. Cape Town was the half-way house between East and West, and in due course North and South—Europe and Africa—met in the interior.

Within fifty years of the establishment of the trading station at the Cape we may discern the origins of most of the socio-political problems that have continued to harass South Africa down to the present time. Slaves had been imported from east and west Africa and from Madagascar, and it was partly from them that the Cape Coloured people, who by 1968 numbered over 1,860,000 of the total 18,800,000 population, were descended. Despite the Company's instructions that the Cape was to be regarded purely as a 'refreshment station' where ships could obtain fresh food, the European population increased naturally and by immigration, and by 1700 cattle farmers had begun to trek into the interior. Three generations later this trekking was to bring them into contact with the African tribes, followed by wars of conquest, so that by 1968 the population of South Africa included 12,750,000 Africans. It is frequently though erroneously stated that there were white men in South Africa before the Africans arrived. But although the men from Europe who began to settle in what is now the Western Province of the Cape in 1652 found only Hottentots and Bushmen, there is clear evidence from the accounts of early Portuguese travellers and from modern archaeological and anthropological investigations, that Africans were living in various parts of what is now the Republic of South Africa from at least 1500.

By 1700, then, European, African, and Coloured already made up the three main elements of South Africa's population. The smaller Asian population was to come much later; the European population was in due course to consist of two main groups, English and Afrikaans. But for good or for ill Western Europe had entered Africa from the south and the process had begun by which, in the fullness of time, the Republic of South Africa was to be established. Within the Republic there is a white population of 3,563,000, which is at least eight times as great as the white population of the rest of Africa south of the Sahara and constitutes the largest single concentration in Africa of people whose ancestors came from Europe. What happens in South Africa, as between white and non-white, is of importance to central and southern Africa and to those countries of Europe that have colonial commitments, past or present, in Africa. It is of importance, too, to Russia and the United States of America, and it is of profound and disturbing importance to the Commonwealth. Finally, it is becoming increasingly clear that what happens in the rest of the world is making an impact on all the inhabitants of South Africa.

To understand what has happened in South Africa we must trace, however briefly, some of the main strands in her history, for unless we do so it will be difficult to grasp present-day policies or arrive at a reasonable evaluation of the situation that exists there and elsewhere in Africa. Without some knowledge of the factors that have made this a multi-racial society it is tempting to apply formulas that might be valid in Europe but may well need to be modified when applied to Africa.

By the end of the fifteenth century Portuguese explorers had discovered the profitable trade route to the East, and for 100 years Portugal was virtually undisputed master of it. Lisbon became the new Venice; and of all the merchants who dealt with Lisbon the Dutch were the most important. At the end of the sixteenth century Philip II of Spain gained control over Portugal, and in an attempt to subdue his recalcitrant Protestant subjects in the Netherlands he closed the harbour of Lisbon to Dutch merchants, hoping thus to destroy the main source of their national wealth. While it is probable that the Dutch would in any case have developed a direct trade with the East, this threat to their religious and national freedom was an additional spur to action. By 1602 they had established the famous Dutch East India Company, the instrument by which they overthrew the might of Spain and freed their consciences along with their commerce.

Like the East India Company in England, the Dutch East India Company was a powerful, monopolistic, chartered company that enjoyed political influence and patronage so long as it increased the shareholders' dividends. Some of its main characteristics were the limitation and destruction of crops in order not to flood the market; ruthless exploitation of its territories of Java, Sumatra and Ceylon; fanatastically high dividends; corruption and bad book-keeping. All these ultimately brought about its fall, but not before it had—without really intending to do so—established a permanent Dutch settlement at the Cape.

In April 1652 the Company sent Jan van Riebeeck, one of its officials, to the Cape to set up a refreshment station at which its ships could get fresh vegetables and meat. His instructions were to confine himself to establishing this station and not to become involved in trouble with the inhabitants. (Throughout its century and a half of rule at the Cape the Company was consistently to regard it as nothing but a refreshment station and an item in the East India ledger.) Jan van Riebeeck found loosely organized nomadic Hottentot tribes, and for a time the Dutch bought cattle from them for copper wire and beads, the traditional currency between Europe and primitive peoples; but soon the questions of grazing rights and of land obtruded themselves. The Hottentots resented the occupation of their pasture lands near Table Mountain and constantly stole from and attacked the Dutch. This provoked reprisals, and two short wars compelled the Hottentots to recognize Dutch occupation. By degrees they accepted the situation and began to hire themselves to the Dutch colonists as farm-labourers and domestic servants. Meanwhile, the Company had imported slaves, chiefly from the East Coast and from Madagascar, and miscegenation between slaves and Hottentots and Europeans gave rise to the Cape Coloured population.

Jan van Riebeeck soon found that the cheapest method of supplying passing ships with fresh produce was to introduce free colonists as farmers and to buy their produce at prices controlled by the Company. Thus it was that, in 1657, the first few non-official Europeans came to settle at the Cape, and soon regarded it as their home. They were styled free burghers, and their number increased steadily though slowly.

Jan van Riebeeck left the Cape in 1662 after ten years of hard and discouraging work. He is regarded today as the founder of European civilization in South Africa, but it is doubtful whether he himself ever regarded the Cape as anything more than a refreshment station. It was some twenty years later that a vigorous successor, Simon van der Stel, first saw the possibilities for settlement. Urged by him, the Company made its only real effort to encourage immigration. Dutch and German immigrants were settled, a new village was established thirty miles from Cape Town, and local government instituted. Most important of all, between 1688 and 1700 about 200 French Huguenots arrived to enrich the social and economic life of the settlement and to become absorbed into the Dutch population. The Company also sent out orphan girls as wives for the colonists, and so the population grew. By 1708 there were about 1,700 Europeans, men, women and children, and about the same number of slaves. But colonization was slow. There was nothing in the history of the Cape comparable to the migrations to the American continent, and the Company was fundamentally opposed to increasing its commitments.

Small as the population was at the beginning of the eighteenth century, it was sufficiently numerous and influential to challenge successfully a clique of high officials who were attempting to corner the Cape market for their private benefit. And it was showing signs of developing characteristics of its own—characteristics that stemmed from the motherland in Europe, but were to be moulded by circumstances into a new pattern until, in later centuries, the name Afrikaner became a description of someone who though European by origin, was neither Dutch nor German nor French. One of these characteristics was a strong sense of individual freedom and a hearty dislike of control by government. This might have been expected from seventeenth-century Calvinists, but while Calvinism in Europe stressed the importance of the individual, its followers were disciplined by fear and persecution into a cohesive body. At the Cape there was no outward compulsion to force the individual to merge his identity in a defensive body. On the contrary, social and economic circumstances were such that the European colonists had every incentive to become undisciplined individualists. Slave labour, plenty of land, and a reasonably fertile climate conspired to produce a leisurely people, accustomed to being obeyed by slaves and Hottentots but themselves not obeying the law, resenting interference, and regarding government at the distant castle in Cape Town as something that should protect but not tax. And by 'protect' they meant that the government should see to it that the farmer had sufficient labour and that prices for farm produce were always at a maximum. As every government in South Africa today knows, the word 'protect' never entirely lost this somewhat specialized meaning.

The increasing demands of the Cape market for meat greatly encouraged cattle-farming. Since the land round Cape Town and Stellenbosch was not suited to ranching on any large scale, the cattle farmers began to move across the Hottentots-Holland Mountains to establish large cattle farms to the east. These farmers were the *trekboere* (trekking farmers). They did not own the huge ranches on which their cattle grazed, because the economical Company, unwilling to spend more money on administering its distant subjects, refused to survey and to grant freehold. The land was on loan, and this system encouraged farmers to over-graze and then move on to new pastures, still more miles away from the government at Cape Town. Only after three or four generations of *trekboere* had followed this nomadic life did government, in the shape of local administration, catch up with them. By then the *trekboere* had come to regard any government at all as interference with a man's personal liberty. They had also acquired a rooted belief that the possession of plenty of land was the natural right of all free men.

These nomadic cattle farmers were of the same Calvinist stock as those who lived near Cape Town and Stellenbosch, but they had even less incentive to maintain corporate discipline and cohesion. They lived a poor life, spiritually, culturally, and materially, and they developed an individual independence of the pioneering kind. What they needed they made for themselves, and they asked for nothing better than to be left alone. Their religion was that of the Old Testament, a harsh and forbidding one. Although Cape Town was in contact, however rare, with ideas that came from Europe, the cattle farmers neither knew nor cared about things beyond their own material wants and the safety of their families and their herds.

During the course of their trekking the cattle farmers came upon the Bushmen. Small of stature, living on wild herbs and game that they killed with poisoned arrows, having only a rudimentary social structure, the Bushmen were unable to adapt themselves, as the Hottentots had done, to the ways of the white man. They were accustomed to hunt where they pleased, and the idea of private ownership of land was utterly foreign to them. They not unnaturally regarded the European farmers as intruders and did their utmost to defend their ancient way of life. But it was a forlorn hope. The cattle farmers organized hunting parties, killed the adult Bushmen and captured the children, whom they used as herdsmen. In one such party 250 Bushmen were killed. What remained of the Bushmen families fled to the semi-desert lands in the north-west, where the remnants of their descendants now live in a reserve, under the protection of the South African Government, their language, customs, and rock paintings being studied by a generation more appreciative of the values of primitive and disappearing cultures.

During the last quarter of the eighteenth century the Dutch trekking farmers came into contact with African tribes who had a more advanced culture than the Bushmen and Hottentots and who numbered millions where the others had numbered thousands. The original home of the southern Bantu or African was probably near the equatorial highlands on the eastern side of Africa, where, possibly 2,000 years ago, Negroes from the Congo and from West Africa mixed with Hamitic stock to form the Bantu people. Migrations caused by pressure of population, tribal wars, and slave-raiding brought the Bantu southwards through the present Tanzania, Malawi, Rhodesia, and Zambia. The migrations were probably spread over hundreds of years, and by the middle of the eighteenth century some of the tribes had reached the Great Fish River in what is now the Eastern Province of the Cape. Like the Europeans, these Africans owned cattle and tilled the soil. They had well-developed social and political institutions according to which the chief was the depositary of tribal law and custom, but in normal circumstances he was no despot, being controlled by the tribal council and the tribe itself. The Africans were heathen; they had no written language; they were haunted by the fear of witchcraft and explained everything in terms of the supernatural. Their social system was based on cattle and the communal ownership of land, and they practised a subsistence economy.

The contact between these virile people and the hardy trek farmers had many important results. It led, eventually, to the conquest and Christianizing of the African, but its more immediate result was innumerable cattle raids which ended periodically in war. There were raids and counter-raids until some minor incident would precipitate a war, in which the African tribe involved would always gain a preliminary victory and then be defeated but not conquered. In fact, typical frontier conditions prevailed for close on 100 years until the middle of the nineteenth century.

Another important result was that the old habit of trekking farther into unoccupied lands could no longer be indulged. There was no longer an apparently endless stretch of unoccupied land before the farmers. The land was in fact occupied by large numbers of Africans who also required grazing-land for their herds of cattle. This was one of the principal reasons that eventually led the Dutch to trek round north-west of the African tribes and on to the highlands of the interior, there to establish independent republics.

By the end of the eighteenth century, when events in Europe altered the current of South African history, the refreshment station had grown into a colony sparsely inhabited by about 30,000 people. There were four districts, the Cape, Stellenbosch, Swellendam, and Graaff-Reinet. In the Cape there were Company's officials and a non-official population that lived by keeping lodging-houses, by fishing, by brickmaking, or by market-gardening. The chief attraction of keeping a lodging-house was the possibilities it afforded for smuggling and for making money from visitors. The Company strictly controlled all forms of commerce; it allowed certain minor participation in local government; it kept down expenses and as a consequence connived at bribery and corruption in its officials.

At Stellenbosch there were well-to-do farmers who cultivated vines and corn, kept sheep and cattle, built the beautiful old Cape Dutch houses that adorn the Cape to this day, and lived the leisurely lives of slave-owners. On the whole they treated their slaves well, and manumission for those who became Christians and literate was relatively frequent. In the Swellendam and Graaff-Reinet districts lived the stock farmers, occupying 6,000 acres or more at a time, trekking on when the need arose, far removed from the influences of the Cape, not so much lawless as a law unto themselves, and asking for nothing more than plenty of land and no interference from government. When the government attempted to enforce existing laws they rebelled and formed two short-lived republics. This was in 1795, and five years later the British Government had to suppress two more rebellions in the same areas.

The non-European population at this time consisted of slaves and non-slaves, the former being more numerous in the west and the latter in the eastern districts where the farmers depended on what Hottentot labour they could get rather than on slaves. The latter were of diverse origin—

West African, East African, Mozambique, and Malay—all of these already tending to merge ethnically to form the Cape Coloured people. There were as yet no Africans within the borders of the colony; but, as we have seen, the great clash between Africa and Europe had already begun.

When the French revolutionary armies invaded Holland in 1795, Britain, by arrangement with the Dutch King, occupied the Cape for the first time. The Company was by now bankrupt, and when the Treaty of Amiens of 1802 provided that the Cape should be restored, it was to the Dutch Republican Government, and not to the Company, that it was handed back. For three years the Cape was ruled by a brilliant Dutch advocate, Jacob de Mist, in accordance with enlightened governmental principles then current in France and Holland. When Napoleon renewed the war against Britain it became clear to the British Government that it would endanger her trade with the East if the Cape were to remain in the hands of an ally of France. She therefore occupied the Cape for the second time in 1806, with no intention now of returning it. In 1815 the Congress of Vienna ratified the cession.

The British Government took a more serious view of its governmental duties than the Dutch Company had done. Government was reorganized; the currency was stabilized; circuit courts were introduced, to the annoyance of frontiersmen who found the courts interfering in what they considered to be purely personal matters such as relations with their Hottentot servants; the salve trade was abolished, and the government tried to overcome the labour shortage by pass laws that restricted the free movement of Hottentots.

Unemployment in Britain after the Napoleonic Wars led to emigration, and 5,000 British settlers arrived in 1820 to settle in the eastern districts. Their advent had a profound effect on the history of the country. It brought to the colony, and to South Africa, a most valuable new element in the population—an element that, because it was English-speaking and had friends and relatives in Britain, compelled the British Government to pay greater attention to the Cape. They had left England at a time when administrative reforms that were to come after the death of Lord Castlereagh were being widely discussed, and it was largely owing to the presence of the settlers and to persistent agitation by individuals among them that a whole series of reforms was instituted at the Cape. The freedom of the Press was achieved in 1827. In the same year a Charter of Justice established the independence of the judiciary and instituted trial by jury. In 1834 slavery was abolished; a Legislative Council, with an official majority, was set up; the old local courts of *Landdrost* and *Heemraden* were abolished, paid magistrates were appointed, and popularly elected municipal councils were instituted. Freedom of internal trade and the right to export surplus produce were granted; new towns were established and roads and bridges were built.

The first thirty years of British rule at the Cape were years of considerable economic expansion and administrative reform. The British Government had, however, done many things which the Dutch inhabitants heartily disliked. The English language had been declared the only official language, and, though this policy was reversed some thirty years later, it left a deep mark on the minds of South Africans. To this day Afrikaans political speakers can be sure of a ready response when they refer to 'old Lord Charles Somerset' and his attempts to suppress the Dutch language. An even greater shock than the suppression of their language was the shock to fundamental beliefs and traditions, more especially of the frontier farmers, involved in British policy. Largely as a result of the persistent advocacy of Dr. Philip of the London Missionary Society, the famous Fiftieth Ordinance was passed in 1828. This Ordinance repealed the previous pass laws and established the principle of equality in the eyes of the law for 'all free persons of colour'. In the twentieth century, white opinion in Africa can with difficulty bring itself even to contemplate the doctrine of racial equality, and it may be imagined with what loathing the frontiersmen of 1828 regarded it.

Further, there had been more Kaffir Wars, as the frontier wars between European and African are called, and the British Government, strongly under the influence of the liberals and the philanthropic movement, and not wishing to extend its commitments, had refused to satisfy the land-hunger of the trek farmers by the annexation of African territory. From about 1834 a few frontier farmers, despairing of obtaining more land on the old cheap terms, began to trek west of the Bantu territories, across the Orange River and on to the highveld of what is now the Orange Free State. They really went to spy out the land, and could report back that there was plenty of excellent grazing-land which seemed to have no one on it. In the same year, 1834, another Kaffir War broke out and farmhouses were destroyed, stock stolen, and people murdered before the Africans could be subdued. The Governor, Sir Benjamin D'Urban, sympathized with the farmers in their plight and annexed a portion of the defeated Africans' land to hand out as farms by way of compensation. But he modified his policy when he found that he could not keep Africans out of the area, and he reversed it after being severely criticized by the government in London. The frontiersmen then realized that nothing more was to be hoped for from a government that refused to help the white at the expense of the black, and so began the Great Trek which was intended to carry them beyond the reach of the British Government.

The Trekkers, in a public statement issued on the eve of departure of one of their groups, complained of the suppression of their language and institutions; of the lack of protection on the frontier; of the unfair way in which the liberation of the slaves had been carried out; of the unjustifiable odium that had been cast upon them by missionaries and other prejudiced persons. They complained that they had no voice in the government that taxed them. Anna Steenkamp, one of the Trekker women, spoke in her diary of the unbiblical policy of equality between black and white, and the phrase conveys some of the genuine horror with which the Dutch emigrant farmers viewed a policy that placed white and black on an equal footing and interfered in the relations between master and servant.

During the decade from 1836 to 1846 something like 10,000 men, women, and children left their homes in the Cape Colony, expressing the hope that the British Government would leave them in peace. They trekked northwards with all their possessions packed on ox-wagons or slung beneath them—beds, furniture, a harmonium where they had one, pots and pans, and, always, the family Bible. The women in long dresses and bonnets travelled in the wagons with the children; the men, in coarse, home-made clothes and with a rifle slung over their shoulders, usually travelled on horseback. All—men, women, and children—took turns at leading the oxen and herding the cattle. They encountered much hardship and danger in the course of their wanderings. Wagons had to be taken to pieces and carried over the difficult mountain passes; there was constant danger from wild animals; and there was the threat of attack by Africans. Usually they trekked in small parties of from twenty to thirty families and agreed to meet when they had reached the promised land; but there were larger parties under elected leaders and the smaller parties eventually attached themselves to these.

The Voortrekkers[1] envisaged an independent republican state in which there would be no equality between black and white. They intended, they said, to obtain land justly by purchase, and to found their state upon principles of religion and justice. After a good deal of quarrelling among the leaders as to where they should settle, Piet Retief, the most intelligent of them, trekked eastwards with his followers towards the present Natal. At that time what is now Natal was ruled by the Zulu under Dingaan. They had been an obscure tribe but had risen to pre-eminence under Dingaan's predecessor, Chaka, a man of outstanding ability although, like Dingaan, he was a ruthless tyrant and slew without mercy all who offended against him or against the laws of the tribe. Against both there is a heavy record of savage and indiscriminate slaughtering of their own subjects and of wiping out other African tribes. They had not even the excuse that might be made for Dingaan's murder of Europeans, who in his eyes threatened the safety of his country.

Having reached Natal, Piet Retief went to meet Dingaan and negotiated for the transfer of land; but the Zulu chief played for time and asked the Trekkers, as an earnest of their good intentions, to recover some stolen

---

[1] *Voor* here means 'in front of', and Voortrekker means pioneer. The word is frequently abbreviated to Trekker.

cattle for him. They did this, and a treaty was drawn up by which the Trekkers were given a large part of Natal. As with most treaties signed with African chiefs, Dingaan probably intended this land for use and not for ownership. But, whatever his intentions, the ease with which the cattle had been recovered by the Europeans, and the fact that, contrary to Retief's instructions, the Trekkers had begun marking out farms for themselves, frightened Dingaan and he determined to kill those people whom he and his people regarded as white wizards. At a royal feast he had Retief and seventy followers murdered, and sent his soldiers to kill all the white people they could find. Vengeance followed about a year later when, on 16 December 1938, the Zulu were decisively defeated at the Battle of Blood River and their country annexed.

Having conquered Natal, with its harbour at Durban, the Trekkers found themselves at odds with the Cape Colony. Merchants at the Cape feared the possible rivalry of Durban, where ships from the United States and from Holland had already begun to put in to trade. Further, though the Zulu had been defeated, the country was by no means settled. There were thousands of wandering, landless Zulu, and cattle-thieving was rife. This led to reprisals and raids, and generally to a state of unrest among African tribes right up to the borders of the Cape Colony. The Governor of the Cape, therefore, persuaded the British Government to annex Natal in 1843, to the anger of the Trekkers, and many of them trekked back over the Drakensberg Mountains to the highveld of the present Free State and Transvaal. British authority followed them once more. In 1848 the Free State was proclaimed the Orange River Sovereignty with a Resident Commissioner to represent the British Government.

British policy with regard to the Trekkers had been vacillating. Like the Dutch Reformed Church, the government had frowned on such a dispersal of its subjects as the Great Trek constituted. To follow up its obviously reluctant subjects with administrative and police machinery would involve enormous expense, and unless it could be justified on such obvious commercial and strategic grounds as that provided by the possession of Durban harbour, it would not be worth it. The new country was sparsely populated by a race of farmers who were antagonistic to British rule and possessed little or no cash income that could be taxed to pay for expenses. At that time, moreover, the existence of minerals, which was later to prove so attractive, was unknown. There was, therefore, no great incentive to Britain to retain her hold over the country occupied by the dispersed Trekkers; and under the re-alignment of parties that followed the repeal of the Corn Laws in Britain, parliament began to regard colonies as undesirable burdens. Accordingly, by the Sand River Convention of 1852. Britain withdrew all claims to exercise authority beyond the Vaal River, and two years later, by the Bloemfontein Convention, she withdrew south of the Orange River. These actions left the two Boer republics, the Orange

Free State and the South African Republic (the Transvaal), independent of British control.

There was virtually complete equality of wealth and condition among the European inhabitants of the two new republics. Wealth consisted of land and stock, and there was certainly enough land for all. The Boer ideal, that when he sat on his *stoep* he should not see the smoke from his nearest neighbours' chimney, could be realized in those spacious days. Twenty or thirty farms in the Free State today would have been lost in the farm of a century ago. It was only later, when the population increased, and when towns were established and minerals discovered, that differences in wealth and status began to appear. But at the time when the Boers were establishing their republics, economic and social equality of all European citizens was reflected in the constitutions they made.

The constitution of the Orange Free State is a good example of what one might call natural democracy. A group of people with practically no book learning, many of them semiliterate, with few examples (in the 1850's) of democratic constitutions to guide them, with a strong sense of individual liberty, and a rough economic and social equality, set up an efficient democratic constitution that contained many of the principles of sound constitutional government. There was an elected *Volksraad* (Legislative Assembly) and an elected president; the judiciary was independent; control of the commandos remained with the elected *Volksraad*; the legislature was supreme and controlled the executive; freedom of the Press and of the individual was guaranteed in the constitution. The constitution of the Transvaal was a rambling document that stressed the popular will but left vague such constitutional questions as the relations between the executive, the legislature, and the judiciary, and it was, moreover, frequently changed by simple resolution of the *Volksraad*. Nevertheless, it was only when gold was discovered and a highly specialized industrial community was superimposed on the agricultural republic, that the constitution failed to work with reasonable smoothness.

Many of the Africans who were living in the Transvaal and Free State were deprived of their rights to occupy land. This was sometimes accompanied by violence and war, but much more frequently it was a silent process comparable to the enclosure movement in England. Much of the land occupied by Europeans was, indeed, vacant land; and frequently land occupied in genuine ignorance that anyone else had a right to it, and farms granted to individuals without the knowledge that Africans were in occupation. The population, African and European, was sparse, and on farms of from 50,000 to 100,000 acres it was quite possible for people to be living on the same land without being aware of one another's existence. Further, possession meant different things to Europeans and to Africans. To the latter it meant use; to the former it meant physical possession, the right to own property and dispose of it at will. In those parts of the republics where there was obvious occupation by Africans, the Boers recognized the authority of the chiefs and left the people in possession of their land under the name of Reserves.

The Great Trek changed the course of the history of southern Africa. It withdrew from the Cape Colony, at a critical period, about a quarter of its Dutch-speaking population, thus leaving British ideas and institutions fuller play in the Cape Colony. In a period of ten years it opened up vast tracts of land to European occupation and established three new political entities, and it thus opened the way to eventual expansion northwards. It brought millions of Africans under the political control of Europeans, and in doing so it deprived many of them of their rights to tribal occupation of land and reduced the areas to which they had previously had free access; it also, in time, brought peace and the rule of law where formerly there had been intertribal warfare and general insecurity.

The Boers established republics whose democratic constitutions were in some ways in advance of those enjoyed by their compatriots in the Cape Colony. But these constitutions were, as seemed natural to the Boers, for Europeans only; when the Cape achieved responsible government it was for all colours. Thus, two radically different policies with regard to non-whites were established in South Africa, and the difference has not yet been composed. The republican tradition in South Africa became firmly established, closely associated with the Afrikaners and opposed to Britain. The Trek thus created a gulf between Britain and the Afrikaners that has not yet been bridged. British policy from the Great Trek until the Boer War bred a deep suspicion in the minds of Afrikaners, and even now the Afrikaner cannot quite shake off the illusion that he is being followed.[2]

Because of their experiences with African tribes, experiences of wars and misconceived treaties, the Boers developed a firm conviction that a policy of equal rights for black and white is contrary to the laws of God and the dictates of common sense. They did not know, what investigations have since revealed, that an African chief did not possess tribal land and had no authority to alienate it for it belonged to the tribe. The British Government, too, acquired territory throughout Africa by hundreds of treaties with African chiefs. Indeed, at one time the Foreign Office provided printed treaty forms for the use of officials and explorers. The Boers made a few such treaties; but whether British or Boer, all the treaties were in reality valueless. In the first place, the chief had no power to alienate land; in the second place, what he thought he was doing was to give the Europeans the usufruct, not the possession, of it. In their ignorance of tribal custom, Europeans of all nations made what they thought were contracts by which the land became theirs, and to this day they all argue that their particular colony was acquired by genuine treaty. What really

[2] For a discussion of the use of the term Afrikaner see chapter 3.

happened was that two totally different conceptions of landownership were in conflict, and neither side knew or recognized the conflict.

Perhaps the most important result of the Great Trek is to be found in the influence it had on the social and political thought of the Afrikaners and in the way it affected their cultural and emotional life. Just before the Battle of Blood River, in which the Zulu were defeated, the Trekkers held their customary religious service, and the preacher, Cilliers, vowed that if victory was granted them, the Afrikaners would every year hold a thanksgiving service on that day. The Day of the Covenant,[3] 16 December, is still celebrated as a national holiday, on which the Afrikaans churches have services in remembrance of the vow made by Cilliers. When the services are over political speeches are made recalling the past and exhorting Afrikaners not to forsake the ways of their forefathers. Voortrekker dress has been revived for such occasions; so too have the folk-dancing, games,[4] and simple folk-tunes of earlier days. Afrikaners regard the Great Trek as the spiritual, cultural, and political event that gave birth to the Afrikaner *volk*. Through the mists of time, as frequently happens, some of the economic facts of the Trek have become overlaid, and the reasons that caused the Trek are idealized in the popular mind.

The tradition of the Great Trek has a strong link with the rise of Afrikaner nationalism and of the Nationalist Party. As the Great Trek itself split the European population of South Africa, so the memories and traditions of the Trek tend to divide Afrikaners and English-speaking South Africans. Politicians are fond of saying this need not be so; but it is a fact. South Africa is full of memories that its citizens cannot yet share with equal pride; and the Great Trek is one of them. The time may yet come when Afrikaners, English-speaking South Africans, and Africans will all be able to find cause for satisfaction in the spread of Western civilization in southern Africa that resulted from the Great Trek. By 1968 there were signs that English—and Afrikaans—speaking white South Africans were beginning to shed some of their exclusiveness towards each other; but the more they did so the more exclusive did each become towards the non-whites.

We left the Cape Colony at 1836. From then it shared in the steady constitutional development that Lord Durham's report on Canada had persuaded British opinion to accept as reasonable. In 1853 representative government was instituted, and in 1872 full responsible government. As we saw, there was no colour bar in the constitution; but franchise qualifications, applicable to all, kept the number of non-European voters small and enabled the European colonists to accustom themselves gradually

---

[3] Until 1952, when it was changed by Act of Parliament, this was called Dingaan's Day.

[4] Folk-games (*volkspeletjies*) had largely died out and were revived in 1914 by Mr. S. H. Pellissier, later Director of Education in the Orange Free State. He had been much influenced by the folk-dancing and singing he had witnessed in Denmark while on a study tour of Europe.

to the idea of a common electoral roll. The Cape Colony thus had an opportunity of showing whether the different elements in a multiracial society could co-operate in running parliamentary institutions. So satisfactory was this experience that in 1910, when the Cape Colony entered into Union with the other South African colonies, Afrikaans- and English-speaking citizens at the Cape were practically unanimous in believing that a common franchise, restricted by educational and property tests for all alike, not only worked well but was the only sane policy. And so convinced were the Cape politicans that this was a sound policy that they were prepared to forgo union rather than abandon their common franchise. We shall see later what the sequel was.

From 1848 the British Government at the Cape gradually abandoned the policy of trying to maintain a peaceful boundary between the Cape Colony and the African tribes. Step by step African territory between the Fish River and the Natal border was annexed, and European magistrates and police were sent in to rule. In most cases the land annexed was reserved for African occupation, and missionaries, schools, hospitals, and other civilizing agencies began their slow and uphill task among Africans.

Although the British Government had, in the 1850's, refused to undertake further commitments, subsequent events and the logical demands on the strongest government in southern Africa brought Britain back into politics north of the Orange River. To begin with, there were many people in the Cape Colony, and even in the Free State and Transvaal, who regretted the balkanization of South Africa and were anxious for some form of federation or union. Sir George Grey, popular in the Free State as well as in the Cape where he was Governor, took soundings in 1856 and found the Free State not unwilling to consider federation. At that stage, however, the British Government, having only recently withdrawn from the Free State, was unwilling to reverse her policy. Thus the first attempt at union came to nothing. The second attempt was made by Lord Carnarvon, Secretary of State for Colonies.

In 1870 diamonds were discovered at Kimberley and a dispute arose as to who owned the area. It was claimed by Waterboer, chief of a mixed Hottentot and half-breed tribe called the Griquas, by the Transvaal, and, with more justice, by the Free State. The negotiations and the arbitration by which the award went to Waterboer, who was then induced to come in under the British wing, left the Transvaal and Free State resentful. Even so, the statesmanlike Brand, President of the Free State, was prepared to discuss the proposals for a federation put forward by Lord Carnarvon; but by this time the Cape had been granted responsible government and the Cape ministers considered that Carnarvon had gone over their heads. His attempt, therefore, was a failure.

A third effort was made in 1877. The Transvaal was in very low water; economically it was on the verge of bankruptcy, politically it was rent by internal and personal disputes, and it was, moreover, having grave difficulty in keeping the peace with its African neighbours. Sir Theophilus Shepstone, acting on behalf of the Imperial Government, went to Pretoria with a bodyguard of twenty-four men and persuaded a majority of the *Volksraad* to accept British rule. On behalf of the British Government he promised that responsible government would be instituted as soon as possible. When, four years later, the promise had not been carried out, the Transvalers rose and fought the Transvaal war of independence. They won a notable victory at the Battle of Majuba Hill, which called forth the tribute of a poem of praise from *Punch*, and Gladstone decided to make peace as quickly as possible. By the Pretoria Convention the Transvaal's independence was restored, but Britain retained the right to veto her foreign policy, a clause that was to cause endless trouble later. The final and most disastrous attempt at federation will be described presently.

The discovery of diamonds in 1870 wrenched South Africa from her agricultural rut and began the process which was to alter the course of her history. Its economic effects were immediate: agricultural prices soared and, for a time, Free State farmers were selling eggs at a pound a dozen. Money and people poured into the country; from the Cape people walked and rode to make their fortunes on the diggings; Africans came out of their reserves in thousands to earn money and, more desirable, guns. It became profitable to build a railway line from the Cape to Kimberley, and African labour was required to do the rough work. Gradually people like Cecil Rhodes, Barney Barnato, and the Beits got control of the mines by buying out the small operators, and established the enormous fortunes that were subsequently used to develop the gold-mines of the Transvaal and to expand the British Empire farther north.

The discovery of gold on the Witwatersrand in 1886 made Kimberley look like a minor boom in a small town. Within a very few years of the discovery there were more foreigners, or Uitlanders, in the Transvaal, concentrated on the Rand, than there were Boers. The construction of railways from the Cape and from Lourenço Marques was rushed through to carry the mining material and the heavy and light goods that the Rand required. The effects were felt throughout South Africa like a seismic disturbance, and in London, where the capital or its exploitation came from, people began to regard the Transvaal in a new light.

Even before the discovery of gold had made the Transvaal a country of world importance the scramble for Africa had begun. Germany, France, Britain, Belgium, and Portugal were competing for African territories, and the Berlin Conference of 1884 had arranged for the peaceful partition of Africa among the European powers. Spheres of influence were demarcated on the map, and often these boundary lines were lines of latitude or longitude that cut through existing tribes. Everywhere treaties were made with chiefs who had little if any understanding of what they were putting their mark to.

To preserve as wide a sphere of influence as possible, Cecil Rhodes, from his base at the Cape, pushed energetically northwards, west of the Transvaal, through Bechuanaland, and on to the Rhodesias. In 1886 part of Bechuanaland was annexed to the Cape Colony, and three years later Rhodes's agents persuaded Lobengula, chief of the Matebele, to grant mining concessions. These were used by those who came to mine for gold as giving them the right to settle, but a Matebele war and a Matebele rebellion had to be fought before the Europeans gained a title to Rhodesia. In doing so they created a barrier around the Transvaal which effectually prevented Germany from joining her eastern and western African territories.

From his capital in Pretoria, some thirty miles from the teeming Rand, president Kruger watched all these goings-on with growing fear and suspicion. His republic had become well off because he was able to tax the Randlords, but he had reason to fear that it would not be able to hold out against the strong combination of capital and Empire. The constitution of the Transvaal was designed to serve an agricultural community and was unable to adjust itself to the new strains to which it was put. Wealth in such great quantity corrupted a public service unable effectively to govern the turbulent and lawless Johannesburg.

It was against this background that Cecil Rhodes, then Prime Minister of the Cape Colony, plotted the final attempt to bring the republics into line with the Cape. Rhodes and Jameson, almost certainly with the know-ledge of Chamberlain, decided to annex the Transvaal by a sudden stroke. The Jameson Raid was ill-conceived and badly executed. The noisy Uitlanders in Johannesburg were undependable, and the success of the Raid would have to depend on a rising in Johannesburg. In fact, the rising was to have been the excuse that would cover Rhodes, as Jameson would then go in to 'restore order'. But the rising never took place and Jameson's force was captured with little trouble by the Transvaal burghers.

The Jameson Raid was a complete failure, but it had far-reaching consequences. Rhodes had to resign from a position in which he had great influence with the Cape Afrikaners, and they and the rest of the Afrikaners now repudiated him as the archetype of finance-imperialism. Kruger very wisely handed Jameson over to the British Government to deal with. He was tried and given a light sentence; actually he did not serve the whole of it. A parliamentary inquiry at Westminster seemed to have but one object, that of protecting the Secretary of State for Colonies, Joseph Chamberlain. The British public was in an imperialist and jingoistic mood and regarded Jameson and Rhodes, not as political adventurers who had endangered the good relations between Great Britain and the Transvaal, but as empire builders who had had bad luck. All these things had the effect of turning the Afrikaners, from the Cape to the Transvaal against Britain and against any idea of peaceful federation. The Raid, and particularly the refusal of the British Government to repudiate it whole-heartedly and unequivocally, destroyed what slender hopes there had been of a peaceful settlement with the Transvaal.[5] In 1899 a conference was held at Bloemfontein between representatives of the Transvaal and of Great Britain; but it failed to arrive at an agreement over the crucial question of Uitlander rights. Kruger could not hand over the vote to the Uitlanders without endangering Boer political power. On the other hand, the Uitlanders were paying taxes and demanded an effective share in calling the tune. It was a position from which, in the atmosphere engendered by the Raid, neither side could extricate itself. Britain sent troops to South Africa, and in October 1899 the Transvaal demanded their withdrawal in an ultimatum. When this was refused, war began and the Free State, bound by treaty, joined the Transvaal.

Afrikaners call the war *Die Engelse oorlog* (the English war), or the second war of independence, the first being the Transvaal war of independence of 1880-1. In England it is called the Boer War, and some people in South Africa call it the Anglo-Boer War. These names are perhaps indicative of the different opinions that exist on the question of the responsibility for the war. In this book the term Boer War is used for the sake of brevity and with no intention of apportioning blame.

Without going into any details of the war, there are a few points that can be made. The Boer War is still within living memory. It took place at the turn of the century, and men who were in their early eighties in 1968 may have taken part, as youngsters of fifteen, in the actual fighting.[6] Women of that age can recall the concentration camps, in which their brothers or sisters or mothers may have died. Children and grandchildren of these people have heard Boer War tales at first hand, tales of heroism and escape, of hunger and privation, of cruelty and of kindness, and in many cases the tales are told with humour and an absence of rancour or bitterness. The first three prime ministers of the Union were Boer War generals—Botha, Hertzog, and Smuts; and Smuts died in 1950. It is therefore only in comparatively recent times that the men who had led the Boers in their times of trouble finally departed from the scene and left the stage to younger men. No wonder, then, that the Boer War occupies a large place in the thinking and politics and culture of the Afrikaner people.

During the first three or four months of the Boer War the British forces were checked and defeated on three main fronts. Then they gathered force and pushed on, leaving the bulk of the Boer forces to waste their

[5] See Jean van der Poel, *The Jameson Raid*, Oxford University Press.
[6] Within a week of the outbreak of war the Grey College School at Bloemfontein, at which many Transvaal and Free State boys studied, was practically emptied of its senior classes. The boys had gone to the war!

energies and limited manpower in besieging Kimberley, Mafeking, and Ladysmith, or, as General Smuts did, to make dramatic but fruitless raids into the Cape Colony. When the sieges had been relieved, the two capitals, Bloemfontein and Pretoria, were captured, but the Boers hung on tenaciously for two years, living on the country, for the most part fighting their battles with ammunition captured from the enemy, and hoping for international intervention. It was a war of attrition, and when Kitchener tried to make contact with his elusive opponents he found that practically every farmhouse in the Free State and Transvaal was a Boer base. Strategically he was bound to destroy these bases, and he decided to burn the farms. Once this decision was taken, women and children could not be left on the bare veld to starve. So they were brought into hastily improvised canvas concentration camps.[7]

In the early days of their establishment the concentration camps were for the most part inefficiently run. There were not enough doctors or hospitals and medical supplies to cope with the women and children from the destroyed farms, let alone those who were suffering from the hardships of following the commandos and had found refuge in the camps. In a country ravaged by war it was difficult to get supplies rapidly to points where they were most urgently needed, and communications were further disrupted as the Boers blew up railway lines. So, when epidemics of typhoid fever and a particularly virulent type of measles broke out, they spread rapidly. Sewage disposal and water supplies presented no problems in a sparsely populated country on isolated farms; but the camps, overcrowded with people unaccustomed to living at such close quarters, were favourable breeding grounds for germs. It must be remembered that the British Tommies themselves were dying by the thousand from fever. Before these epidemics finally subsided about 26,000 women and children had died.

When news of the conditions in the camps reached the Cape and Britain there was a wave of indignation and the British Government sent a Ladies' Committee to investigate. As more medical supplies and doctors were sent out and as the epidemics receded, conditions improved. Camp schools were established and Dutch Reformed ministers from the Cape were allowed to minister to the spiritual needs of the people. The women themselves showed great courage and adjured their menfolk not to surrender or to give up the struggle on their account; and there is, in fact, evidence that the Boers were able to continue fighting in the knowledge

---

[7] The most authoritative account of the origins of Boer War is J. S. Marais, *The Fall of Kruger's Republic*. Lionel Curtiss, *With Milner in South Africa*, is a lively and statesmanlike commentary on the war and condemns the burning of farms. A. C. Martin gives a well-documented account, in *The Concentration Camps, 1900–1902*, that destroys many myths. Victor Pohl's *Adventures of a Boer Family* and Margaret Marquard's *Letters from a Boer Parsonage*, contain charming accounts, given without rancour, of how the war affected individual families in small Free State villages.

that their women and children were being looked after. General Botha expressed his thankfulness that so many Boer families were in British hands; and President Steyn used the improved conditions in the camps as an argument to encourage the burghers to fight on.[8] Nevertheless, the burning of farms and the hardships of the concentration camps left a deep mark on the Afrikaner people.

By the beginning of 1902 it was evident that the Boers could not hold out much longer. In May final negotiations took place and the treaty of Vereeniging was signed on 31 May 1902. (On the same date, eight years later, the Union of South Africa came into being.) The terms of the treaty were generous. Britain promised to grant responsible government as soon as the country was settled; the equality of the Dutch language, as it then still was, with English was recognized; the question of the non-European franchise was to be left until after the grant of responsible government; and Britain agreed to help in the economic reconstruction of the country. These promises were faithfully kept. By 1906 and 1907 the Transvaal and the Free State were granted responsible government, and the country recovered remarkably quickly from the ravages of war. Milner, whose pre-war policy had natuarlly been unpopular with the Boers, was mainly responsible for the efficient way in which administration was reorganized even while the fighting was still going on.

The way was now open for another move to combine the four self-governing colonies in South Africa, and in 1908 a National Convention met at Durban to discuss closer union. Though all parties were agreed on most of the terms of a constitution, there were various obstacles to be overcome. Union, rather than federation, was decided on and parliament was to be sovereign. But, as a compromise to allay the fears of the two smaller colonies of Natal and the Free State, provincial councils were given powers that could not be altered by Parliament until ten years after union, and among these powers was the control of primary and secondary education. The question of the franchise was the most difficult of all. The Cape, with its liberal tradition, wanted to retain the Cape franchise, which had no colour bar; the Transvaal and Free State refused to grant the vote to non-Europeans. Eventually it was decided to leave the franchise laws of the four states as they were and to satisfy the Cape delegates by entrenching the Cape franchise in a clause which provided that it could be altered only by a two-thirds majority of both Houses of Parliament sitting together.

When the National Convention had reached finality the draft Act was taken to Westminster where it was passed by the British Parliament as the South Africa Act, 1909. By May of 1910 Union was an accomplished fact.

Much of the history of South Africa since 1910 will become apparent in the course of the subsequent chapters, and a few main facts only need be

[8] See Walker, *History of South Africa*, p. 499.

told here. She was involved in two world wars, both of which interrupted normal life, and at the same time enormously accelerated development. In neither world war was the European population united.

When the First World War broke out in 1914 General Botha was Prime Minister. A portion of the Afrikaner people had already broken away from the leadership of Botha and Smuts and, under Hertzog, had formed the Nationalist Party whose slogan was 'South Africa First', in opposition to Botha's policy of 'conciliation'.[9] When parliament approved the government's policy of invading South-West Africa, then a Germany colony, the Nationalist Party condemned the action and found considerable support in the Free State and Transvaal. Many Boer War leaders— de la Rey, Beyers, de Wet, among others—organized protests against participation in 'England's wars.' Officers in the Defence Force and in the burgher commandos openly declared that they would not obey instructions to fight, and some resigned their commissions. Maritz, the officer in charge of the troops nearest to the South-West Africa border, was treasonably in touch with the German Command, and in due course he went over to the enemy and rebellion broke out in the Union.

Lack of organization or of cohesion among the leaders, who were all experienced soldiers, proves that the Rebellion was not premeditated. It was, rather, a spontaneous rising with a vague hope of regaining the independence lost twelve years earlier. Afrikaner nationalists refer to the event as *die gewapende protes*—the armed protest. Legally it was rebellion, participation in which was punished; but there is evidence that many of the rank-and-file did not intend anything more than a protest against government policy. Moreover, when the rebels of today easily become the rulers of tomorrow, sharp legal distinctions become blurred. In 1967 Parliament decided to include former rebels among those eligible for war veterans' pensions.

Neither de Wet nor Beyers had any real plans, and Hertzog, political leader of the Nationalist Party, condemned rebellion. The magic of de Wet's name attracted some of his old burghers and many young bloods; but the Rebellion was not widely supported and there were probably not more than 12,000 rebels all told. On the other hand, Botha soon had 40,000 men in the field, most of them Afrikaners, and by December 1914 the Rebellion was over.[10] General de Wet was captured and sentenced to imprisonment, but was soon released on parole and allowed to live on his farm.

Botha now turned his attention to South-West Africa, which he took in

---

[9] See chapter 7.

[10] An illustration of how close to the Boer War all these men, on both sides, were, is the story of General Botha on the morning of the Battle of Mushroom Valley, where he defeated de Wet. He was waiting anxiously for the expected attack, and when he saw de Wet's commando in the distance he said to one of his officers: 'Here they come. Here come the English.'

1915 and which has remained ever since to trouble South Africa's international relations. After German South-West came German East Africa. Troops were sent to join the rather mixed forces that were operating there, and General Smuts himself went to conduct an exhausting and fruitless campaign against von Lettow, a campaign about which the two opponents swapped yarns at a dinner party in London after the war.[11]

Thousands of South Africans volunteered and went to England to join various British regiments and the Royal Flying Corps, as it was called until 1 April 1918. A South African Brigade was recruited and sent to France, where it distinguished itself at Delville Wood. The Cape Coloured Corps was sent overseas and 7,000 Africans went as a Labour Corps. Out of a possible total of 685,000 European men of fighting age 136,000 enrolled for service and 76,000 went overseas.[12]

Between the two world wars industrialization took place at a rapid rate, too rapid for South Africa to be able to adapt her social economy with comfort. The balance of European population shifted from country to town; the number of manufacturing establishments increased from 2,000 to 9,000 and their output quadrupled; exports and imports doubled; the railway network increased by 25 per cent, even though the main lines from the ports to the mines had all been laid before Union; and banking, agricultural production, revenue and expenditure, the public debt, and the public service establishment, all kept pace with this industrial expansion. Housing and town-planning lagged far behind.

In political life, too, changes had taken place. The Nationalist Party came to power with the aid of the Labour Party in 1924. When, at the Imperial Conferences of 1926 and 1930, Hertzog completed the work that Botha and Smuts had begun and secured beyond any doubt the independence of South Africa as a member of the British Commonwealth, he declared that he had now done for the Afrikaner people what he had set out to do in 1912, and that, as far as he was concerned, a republic was neither necessary nor desirable. The extreme Nationalist wing under Malan would not accept this doctrine, and Hertzog's position became increasingly difficult. On the other hand, there was no longer any reason why he and Smuts should not pull together, and they formed the United Party with Hertzog as leader, a wise piece of self-effacement on the part of Smuts. Malan remained in the new party for a brief spell and then left it to lead the so-called 'Purified' Nationalists, and at the other extreme a small group of ultra-British people, who considered that Smuts had gone too far towards the Afrikaner side, left his party and formed the Dominion

---

[11] When the writer was introduced as 'a fellow-countryman of General Smuts' to von Lettow's youngest daughter, she remarked: 'General Smuts and my father were great friends.'

[12] See Walker, *A History of South Africa*, p. 565, note.

Party. That the union of the two big parties was popular was shown by the next general election when the United Party won an overwhelming victory.

For the next seven years there was continued debate as to whether the Union could, and would, remain neutral if Britain went to war. When the test came, in September 1939, Hertzog opposed South Africa's entry into the war and proposed a benevolent neutrality, while Smuts favoured immediate participation and carried the day with a majority of thirteen votes. Hertzog then asked for a dissolution to test the feeling of the country, but the Governor-General, advised by what was now the strongest party under Smuts, refused. For a few weeks emotions ran high and the atmosphere seemed favourable for a repetition of the events of 1914. The Nationalists were jubilant that Hertzog should have shown himself to be, as they put it, a 'true Afrikaner' and had, in effect, rejoined the Purified Nationalist Party; but as we shall see in a subsequent chapter, reunion between the Hertzogites and the Malanites did not take place. There was no rebellion, partly because Smuts acted with great wisdom and circumspection and did not provoke trouble, partly because rebellion is not a step lightly taken, and partly because, in 1939, many Nationalists, in company with many people in other countries, backed Hitler's highly organized Germany to win, and nurtured the illusion that a republic might well be snatched from such a situation.

Once more, therefore, South Africa was engaged in a life-and-death struggle as a partner of Great Britain; and once more she was divided on that very issue. All the moral and political authority of a considerable opposition was used to hamper the war effort. One, among many, of the serious results of this was that throughout the war there was never an effective alternative war government. Criticism of war policy was, therefore, never really responsible and the government, unable for security reasons to take the opposition into its confidence, was deprived of all effective criticism.

South Africa's contribution to the common war effort was on a much larger scale than in 1914–18. Where her airmen had, in the first war, joined the Royal Air Force, she now had a large and efficient air force of her own, and South Africa became a training ground for the R.A.F. Two full divisions at a time were put into the field and others existed in skeleton form. The so-called 'little ships' operated round the coasts and in the Mediterranean, where they gave gallant service on the famous 'Alex-Matruh–Tobruk' run. And the graves of South Africans that are scattered over the Middle East, the Balkans, Austria, Germany, France, Italy, Poland, and wherever else British troops fought or British airmen flew, testify to the number of South Africans that were to be found in British units. A South African division assisted in the conquest of Abyssinia and of North Africa, and a brigade was sent to take Madagascar. Most of one division was captured or killed at Tobruk,[13] and after North Africa a South African division and many Air Force squadrons operated in Italy.[14]

South African industry, too, was geared to the general war effort, making boots and bombs for her allies as well as for her own troops; and agricultural products and manufactured foods were used to supply the hundreds of thousands of Allied troops that steamed round the Cape to the East and to Egypt. The Cape route served a highly important strategic purpose, and there must be many a Briton, or American, or Australian, or New Zealander, or Indian, who recalls the hospitality he received at Cape Town and Durban. Women played an important part, both in the services and by releasing men from industry and the professions in order to fight. Finally, 45,000 Cape Coloured and 80,000 Africans served wherever South African forces were to be found—as transport drivers, stretcher-bearers, hospital orderlies, gunners, batmen, and as sailors in the 'little ships'; and they earned high praise and many medals for devotion to duty, for courage under fire, and for gallantry. Many of them were wounded and taken prisoner, and 2,500 gave their lives for their country.

Smuts represented South Africa at the San Fransisco Conference and was one of the few people there who had also been present at Versailles at the end of the First World War. Three years later his party was narrowly defeated by a combination of the Nationalist and Afrikaner parties in the general election of 1948. His defeat, and his death two years later, mark the end of one phase of more than fifty years of South African history and the beginning of another and even more turbulent period.

The coming to power of a coalition of the Nationalist and Afrikaner parties in 1948, strengthened by their merging under the title of Nationalist Party[15] in 1951, meant that for the first time since Union a purely Afrikaans-speaking party was in power. Afrikaners had had independent republics for fifty years before the end of the Boer War, and it took another fifty years before they regained at the polling-booth what the Boers had lost on the battlefield. They had lost two economically and politically

---

[13] The story of the fall of Tobruk has been told in *Crisis in the Desert*, one volume of the official war history of the Union. Two further volumes in the uncompleted official war history are *The Sidi Rezeg Battles, 1941* and *The War in the Southern Oceans*.

[14] It is an interesting commentary on South African history to note that when, in 1955, the Grey College at Bloemfontein celebrated the centenary of its foundation by Sir George Grey—a British governor when Bloemfontein was the capital of the Orange Free State Republic—a memorial was unveiled to past pupils who had lost their lives in three wars— the Boer War, when they fought against Britain, and two world wars, when they fought with Britain against Germany.

[15] The Afrikaans title is *Die Nasionale Party* and the translation habitually used by that party is 'The National Party'. This is inaccurate. When the word 'National' is used in conjunction with words such as 'Government' or 'Party' the connotation in English usage is that the party or government represents all the population or political groups in the country. This is patently not the case with *Die Nasionale Party* and it is misleading to call it The National Party.

weak republics and they had gained the Union of South Africa. This was a notable achievement of political power by the Nationalists, marred only by the knowledge that their party did not yet have the support of the majority of voters and that it was the vagaries of the South African electoral system that had given them victory; moreover, they knew that about one-quarter of Afrikans-speaking South Africans had voted against their party. Nevertheless, Afrikaner nationalism was in effective political control of government; and subsequent elections were to increase their parliamentary majority.

On 20 January 1960 Dr. Verwoerd announced in parliament that there would be a referendum of all white voters on whether South Africa should become a republic. Two weeks later, on 3 February, the British Prime Minister, Mr. Harold Macmillan, made his famous 'winds of change' speech to both houses of the Union Parliament. By this speech Mr. Macmillan was widely interpreted as having served notice to South Africa that her racial policies were not acceptable to the West, and that if the West had to choose between the friendship of two hundred million blacks and four million whites, there would be no question of how Britain would choose. The Nationalist Party Press drew the conclusion that the whites could no longer depend on British sympathy and should unite to defend their right to a separate and independent existence. The opposition Press and the non-white leaders made a different inference: that South Africa should modify her racial policies, though the various opposition parties differed markedly on what the extent of such modification should be.

As if to give point to Mr. Macmillan's speech, the first half of 1960 witnessed race disturbances on a scale not previously known in South Africa. In East Pondoland, tribesmen revolted against the rule of chiefs and headmen nominated by the government under the Bantu Authorities Act. The revolt took the form of hut-burning, the murder of those who collaborated with the authorities, and boycotting of stores owned by whites; and it required strongly armed police and military detachments to restore an uneasy peace. During March and April the event known to the world by the name of Sharpeville took place. In most of the large urban centres Africans, led by the Pan African Congress, demonstrated against the pass laws by handing in their reference books (the new name for passes) to the nearest police station and asking to be arrested. The police were clearly unable to comply with this request and made the mistake of arresting a few of the leaders only, thus angering the crowds who demanded their release. In a number of towns the police were unable, and indeed lacked the authority and the experience, to deal with large but non-violent demonstrations. There is evidence that at both Langa and Sharpeville the crowds that gathered did so expecting to be addressed by someone in authority. At Langa they were given three minutes to disperse before a baton charge was ordered; at Sharpeville the police opened fire, and subsequent judicial inquiry established that it had been unnecessary to do so but was unable to discover who had given the order that resulted in the death of 69 Africans.

The African National Congress, which had held aloof from the demonstrations, now called for a day of mourning to be observed on 28 March. Hundreds of thousands of Africans stayed away from work and in many centres industry came to a temporary standstill. Two days later the government proclaimed a state of emergency which enabled it to mobilize the armed forces, to ban all public meetings, to arrest people without bringing them to trial, and to make it an offence to publish the names of those arrested. In pre-dawn raids over 1,800 non-white and close to 100 white persons were detained, and the number subsequently rose to close on 20,000. These arrests provoked further demonstrations, and in Cape Town a crowd of about 30,000 Africans marched to the centre of the city to demand the release of their leaders. The march was led by a young African student, Mr. Philip Kgosana, and all eye-witness accounts agree that it was a peaceful and unarmed procession, completely under control. To the authorities, and to many whites, it was an alarming sight and seemed to constitute a threat. The Deputy Commissioner of Police parleyed with Mr. Kgosana, who undertook to disperse the crowd if he was granted an interview with the Minister of Justice. The evidence on what precisely took place is conflicting, but Mr. Kgosana told the crowd to go home quietly, which it did. The Minister refused to see him but instructed the Secretary for Justice to inverview a deputation; and when Mr. Kgosana arrived for the interview he was detained under the emergency regulations. Once the crowd had reached their homes, military and police cordons were thrown round the African townships. On 8 April the government banned the African National Congress and the Pan African Congress as unlawful organizations.[16]

The events just described came as a shock to the white population of South Africa, and the effects of this are mentioned in subsequent chapters. It should be noted here, however, that there was a great deal of public anger against a system of administration that had provoked such demonstrations and at the way in which the situation, once it had arisen, was handled. There was, too, much practical sympathy for those Africans who had suffered: the Black Sash, the Liberal Party, the Coloured People's Organization, the Moslem community, and Red Cross collected food and money to relieve distress, and the Black Sash organized a transport system

---

[16] The leader of the P.A.C., Mr. Robert Sobukwe, was found guilty of incitement to break the pass laws and sentenced to three years imprisonment. Before his sentence had expired parliament passed an amendment to the General Law which enabled it to decide annually to continue the detention of someone who had served a sentence for a political crime. Since 1963 Mr. Sobukwe has six times been sentenced by resolution of parliament without being charged or tried, solely at the request of the Minister of Justice.

for wives to visit husbands who had been detained. In parliament the opposition parties, and more particularly the Progressive Party, took every opportunity to expose facts and to make the country aware of the true nature of the situation.

The five years after 1961 were marked by violence and by attempts at sabotage by disrupting public communications. For the most part these were amateurish and unco-ordinated though they were, of course, potentially dangerous to life and public order. Non-white organizations, declared unlawful and whose leaders were in gaol, went underground to reappear under such names as Poqo (which means 'only' or 'pure') and the African Resistance Movement. In 1962 serious riots took place at Paarl when African and Coloured men marched on the town, destroyed a few shops and houses by fire, and murdered two white people. Five non-whites were shot in the riot. A one-man judicial enquiry found that the riots were instigated by Poqo, but it seems likely that living conditions in the Paarl locations were an important factor.

The best-known of these underground movements was the Spear of the Nation whose secret headquarters at Rivonia, near Johannesburg, were raided by the police in 1963 uncovering plans for extensive sabotage, guerrilla warfare, and ultimate revolution. In 1964 John Harris, a schoolmaster and a banned person, left a bomb to explode on the Johannesburg railway station. An elderly woman was killed and a number of people were injured, and Harris was sentenced to death. In 1966 Mr. Abram Fischer, a well-known Johannesburg Q.C. who had defended many of those accused of so-called political crimes, was found guilty on a number of charges, including sabotage and furthering the aims of communism, and sentenced to life imprisonment. Altogether, by the end of 1966 some 3,500 Africans, 130 whites, 90 Asians, and 75 Coloured had been arrested on charges of sabotage or belonging to an unlawful organization. More than one-third were released without trial and one-fifth were found not guilty. Most of those found guilty were heavily punished, but a few managed to escape by fleeing the country. The legal defence of practically all the accused was undertaken by a voluntary organization known as Defence and Aid. This body was declared to be an unlawful organization by the Minister of Justice in 1966.

The emergency in 1960 of necessity postponed the referendum on the republic and this was eventually held on 5 October. The white voters were asked the straightforward question whether or not they were in favour of a republic. A majority of about 74,000 some 4 per cent of the white electorate, voted in favour of it, and in April 1961 the South Africa Act was amended by parliament to substitute a president for the crown as head of the state. At the conference of Commonwealth prime ministers, held in London in March 1961, Dr. Verwoerd had formally applied for continued membership of the Commonwealth despite South Africa's decision to become a republic. The conference used the occasion for a full discussion of South Africa's treatment of her non-white citizens, and though accounts of what actually happened differ, Dr. Verwoerd eventually withdrew the application. The result was that, on 31 May 1961, the Republic of South Africa came into being and South Africa ceased to be a member of the Commonwealth. The constitutional ties that had existed between Britain and South Africa since 1806 were broken.

The purpose of this book is not to present a history of South Africa but to examinte contemporary conditions and policies and to introduce only such historical background as seems necessary for that purpose. The two decades after 1948 are full of incident and some of the stirring events are described in later chapters where they more rightly belong. This historical introduction may well be concluded by noting some of the main threads that run through the period.

The prime objective of Afrikaner nationalism after 1948 was to consolidate the hold on political power that it had at last won by the general election of that year. The Nationalist Party in 1948 represented a minority of enfranchised South Africans who were themselves only a small minority of the total population. The government was, thus, narrowly based and the short-term threat to its power lay in the more broadly-based white opposition parties together with the small number of white parliamentary representatives of African and Coloured voters. The Nationalist Party dealt with this threat by depriving Africans and Coloured of representation and persuading ever-increasing majorities of white voters that it was the only party that could be depended on to 'safeguard white interests'.

Non-white South Africans could clearly not be expected to acquiesce in policies that gave a monopoly of political control to the whites. Herein lay the long-term threat to the political power of Afrikaner nationalism. Tight police control and suppression of non-white political organizations could contain such a threat for a limited time only, but in the long run more positive policies would be called for.

These two forces, and the opposing forces they evoked, make a recognizable pattern: the determined efforts of Afrikaner nationalism to consolidate its power and the struggle of its opponents to bring about a broader South Africanism; and, in the second place, the efforts of the majority of white South Africans to retain political control and the growth of extra-parliamentary non-white opposition, supported by a minority of whites, to bring about a greater spread of political power. Subsequent chapters will show that most of what happened in South Africa after 1948 fits into this pattern.

2

THE PEOPLE

THE expression 'a house divided against itself' is more applicable to South Africa than it is to any other country. Disraeli's 'two nations' become, in South Africa, at least five; and these are rent by subdivision and internal dissension. The history of South Africa is the story of strife between the various groups composing the political union. There is no single instance where the population of South Africa was united during a great crisis. Until 1910, when Union was established, the story is one of war between tribe and tribe, between black and white, and between English and Afrikaner. Political union brought the warring tribes, white and black, under one central government; but in all international crises between 1910 and 1961 the country was sorely divided against itself. There were, it is true, notable examples of co-operation between groups or individuals of the different 'nations'; but there was no national front, no co-operation on a national scale. Economically, everything that was achieved in agriculture, in mining, in transport, and in industry was the result of European skill, capital, and organization combined with non-European labour. The different 'nations' combined to that extent, but, politically and socially, the divisions remained as obstacles to the real union that was hopefully implied in the original title: Union of South Africa. In 1961 the title was changed to the Republic of South Africa, and it was confidently predicted that this would unify the white population. It is arguable that it has done that to some small extent; but in terms of total population South Africa is more divided than ever.

In a final chapter the whole question of what prospects there may be for a resolution of these differences and for the development of a genuine union will be discussed. It is a question of importance to Africa and to the world, no less than to South Africa. But before we can consider the question we must know more of the different nations that constitute the population of South Africa. We must consider the separate factors that make up the final equation.

A variety of different headings may be used to describe the people of a country such as Britain. They may be described as 'rural' and 'urban', or as 'industrial' and 'agricultural', or according to geographical regions. Though the word is no longer fashionable the population could be divided into upper, middle, and lower 'classes'. When you have described the people of Britain under these or any other convenient subheadings you have not denied the essential unity of the people as British. What social differences and distinctions there may be in the way of language, of customs, of amusements are picturesque survivals rather than essential differences.

In South Africa the situation is different. You may indeed describe the population according to regions, or classes, or occupations; but it would be unrealistic not to subdivide these divisions into European, African, Coloured, and Asian. In the sense that all who live in Durban enjoy the same climate, are subject to the same physical wants, and would show similar physical and psychological reactions to aerial bombing or to the plague—in that sense you may speak of the 'people of Durban'. But to regard this as an expression of common citizenship is misleading. It may be argued that what matters is not the differences between human beings but the essential similarities. To ignore these differences in an account of South Africa would be to describe things as no doubt they should be, but not as they in fact are.

THE AFRICAN

Africans are to be met with everywhere in South Africa. There is no farm or factory or town where they cannot be found. Where building and road-making are in progress, where European-owned shops and offices are run, where ships are being loaded and unloaded, there the African will be. The traveller by train will see Africans at every station and siding; the traveller by road will, from time to time, pass an African who is walking to a town or city hundreds of miles away. And when the traveller stays at an hotel for the night he will probably find Africans waiting on him at table and waking him with an early-morning cup of tea.

The Africans of South Africa form part of a group of about seventy million people who live in the southern half of Africa and speak one of about 200 related Bantu languages or dialects. They and the inhabitants of Lesotho, Swaziland, and Botswana are called the southern Bantu, as distinct from the western group who live in French Equatorial Africa, the Cameroons, the Congo, and Angola, and from the eastern group who inhabit the regions round the great lakes of the Rift Valley.

To generalize about 'the African' is of as doubtful value as it is to generalize about 'the mysterious East' or 'the Englishman' or the inhabitants of the United States of America. Africans are individuals, each with his or her own personality, likes and dislikes, moods and hopes and fears, reacting in various ways to external circumstances, social life, and other individuals. In general they are, possibly, more conservative than Europeans, because they are more closely bound by convention and tribal tradition; but any theory or policy that acts on the false assumption that Africans are a mass rather than a group of individuals would be wrong. They have dark skins, varying from black to light brown; it is conventional to call them 'black', and about as accurate as calling Europeans 'white'. Although not Negroes, they have Negroid features, such as thick lips, flat noses, and short, black, frizzy hair. This latter characteristic is general, while other features vary considerably from tribe to tribe and from person to person, depending partly on the amount of Hamitic blood that is present.

Africans who live in or near white towns wear European clothes, in all stages of respectability or raggedness. In African Reserves or in white villages near Reserves they still frequently, though not by any means invariably, wear a blanket as a general cloak over a pair of trousers or a short skirt. African women in the Reserves dress picturesquely in brightly coloured blankets and beads, with a gay *doek* (scarf) wound round their heads. The blankets and scarves are of European manufacture, the former made specially for the African market. But European dress is rapidly ousting any other.

There are in the Republic some hundreds of African tribes divided into four main language groups. The Xhosa, Zulu, and Swazi belong to the Nguni group; the northern and southern Sotho, the Tswana-speaking tribes of Botswana, and various tribes of the western Transvaal belong to the Sotho group; the Venda and Tsonga are two smaller separate groups. About half a million Africans have not yet been officially classified.

The Xhosa and the Zulu have different languages, but they can understand each other without much difficulty. It would require study and practice, however, for members of one language group to understand those of another. When educated Africans from different parts of the country meet in conference they most often speak English, and they use English in their professional or political contacts with whites. At the domestic service and master-servant level their medium is usually English or Afrikaans, depending on the home language of the employer; sometimes, as is the case on many farms, it may be a Bantu language, and sometimes it is a hybrid called 'kitchen kaffir'. A more or less regularized version of this, called 'Fanakolo', is used as the lingua franca on the gold-mines, where many languages from southern (not only South) Africa are represented. It serves a useful purpose, but is deplored by educated Africans.

There are parts where the use of a Bantu language by whites is fairly common. Traders in the Transkei and in Zululand, and people who grow up on farms and villages bordering on Lesotho or a Reserve, learn the language of their vicinity through early contact with African servants. In Natal particularly there seems to be a tradition that farmers learn to speak Zulu. During the last war it was said that when that renowned regiment, the Natal Carbineers, really became excited its officers and men lapsed into Zulu, and when their signallers suspected enemy interception they used a Zulu code.

Prior to European penetration into southern Africa no Bantu language had a written alphabet. That there is a growing literature in all the major languages is due primarily to the missionaries who reduced the languages to writing. It is due also to African and European scholars and authors, chiefly at the universities, who have produced grammars and dictionaries and have encouraged the publication of translated and of original work. After the passing of the Bantu Education Act of 1953 the Department of Bantu Education laid great stress on the use of the mother tongue in African schools and set about creating Bantu terminologies in all subjects.

Education for Africans is neither compulsory nor free, and even official estimates differ about the number of children of a school-going age who do not attend school. It is probable that between 20 and 25 per cent receive no schooling and grow up illiterate. Of those who do go to school the large majority leave before or immediately after standard II (about the age of 10) and an unknown number of those have so little hold on literacy that they become lapsed literates. They and the illiterates may later acquire literacy in towns where their friends or interested whites organize adult classes.[1] The extent of illiteracy and the number of Africans who are ignorant of both official languages of the Republic are matters of guess work. In 1959 Dr. Eiselen, then Secretary for Bantu Administration and Development, said that the number of African literates had risen to 35 per cent of the population.[2] By 1968 it was probably 50 per cent.

Literacy, whether in a Bantu or a European language, is about twice as high in urban as it is in rural areas. With the great mobility of African labour it is probable that about half the African adult population is able to understand spoken English or Afrikaans, or both, often at a very elementary level. It is evident that the use of Afrikaans is increasing, and there are strong economic reasons for learning English and Afrikaans. The Bantu languages are those of a tribal peasant culture, flexible and rich in homely idiom and vocabulary. But if Africans are to learn the industrial and scientific and commercial arts of the European it seems probable that they will, for the foreseeable future, do so through the medium of English or Afrikaans.

The fact that two-thirds of the population of the Republic have a Bantu language as their mother tongue is one of those things that make it unreal, for the present at any rate to speak about 'the people of the Republic' in the way one would about a country with a homogenous population. It is also one of the things that makes administration difficult and complicates social and industrial life. Political and administrative power rests with the white group; it is the whites who are the employers and control

---

[1] Night Schools Associations in Cape Town and elsewhere, run by white volunteers, operated under an annual permit until 1967 when it was refused and the schools had to close down. The existence of the schools—white teachers and adult non-white pupils—was contrary to government policy.

[2] See *Optima*, March 1959.

the economy. Many white officials who have to deal almost exclusively with Africans are proficient in a Bantu language and in some government departments officials are paid a bonus if they are able to speak one; but it would be a counsel of perfection to suggest that, since Europeans rule Africans, they should know the language of those they aspire to govern. That would be reasonable in an African colony where the only whites are officials and missionaries. In South Africa, however, apart from a comparatively small body of officials, contact between white and black is limited and intermittent, and there is neither the moral nor the economic urge to acquire a Bantu language. This has many disadvantages, and misunderstanding, hardship, and injustice too often result from ignorance on both sides. Nor is it merely a matter of linguistics. Closely associated with speech are gestures, customs, and manners. A turn of speech demanded by good manners in one language may be akin to an insult in another. A courteous gesture by a European may well offend against an African custom. These things, however superficial they may be, illustrate the reality of the barriers between Africans and the rest of the population of South Africa.

Native Reserves

The Bureau of Statistics estimated that the total population of South Africa in 1967 was 18,733,000 of whom 12,750,000 were Africans, grouped, as we have seen, not in one but in many tribes and with no one common Bantu language, about one-third of them living in tribal Reserves—that is, in land set aside by parliament where Africans only may occupy or own land. These Reserves, it should be realized, are for the most part the shrunken remnant of land once owned by the different tribes, but conquered by the white man during the nineteenth century wars. The rest of the African population is to be found in the towns and on European-owned farms outside the Reserves, the vast majority of them in the employ of whites.

It would be a mistake, however, to regard the population of the Reserves and the African population outside the Reserves as in any way static. There may be Africans who have never left their Reserves, and there are many Africans living in towns who have never seen a Reserve. But there is a constant coming and going between the Reserves and the European areas, and this is in spite of legal restrictions on freedom of movement. Among many tribes a young man is not regarded as properly grown up unless he has had a spell at the mines or in a white town, preferably in a large city. This is not merely a matter of social convention or of curiosity to 'see the world'. The economy of the Reserves is largely a simple agricultural subsistence economy that cannot supply the cash or food that the people in them need, so that the African must take work in European areas in order to earn money. On the other hand, the white man cannot run his economy without African labour, and a constant flow takes place between the Reserves and the white areas.

There is a tendency for people unacquainted with South African conditions to think of the Reserves as places where Africans have plenty of room and can live the simple life at their own unhurried pace, tilling the soil and watching their cattle grow fat; places where African culture and tradition can develop uncontaminated by European influences; and, above all, places to which an African can retire after having worked in white areas, a haven of rest for the aged and weary. The reality is different.

The Reserves are, in part, those areas in which African tribes were living when they were originally conquered by the whites. After each conquest boundaries were fixed by the conqueror, who thenceforth occupied some of the land previously owned by the tribes. In this way the amount of land available for tribal use shrank after each of the innumerable wars between white settlers and African tribes. But peace and European medicine tended to increase the African population, so that pressure on land became ever greater. It was a process by no means confined to South Africa. It has taken place wherever in Africa there was any considerable European settlement. What chiefly distinguishes South Africa from the Rhodesias and East Africa is that, in the Republic, there are many more whites in proportion to the total population than there are elsewhere.

By the time that Union was established it had long been traditional among Europeans in South Africa to regard territorial segregation of white and African as a 'natural' policy. That is to say, it was generally accepted that there should be areas where Africans might own land, individually or tribally, and other areas where they might live and work, but might not own land. In 1913 parliament regularized this territorial segregation by the Land Act, which demarcated the then existing tribal areas and made provision for the purchase by government of additional land. But white public opinion was opposed to the purchase of more land for Africans, and various commissions attempted in vain to demarcate further areas. Eventually in 1936, parliament passed the Native Trust and Land Act which provided for the purchase by the Native Trust Fund of a maximum of 7,250,000 morgen[3] of land additional, and if possible adjacent, to the then existing Reserves. Between 1936 and 1967, 5,708,497 morgen were purchased under the Act, bringing the total area of the Reserves to just over 18,500,000 morgen. When the full amount of land has been bought the Reserves will occupy about 65,000 square miles, 13·7 per cent of the total area of the Republic. In the remaining 86·3 per cent Africans are not entitled to own land.[2]

The overwhelming majority of Africans in the Reserves depends on

---

[3] The morgen is a South African measure of area and is equal to 2¼ acres.
[4] Figures given by Mr. G. F. van L. Froneman, M.P., in a paper read at Stellenbosch on 7 October 1967.

some form of agriculture for a living. As a living it is primitive and poor. About 94 per cent live on communally held land, the remaining 6 per cent on individual holdings, chiefly in the Transkei and the Ciskei. The chief usually allocates land for cultivation, and grazing-land is common. There is little fencing; the soil is scratched rather than ploughed; only poor seed can be afforded, and there is an almost complete absence of proper methods of preparing the soil.

There are other factors that account for the low productivity of the Reserves. A very considerable one is that at any one time as many as 50–60 per cent of adult males may be absent, working in white areas. In addition, overstocking is ruining the land and is extremely difficult to combat. Africans are traditionally a cattle people who regard quantity as more important than quality, and in pre-European days there was plenty of land for the cattle population. They have always regarded cattle in a socio-religious light: they are the visible signs of tribal and individual wealth and importance, and they are slaughtered for ceremonial purposes, at deaths or weddings, or for fertility rites. Most important of all, they are used as *lobolo*—that is, as the customary gift to the bride's parents in the African marriage dowry system. There is thus a strong inclination to increase the cattle population and to resist all well-meant attempts by government to improve strains. The result is overstocking which has reduced some parts of the Reserves to semi-desert conditions.

Here and there in the Reserves there are small signs that government attempts to improve standards of agriculture are bearing fruit. Agricultural schools operate, and trained demonstrators fight an uphill battle against conservatism and superstition. Too often the agriculture school is an oasis of sound agricultural practice waging a desperate war against the encroaching desert of bad agriculture and overstocking. On the whole the Reserves are poverty-stricken areas, incapable of standing up to the periodic draughts and floods of South Africa, and unable to support the existing population. They are, in fact, vast rural slums whose chief export is their manpower, which goes to the mines and factories and farms to earn enough money to pay taxes and to support the families in the Reserves. This is ironic, since it has long been the custom in South Africa to regard low wages for Africans as justified on the grounds that the African has one foot in the Reserves and that his labour in white areas is really only a part-time occupation. That was, probably, the case in the late nineteenth century. It is no longer the case.

In the Reserves tribal loyalty is still strong. A man prides himself on being a Zulu, a Fingo, or a Xhosa, and tends to look down on other tribes. Tribal fights still take place in the Reserves and on the mines, where tribes are usually separately housed. With tribal loyalty go the conceptions of chieftainship and tribal customs, such as initiation ceremonies and *lobolo*. These retain a powerful hold over African imagination even where contact with the disruptive forces of Western civilization has been closest; but there is little doubt that such contact has weakened tribalism generally and that loyalty to chiefs and observance of tribal customs are gradually giving way to loyalties and customs with a stronger survival value.

This decay of tribalism is regretted by many Europeans and Africans, and there are Europeans who hold that every effort should be made to restore tribalism and tribal life. Seeing the devastating effects on the fabric of African social life of the clash between European and African cultures, they regard a return to tribalism as the only safe cure. The normal discipline and sanctions of tribal life tend to disappear under the impact of European civilization, and for a great many Africans nothing has yet adequately taken the place of those sanctions. But contact with a more advanced civilization has doomed tribalism.

The idea of setting aside separate areas for white and black occupation is common to the whole of southern Africa. Until independence it was to be found in Zambia, East Africa, Malawi, and Botswana, as well as in South Africa; and it is still the practice in Rhodesia. It is a policy that is employed both nationally and locally; that is, there are national Reserves, and in urban areas there are African and white townships side by side. The historical reasons for national Reserves are probably different from those to which separate urban townships owe their existence. Social habits, different standards of living, and the general disinclination of both races to mix socially are enough to explain the separate townships, though they do not explain the vast differences in social amenities that exist in those townships.

National Reserves for African tribes are, historically, the product of administrative convenience and the liberalism usually associated with the missionaries. For many years after the first clashes between white settlers and African tribes the policy of the whites was to establish a clear boundary between their country and that of the tribe involved. Each war was succeeded by a boundary settlement. Towards the middle of the nineteenth century, however, European policy changed to one of annexation. It is true to say that, with a few minor exceptions, this change was not dictated by a desire to annex land for white occupation. The new policy was instituted in despair of being able to maintain peace by any other means. Sir Harry Smith, Governor of the Cape, originated it in South Africa. The British Colonial Office, strongly under the influence of missionary opinion, would not agree to annexation purely for white occupation. Hence, though white magistrates and police were sent into the annexed territories to rule, the land itself was reserved for African occupation. Traders and missionaries only were allowed in and the white administration confined iself to maintaining peace and to giving general support to the missionaries in their civilizing efforts.

Had South Africa remained an agricultural community, largely and sparsely inhabited by cattle farmers, this policy of reserves for black and white might have provided a reasonable solution to many interracial problems. The earliest missionaries, most notably Dr. Philip in the 1830's, saw clearly that the Africans were not yet able to compete against the superior weapons and organization of Western civilization. They advocated territorial segregation in the interests of the African. It was a valid policy at the time and, in the circumstances, a policy dictated by humanitarian beliefs, as they considered that while in the sight of God Africans and Europeans were equal, in all other respects Africans were the weaker and required protection.

When the times and the circumstances changed—that is, when the discovery of diamonds and gold shattered the subsistence economy of South Africa by setting her firmly on the path of industrialization—the policy of territorial segregation began to lose much of its original validity. So far from wanting Africans to stay in their Reserves, European governments in South Africa urged them to come into the white areas to work. In the Cape Colony Cecil Rhodes introduced a money tax on Africans in the Reserves to force them to seek cash wages.

When the gold-mines needed African labour they set up agencies in all African areas to recruit it. Two world wars hastened this industrial revolution. The growth of secondary industries increased the demand for labour and for agricultural produce; and the sub-division of the large farms of the nineteenth century increased the demand for agricultural labour. The result is that agriculture, mines, and industries all clamour for African labour. Elaborate machinery exists for recruiting it, and farmers complain that their labour is 'stolen' either by the more attractive terms offered by industry or by other farmers, from distant districts, who come by lorry at night to entice their African workers away. With all these demands for African labour, more than half the African population no longer have any but the most tenuous connexion with Reserves. They have become permanently alienated from their old tribal lands, and if they did want to return to their original Reserve there would be no room for them in those agriculturally overcrowded slums.

While, therefore, the original intention behind the establishment of the Reserves was sound enough, much of the reason for their existence has disappeared. The conditions that made the system workable have altered, namely a comparatively small agricultural population, plenty of grazing-land, and a subsistence economy. Population of man and beast has increased while grazing-land has not increased proportionately; and industrialization and a money economy have supervened.

The conception of Native Reserves has a tenacious hold on South African thinking. There is a persistent cry from many Africans for more land to be added to the Reserves. Europeans from the major political parties are practically unanimous is accepting the Reserves as part of the natural order of things. For decades there has been talk of 'rehabilitating the Reserves'. The Tomlinson Commission[5] reported in 1954 that land in the Reserves was deteriorating at an alarming rate and that it would cost—at that date—R70,000,000 to stabilize it, that is, to prevent further deterioration; after stabilization would come the even more costly process of rehabilitation. The Commission added that large areas would become irredeemable if not stabilized within ten years. While governments, past and present, have spent money on soil conservation in the Reserves, not one-quarter of the amount required has been available, and by 1957 only one-seventh of the land had been stabilized. Ten years later stabilization was far from keeping pace with deterioration, and it is against this background that policies affecting the Reserves must be examined.

The Nationalist Party regards the Reserves as the 'national home' of the African within which he can develop self-government and may occupy any position or practice any profession of which he is capable; outside the Reserves Africans are temporary workers, migrants, and have no political rights. Such, in broad outline, is the policy of the Nationalist Party, and the most important question in South Africa is whether such a policy can succeed.

The Tomlinson Commission Report may be regarded as the blueprint of this policy. After a thorough investigation the Commission made recommendations which, if implemented, would by the end of the twentieth century enable the Reserves to carry a population of 14,000,000 Africans out of a total estimated population of 21,000,000. The Commission drew a rough plan showing seven proposed African territories, and it is significant that the plan included the then High Commission Territories which were administered by the United Kingdom and have since become independent states. The recommendations aimed at producing economically viable areas in which agriculture and industry would be properly integrated. The Report postulated extensive soil-conservation schemes, the establishment of industries within the Reserves, and the expenditure over a period of ten years of more than R200,000,000. Finally, the Commission maintained that a modern industrial economy was not compatible with tribalism and rule by chiefs, that a revision of land tenure to provide for private ownership of land was essential, and that 'white' capital and enterprise were necessary for carrying out the proposals.

The Tomlinson Report created an immense stir in South Africa. Statements were issued, pamphlets were printed, and conferences were summoned. The largest conference, representing practically every aspect

---

[5] The full name of this important commission is the Commission for the Socio-Economic Development of the Bantu Areas within the Union of South Africa, under the chairmanship of Professor F. R. Tomlinson. The Commission was appointed in 1951 and reported in 1954. The full report is voluminous and a summary only was published.

of Afrikaner thought, was enthusiastically in favour of the implementation of the Report. Here, it was felt, was the answer to those who had maintained that apartheid was purely negative and designed to prevent the African from progressing. Here was a positive plan, recommended by experts who favoured apartheid. True, it would cost a good deal of money, but the white population must be called upon to make the necessary sacrifices so that a just settlement of the vexed racial problem could be achieved.

There were other voices. Industrialists and farmers were fearful of their labour supply and their markets. Might not industries inside the Reserves, where labour was cheap, prove unbeatable competitors? Economists pointed out that the Reserves are fragmented, that their water supply is inadequate, their equipment of mechanical transport meagre, and their distance from the required raw materials for industry considerable. In fact, all they have is a labour supply, and to make good the deficiencies would require much more than the R200,000,000 suggested, capital which could in any case be more fruitfully employed elsewhere.

The greatest blow to the enthusiasm generated by the Tomlinson recommendations came from an unexpected source. Dr. H. F. Verwoerd, then Minister of Native Affairs, issued a White Paper which revealed considerable disagreement with the main postulates of the Report. The amount of money the taxpayer would be called upon to supply, he said, had been exaggerated and it was possible to carry out all the recommendations on about one-quarter of that amount. Moreover, 'white' capital' would not be allowed inside the Reserves but only on the peripheries, and the industries set up there would draw their labour from within the Reserves. Further, though the Commission might regard tribalism as incompatible with a modern economy, it was the government's firm intention to revive and strengthen tribalism, to bolster the power of the chiefs, and not to allow private ownership of land in the Reserves. Finally, the White Paper rejected the Commission's recommendation that, in order to consolidate the Reserves, more land should be purchased than the $7\frac{1}{4}$ million morgen still to be acquired under the 1936 Act.

The White Paper knocked away the props that had supported the Tomlinson recommendations, though this fact was either unnoticed or ignored by many of those who wished to continue regarding the Reserves as a national home for Africans. At the beginning of 1959 Dr. Verwoerd, by then Prime Minister, made a significant speech in parliament which gave fresh impetus to the policy of the Nationalist Party. In what the Nationalist Press acclaimed as a 'new vision' of positive apartheid, the Prime Minister envisaged eight separate Bantu states, which he compared to colonies, and suggested that they would be given progressive self-government, leading to ultimate independence, with the possibility of an eventual commonwealth of white and black states. To this end his government proposed to press on with the policy of creating Bantu authorities that could assume increasing powers, of buying land to the limit of the 1936 Act, and of encouraging African enterprise. In this speech, as in the White Paper, the Prime Minister failed to come to grips with economic realities, and he and his new Minister of Bantu Administration and Development, Mr. M. D. de Wet Nel, subsequently stressed the importance of reviving that tribalism which the Tomlinson Report held to be incompatible with a modern economy.

Since its enunciation in 1959 the Nationalist Party has officially adhered to the policy of Bantu homelands that are to be ripened for self-government. Indeed, the theory has been developed and refined, and some progress has been made in consolidating the scattered and fragmented Reserves by further purchase of land under the 1936 Act. Moreover, there has been a significant though cautious departure from the policy of the White Paper on the Tomlinson Report—that no 'white' capital would be admitted into the Reserves and that there would be no departure from tribalism. In August 1967 it was announced that a group of industrialists was to visit some of the Reserves to investigate the possibility of investing money there. It was however stressed that such investment would have to be through the Bantu Development Corporation (a government body) and not simply on individual choice.

That practice has lagged behind theory, however, became clear in October 1967 when the South African Bureau of Racial Affairs (SABRA)[6] devoted its annual conference to a discussion of the consolidation of Bantu homelands. The leading intellectuals of SABRA argued strongly that scattered and fragmented Reserves could never be regarded as an adequate basis for an independent homeland, and they urged that more land than that contemplated under the 1936 Act should be bought. The government reply, through the Deputy Minister of Bantu Development, was that no additional land would be bought and that, in any case, there was no money available at that time for such a purpose. The Deputy Minister was being realistic. Taxation to enable the government to buy more land for Africans would not be popular with the white electorate. Furthermore, in regard to industrial development of the Reserves, the Tomlinson Commission had estimated that, by about 1980, the Reserves could hold 9 million people provided that 20,000 new industrial jobs were created during each of the preceding twenty or thirty years. By 1968, 40,000 jobs had been created, leaving a shortfall of 94,000 jobs. It should be noted, moreover, that these were in border industries and not, as the Commission had recommended, inside the Reserves.

The idea of border industries derives from two theories. In the late twenties the theory that industry should be decentralized was popular among Nationalists because it would give economic stimulus to less

[6] See pp. 185–6 for an account of this body.

densely populated areas and, in doing so, would reduce the political influence of large anti-nationalist urban areas in favour of rural areas where Nationalist political strength lay. More recently this theory was combined with the hope that the recommendations of the Tomlinson Commission for industrializing the Reserves could be by-passed by establishing industries on their borders. Since the location of industry depends on economic rather than on political factors, the border industry policy has in practice meant encouraging new industries in those areas where a Reserve happens to border on an established industrial centre such as Durban, East London, or Pretoria. Valuable as the new industries are, they are not what the Tomlinson Commission recommended, namely, industries within the Reserves that would help to give the future Bantustans a viable economy. Border industries cannot be owned by Africans because they are outside the Reserves where, alone, Africans may own land.

The practical administration of the Reserves will be described in chapter 5. Meanwhile it may be noted that whatever the theories may be, the fact is that the Reserves no longer are what they were originally intended to be. They have become, in actual practice, reservoirs of labour for the rest of South Africa. Their existence enables people to argue that 'the Natives have their own lands where they can develop at their own pace', and to regard it as reasonable that, in white areas, they need have no political representation or civil rights. For years the existence of the Reserves has made it possible for governments and local authorities to think of urban housing for Africans as something temporary in which it would be unwise to invest too much capital, and which may be fully provided for by the creation of 'bachelor barracks'. Finally, the existence of the Reserves has enabled governments to throw most of the financial burden of developing a backward area on the Africans themselves, although African poverty is such that African taxation cannot hope to keep pace with deterioration in the Reserves.

Nor can the old argument that the Reserves afford a refuge for the African and a protection against competition with the better-equipped European hold water against the economic facts. Africans are an integral part of South Africa. Whether they live in a Reserve or in a white area their livelihood depends on the economy of South Africa, not on the economy of the Reserves. The economy of the Reserves, in short, cannot be isolated, as the conception of tribal lands cannot be reconciled with a modern industrial economy; and tribalism received its death-blow with industrialization. If the Reserves were to perform their earlier function of cushioning the impact of Western civilization on a primitive subsistence economy, there would be some excuse for them. As it is, they fail to protect the African, they ensure that large areas of potentially valuable land shall be badly farmed, and they act as a will-o'-the-wisp to all shades of political thinking. On the other hand, the African has proved to be a good industrial worker, while he has not, except under white management, proved to be anything but an indifferent farmer. So far from needing protection, therefore, his value to his country and to himself is far greater as an industrial worker than it is as a so-called independent agriculturist.

A progressive and rationally conducted abolition of Reserves—a process of de-reservation—would do much to improve the economy of the country; it would clear the political air of much cloudy thinking; and it would benefit the African. Such a process of national slum clearance would cost a great deal of money; but it would be money better spent than that spent on purchasing more land to be wastefully farmed. A policy of this kind would, of course, have to be applied consciously and slowly, with safeguards against exploitation and land speculation; it would have to include a national housing policy; it would have to overcome, with proper safeguards, the opposition of white trade unions and of Africans themselves; and it would have to include the gradual extension of political and civil rights to Africans.

To state these conditions may seem to condemn the suggestion outright as unrealistic and impracticable. Nevertheless, the conclusion from the facts seems inescapable that some such policy will prove to be the only real alternative to racial strife that will reduce the country to the state where neither white nor black will be able to maintain a reasonable standard of living. Attempts to disguise the alternatives by calling the Reserves 'colonies' to which 'self-government' should be extended, only lead to still greater confusion.

Urban Areas

In 1911, when the first Union-wide census was taken, the African population in white urban areas was half a million; by 1967 it had increased to close on $3\frac{1}{2}$ million. A feature of this change is that the urban female population increased much more rapidly than the male. In 1911 African females formed 19·2 per cent of the total African urban population; in 1950 they formed about 36 per cent, and by 1960 they were 46 per cent of the total, a measure of the increasing stabilization of the African urban population. In 1911 African labour in the towns was predominantly migrant and temporary; but it became increasingly a permanent feature of urban life.

The influx from rural to urban areas is, of course, not a phenomenon confined either to Africans or to South Africa. It is one of the major social characteristics of industrialization and of the twentieth century. In 1911 a minority of whites in Soth Africa lived in towns; by 1960 a majority were urban dwellers. From 1921 there was a steady flow of all races in South Africa from the country to the towns. Orlando, an African township near

Johannesburg, did not exist in 1921. By 1936 it had a population of 10,000, in 1946 this had increased to 58,000,[7] and in 1960 to 66,000.[8]

Urban population in South Africa is concentrated in the large industrial, commercial, and mining centres. Of 634 towns and villages officially listed, only 144 have populations of more than 5,000 of all races, and only 77 have populations exceeding 10,000. According to the official figures for 1960 the total urban population was 5,397,000, and of these, 2,717,000 (or more than half) were concentrated in the major centres of Cape Town, Durban, and the Witwatersrand. The Witwatersrand alone had 1,665,000, or nearly one-third of the total urban population, and included in the Witwatersrand figure are 949,000 Africans, or more than 40 per cent of the total urban African population. It is in these towns that the increase of African population has been the most startling and has caused the greatest concern to local authorities and to the central government.

Africans living in or near to white towns are employed in a variety of ways. In round numbers, 556,000 are in mining and quarrying; 475,000 in manufacturing industries; 122,000 in construction; 136,000 in trade and commerce; 103,000 in transport and communication; 330,000[9] in central, provincial, and local public services; and smaller numbers in other industries and in the professions.

The rapid growth of the African urban population created the same kind of housing and administrative problems that faced the industrial towns of Britain in the nineteenth and twentieth centuries. And the result of the inability of local authorities to provide a solution for the housing problems was, as in Britain, the growth of slums. In pre-industrial days in South Africa there were always a small number of Africans in urban areas, apart from the gold-mines, employed chiefly as domestic servants. When they were not provided with quarters by their employers they constructed small houses for themselves in locations near to the towns. This residential segregation is part of the traditional policy of South Africa; and, when the first influx into towns began, the principle was embodied in legislation by parliament, which tried to control the situation.

The most important of these Acts of Parliament was the Natives (Urban Areas) Act of 1923 as amended from time to time and consolidated in 1945. It empowered local authorities to establish locations and to make regulations governing them and controlling the entry into and residence in such locations; it placed the responsibility for housing on local authorities; and it compelled them to appoint managers of locations, to set up Native advisory boards, and to keep a separate Native revenue account.

By 1939 the problem of urban housing for Africans had reached critical

[7] *Population Census*, 1946, Vol. I, U.G.51/1949.

[8] *Population Census*, 1960. R.P. No. 62/1963.

[9] There is an overlap between this figure and that for transport and communication. The figures are for 1965, the latest available, and are from the *Statistical Year Book* for 1966.

dimensions. About half the urban population lived in controlled locations while some of the other half found accommodation with their domestic employers or in mining or industrial compounds. The remainder squatted illegally on or near municipal land, where they erected 'pondokkies' of packing-cases, sheets of galvanized iron, petrol-tins, sacking and any other material they could find. Neither these shanty towns nor many of the controlled locations had any of the amenities of civilized living, such as water-borne sewage, electric light, or running water laid on to the houses. With few exceptions the houses themselves were poorly constructed, lacked proper ventilation and heating, and were always hopelessly over-crowded.

During the 1939–45 War urbanization of all races increased rapidly and building practically ceased. Africans flocking to the towns first of all overcrowded the already occupied accommodation and then squatted on vacant land, where shanty towns sprang up overnight. Municipal or government efforts to prevent this, or to exercise some form of control, merely exacerbated the feelings of the Africans who considered that the whites did nothing to assist them to establish homes from which they could go to work—for the whites—and did everything to harry and discourage them once they had constructed their pitiful shanties. In many of the established locations, as well as in the shanty towns, social and health facilities were almost entirely lacking; 60 per cent of the children at a conservative estimate were debarred from school because there were no facilities for them. Both parents had to earn, and the total result was the growth of an illiterate, untrained class with lawless elements that preyed on black and whites alike. In the largest cities of the Union administration had virtually broken down in so far as the African population was concerned; to say the least, it had failed to keep pace with the demands made on it.

Though, as will be seen presently, great improvements were made, some of the conditions just described continued to exist. In such anti-social conditions African family life, the discipline of tribal traditions, the customary good manners and natural dignity of the African were bound to deteriorate. In their place came a host of municipal regulations restricting the manufacture of kaffir beer, controlling freedom of movement, pro-hibiting one thing after the other. In the interests of law and order the police had to carry out these regulations; and the easiest and safest way to do that is by mass raids, when a body of armed police moves into an an area. It is also, to the inhabitants, the most alarming and exasperating way.

An astonishing feature of this situation is that comparatively few Africans become real criminals. It is equally astonishing that, in the midst of such poverty and under the weight of such administrative regulation, Africans are able to maintain high standards of conduct and behaviour; and it is surprising that the proverbial African patience, good humour, and tolerance do not more frequently break down under the strain. About 370,000 Africans are convicted each year for contravention of supervision and control regulations, and until the early 1960's there was an increasing number of sporadic outbursts of violence that took the form of stoning police cars when locations were raided and of the destruction of buses and the burning of schools. Increasingly, too, angry women took part in these demonstrations. In 1959 the authorities, aware of mounting discontent, bought a number of Saracens for police use in riots and, generally, tightened policy and security control so effectively that peaceful or violent opposition, on the part of Africans, to government policy, became extremely hazardous.[10]

It is worth while looking in some detail at the failure of the local authorities of the large urban areas to keep pace with the housing needs of Africans. The story illustrates very clearly some of the factors that operate in a multiracial society that has become industrialized. Probably the main reason why the problem of urban housing for Africans was allowed to reach the dimensions of a national crisis was the absence of a definite Native policy. Just as, on a national scale, the idea of Reserves continues to exercise a baleful influence on political thinking, so the idea that Africans working in urban areas are migrants fogs economic thinking. Acting on this assumption, municipal authorities were, at first, reluctant to spend money on what they regarded as temporary housing. When, at last, the public began to realize that locations were likely to be permanent, housing had already lagged far behind actual needs. In an attempt to meet the situation, the government instituted sub-economic loans, and by 1939 more than R10,000,000 had been borrowed by local authorities for African housing; and a few municipalities, such as Johannesburg, floated additional loans on their own credit. By 1947, however, the situation was out of hand. In that year the Department of Native Affairs estimated that 154,000 houses were needed for urban and peri-urban Africans; but, since few local authorities had any accurate idea of how many Africans were living in their area, this number was a serious under-estimate. Moreover, building costs had risen steeply during the war, and in the post-war years local authorities and central government haggled about the amount of loss each could be expected to bear on sub-economic housing. Meanwhile, in spite of preventive regulations, Africans were still moving into the towns and cities in large numbers to meet the needs of an expanding industry.

Another reason for the failure to deal with this problem is to be found in the wage structure in South Africa and in colour-bar habits and regulations. Africans are, by social customs, by trade union action, and by law,

[10] Harry Bloom's well-known novel, *Episode*, illustrates how inflammable a racial situation can become when large numbers of Africans are congregated in slum-like and overcrowded urban locations and are harried by control regulations. After selling freely for some years, *Episode* was banned by the Government at the beginning of 1961.

debarred from entering most skilled occupations. In the building trade unskilled wages of Africans are about one-sixth of the white skilled wages. (In the Cape Province the ratio of unskilled to skilled wages is higher, and moreover a large proportion of skilled work is performed by Coloured—as distinct from African—labour.) Most local authorities used white skilled labour on their housing schemes. They were not compelled to do so by law but were afraid of the white trade unions; whites have votes, Africans do not. The resulting costs of African houses were too high to bear an economic rent for, in effect, houses were (and in some cases still are) built by skilled workers earning six times as much as the Africans for whom the houses were intended. No local authority can follow such a policy for long, and the available money does not go far. The obvious remedy is to train African building workers, a policy which white workers have strenuously opposed for fear that Africans will work at a lower rate and undercut white wages.

The Nationalist Party came to power in 1948 and inherited the chaotic conditions described above, and it is greatly to their credit that, once they had found their feet, they tackled the problems of urban housing with energy and practical skill. There is a certain irony, inseparable from South African affairs, in the fact that the government that was instrumental in building more permanent houses for urban Africans than any previous government, was drawn from a political party whose programme expressed most strongly the prevalent South African assumptions that urban Africans are migrants and that Africans should not be allowed to compete with white skilled labour. Faced with the horrible reality of shanty towns, squatters' camps, and overcrowded locations, the government jettisoned some of its theories and, in 1959, the Minister of Bantu Administration and Development was able to announce that in the previous eight years 500,000 Africans had been housed in 100,000 family units. Despite the fact that since 1959 building had proceeded at a good pace, the Minister of Community Development estimated that at the beginning of 1966 there was a shortage of 42,800 houses for urban Africans.

Commencing in 1950, the government introduced a series of legislative and administrative measures to enable it to carry out a more effective housing policy. Under the so-called site-and-service scheme, large new African townships were planned; and when water, light, and sewerage had been laid on, sites were rented to Africans who could either build their own houses or have them built cheaply with borrowed money made available from government sources. Since the new townships were sited at some distance from the white city where most Africans worked, additional and subsidized transport was provided, the subsidy coming from a newly imposed tax on employers of African labour in the large cities. This tax, known as the Native Services Levy, consists of 25 cents a month for every African employed in commerce and industry.

The new sites were intelligently planned and made provision for schools, churches, public buildings, a market place, a shopping centre, and playing-fields. In its desire to revive tribalism, the government insisted that the new townships should be ethnically zoned and that Zulu, Xhosa, Sotho, and so on should each live in their own areas. The arguments were that this would facilitate mother-tongue education; that it would give new-comers a more familiar and surer base, much needed in the bewildering life of the city; that it would enable tribal chiefs to maintain contact with their subjects; and that it would eventually make it possible to apply tribal law in urban areas. There is, of course, some substance in these arguments; but there are strong counter-arguments. If tribalism finds it difficult to accommodate itself to a modern economy in the Reserves, it will find it impossible to do so in the cities; many Africans (and the number is increasing) have become permanent urban dwellers and have lost all effective contact, or desire for contact, with the Reserves; many inter-tribal marriages take place in the cities and the offspring of such marriages would find it difficult to say to which tribe they belonged; city life promotes an intertribal or non-tribal society, and to keep such a society apart by artificial zoning is likely to lead to tribal clashes such as occurred in African townships in Johannesburg in 1957, when forty Africans were killed and scores were injured.

In its housing policy the government cut across another cherished South African tradition by training and employing teams of African building workers to erect houses and schools at a cost far below what would have been possible with white workers. It also had to cajole, threaten, and dragoon reluctant local authorities not only to accept their responsibilities but to do so on terms which they disliked. Ministers frequently complained that opposition to government policy was obstructionism based on party-political rather than on rational grounds. It is true that, with the exception of Pretoria, Bloemfontein, and one or two Reef towns, the big urban centres normally have city councils in which the majority are opposed to the Nationalist Party. But opposition to government policy was not entirely due to that. There are more solid grounds on which that policy might be considered objectionable. The insistence on ethnic grouping, against the advice and wishes of the city councils, is one. Again, in the desire to separate black and white by the greatest possible distance, the new town-ships were sited so far from the centres they served that, despite sub-sidized transport, the added costs in time and money were a heavy burden on workers and industry and commerce. Moreover, where a new township adjoined a main road, the government insisted that a 500-yard strip of so-called green belt should be left vacant, thus adding to the cost of land which the local authority had to buy.

There are two even more serious objections. In the first place, Africans cannot obtain freehold in the new urban locations. It is as if the government, having recognized the *fact* that the urban African population is either permanent or becoming so, refused to relinquish the apartheid *theory* that urban Africans are migrants. It is difficult to understand, except on ideological grounds, why it missed this golden opportunity of promoting a more stabilized urban community and of gaining the goodwill of thousands of Africans by granting freehold rights. In doing so, it would only have been making a virtue of necessity.

Moreover, while there was everything to be said for the new townships so long as they were intended to meet the genuine needs of shanty towns and squatter populations, in Johannesburg they were also used to accommodate Africans who had been living in areas in which they had long-established rights, including freehold, but which were zoned as white areas under the Group Areas Act. To many people this action seemed uncomfortably like the story of Naboth's vineyard.

Despite the government's notable achievements in the housing of urban Africans, the problem of slums and shanty towns remained. The Tomlinson Commission estimated that in 1951 there was a shortage of 167,000 family dwellings, and that during the next ten years an additional 185,000 would be required. Of this total of some 353,000 houses, possibly 130,000 had been built by 1961; and even if that rate were increased full urban housing needs could not be met before 1980. It may therefore safely be assumed that at least half the African urban population in South Africa still lives in slums where the survival of human values is a cause for wonder.

In those urban locations where the devastating effects of housing shortage were not so great, there had sprung up a new African society, distinct from tribal life and imperfectly modelled on European social life, but full of an unstable vigour that is neither tribal nor European.[11] All the large Christian communities have churches in the locations: and Africans have churches of their own that are, however vaguely, based on European models. Cinemas, schools, sports clubs, shops and cafés, burial societies, debating clubs—all these familiar features of European urban life have established themselves in the African townships, and social distinctions based on possessions and occupation have become marked in African urban society. Superficially the location may look like a poorer replica of the white town; but there are important differences. With few exceptions, Africans may not own land in white areas, so they can never look forward, as the white man does, to complete home ownership. Again, since most local authorities have striven to make the locations financially self-sufficient and not a burden on the white rates, social services are either nonexistent or poor; frequently they are the result of the efforts of philanthropically minded whites. Finally, Africans are subject to a number of restrictive regulations that do not apply to whites. For example, an

[11] Anthony Sampson, in his book *Drum*, gives a lively account of this new urban society about which white South Africa knows very little.

African who wishes to be outside the boundary of the location after a specified time at night must have a permit; the absence of such a permit may lead to summary arrest.

African communities living in urban areas have their own social problems. Tribal life is based on kinship; urban life, modelled on Western ideas, is based on the family. Problems of social relationships, of parental authority, of morals, that do not arise in tribal life, have all made their appearance under urban conditions. In tribal life your neighbour is your kinsman; in an urban township he is almost certainly not. The marriage of your children follows, in tribal custom, a well-marked routine; these traditional forms break down under the strains of urban life. The status of men, women, and children is clearly established in tribal life; each has his or her appointed place and tasks. In urban conditions these relationships are modified by external conditions and by terms of employment. Whites are apt to think simply of 'the African' in the mass, not realizing that these urban townships are living communities of individuals whose social customs have been profoundly shaken by their new environment and who are having to adjust themselves both to European habits and to the new African society in which they find themselves. And their tribal customs have provided them with no rules to guide them in this new and uncharted situation.

Africans on European farms

In 1960 there were about 2,120,000 Africans living on white farms, slightly less than half of them being female. There are African farm labourers in all districts of the Republic, but the number in relation to the white farming population varies from province to province. In Natal there are about 16 Africans, of both sexes and all ages, to 1 white; in the Transvaal the ratio is 6 to 1, in the Free State 7 to 1, and in the Cape Province about 2 to 1. In the Cape there are 403,000 Africans on white farms and 312,000 Coloured workers, so that the ratio of Coloured and African to white is about 3·5 to 1. These are averages, and the ratios will vary from district to district, depending on the kind of farming—whether it is sheep-farming, or grain-farming, or more intensive cultivation. There is such variety of farming in South Africa that we cannot generalize about numbers, conditions of service, housing, or wages, and the following description is intended merely as a reasonably accurate general picture.

There are two main systems, with plenty of local varieties, by which African farm labour is employed. The one is for a regular monthly wage plus payment in kind; the other is a system of labour-tenancy in which there is no cash wage: the African works a fixed number of days in the year in return for the right to live on the farm, to graze cattle, and to cultivate land. On most Cape and Free State farms, and in parts of the Transvaal and Natal, the first system is in vogue. It is notoriously difficult, however, to give anything but a misleading picture of farm-labour wages in cash and in kind. It might be thought that cash wages, at any rate, would be easy enough to discover; but conditions vary so greatly that it is impossible to talk about an average cash wage. When it comes to wages in kind, the difficulties of giving a general picture are wellnigh insuperable. Wages in kind may consist of rations (usually maize, skimmed milk, and occasionally meat), grazing-land, arable land, living-space. It is clear that the value of these, either to the farmer or to the labourer, will depend on climate, fertility of soil, the price of land, the kind of stock grazed, and many other factors of that kind. The Minister of Native Affairs said, in the House of Assembly on 24 July 1958, that the head of a family on a farm earned on an average R13·00 a month in cash and kind and that his wife and children might earn another R4·50. This statement is comparatively of little value unless it is known what district the Minister had in mind. Of more value are the figures given by Miss Margaret Roberts from the survey she carried out in the Albany and Bathurst districts of the Eastern province.[12] She found that the average on 71 farms, in cash and kind, for a family of 6·5 persons, was R214·00 per annum.

While these figures are given to show the order of magnitude of farm wages, the reader is warned again that they have no general validity. All that may safely be said is that African farm wages are lower than urban wages and that, by any standards, they are inadequate. This is amply borne out by the lengths to which farmers and the authorities go to make good the perennial shortage of African farm labour that exists in certain districts. One of the steps taken by government is the system of farm gaols. A group of farmers build a gaol according to official specifications and hand it over to the Department of Prisons, and in return, the farmers are entitled to hire prison labour at a tariff determined by the Commissioner of Prisons; this is revised from time to time and adjusted to the circumstances of the district in which the prison is located. The prison authorities claim that the system prevents overcrowding in city gaols and provides healthful outdoor employment for prisoners, under strict official supervision.

A system, used chiefly in the Transvaal, that is open to abuse and to severe criticism is that by which farmers may recruit prison labour, as it were, at source. A farmer may interview an African prisoner serving a light sentence and, with the prisoner's consent, employ him at current wages for the remainder of his sentence. Conditions are laid down for the protection of the prisoner but there is no adequate check on the possible use of force to obtain the prisoner's consent. Moreover, it had become customary, by a departmental extension of the system, for the police to give an arrested African the choice of being tried or of going to work on a farm. In other words, the mere fact of arrest could be taken as proof of

[12] *Labour in the Farm Economy*, South African Institute of Race Relations, 1959.

guilt. When it is remembered that there are a large number of statutory offences for which an African may at any time be arrested it will be realized how wide open to abuses such a system is. That it was in fact grossly abused came to light in the first half of 1959, largely through the efforts of a Johannesburg solicitor and the Black Sash.[13] It was then revealed that innocent Africans were being arrested in Johannesburg and, with no trial, sent to work on maize and potato farms in the Bethal and other districts, in some cases under appalling living conditions and subject to masters and African overseers who used physical violence to make them work harder. It was also found that a few unscrupulous employers used illegal means, including force and the destruction of their papers, to retain men after their sentences had expired. It was only by applying for writs of *habeas corpus* that relatives of those who had been spirited away were able to bring the matter to court and to secure a release. Under the public uproar that followed these disclosures this system of what was virtually kidnapping was stopped.

In parts of the Transvaal and Natal labour-tenancy is still common. The African labourer contracts to work without any cash wage for either 90 or 180 days, either continuously or for two days a week. In exchange, he and his family live on the farm and may graze cattle and plough land, the quantities varying with different conditions, but being, in any case, larger than where a cash wage is paid. He is, in fact, selling part of his labour for the right to occupy land. This system is wasteful of labour since, on the ninety-day basis, a farmer has roughly four times more labour on his farm at any given time than he actually needs. Nevertheless it is popular, particularly on large farms where a few morgen more or less do not matter to the farmer, because it involves no cash outlay. Since the Reserves are overcrowded, the system provides access to land for Africans who want to farm and thus reduces the pressure on the Reserves. It remains, however, an economic makeshift.

The part played by the system of payment for labour, either in part or in whole, by grazing and cultivation rights, may be gathered from the following facts about African agriculture on white-owned farms.[14]

Owned by Africans on white farms	1955	1961
Head of cattle	1,295,000	1,239,000
Woolled sheep	185,000	214,000
Non-woolled sheep	158,000	129,000
Goats	601,000	501,000

In 1955 Africans on white farms owned 300,000 horses, mules, and donkeys, 165,000 pigs, 1,760,000 poultry. There are no figures for 1961. Africans on white farms produced for themselves as follows:

[13] For an account of this women's organization see pp. 184–5.
[14] *Agricultural Census Report No. 24*, of 1955, and *Statistical Yearbook 1966*.

	1955	1961
Maize (200 lb bags)	3,168,920	3,052,570
Kaffir corn	262,930	384,890
Wheat	19,000	36,770

In 1955 Africans on white farms produced 872,000 lb of wool, 870,000 lb groundnuts, and unspecified quantities of vegetables, such as peas, beans, and potatoes. There are no figures for 1961.

Under the supervision of the farmer, Africans do all the farm work. Milking, ploughing, fencing, dam-making, gardening, shearing, reaping, are all in the day's work. There is practically no specialization, except that an African with an aptitude for machinery may be given all the jobs demanding elementary mechanical knowledge. Transvaal farmers some years ago asked that Africans should be allowed to obtain a motor-driving licence *even if they are illiterate*—a sign of the increasing mechanization of farming, of the dependence of the white farmer on African labour in spite of mechanization, and a reflection on the state of literacy among Africans.

For Africans social life on a farm is much more like life in the Reserves than in towns, which is one of the reasons why young men like to seek their fortunes in the towns. African and white children frequently play together on farms and become firm friends until they are separated at the age of 7 or 8, often to find their paths cross years later, in very different circumstances.[15] Tribal customs and superstitutions have a stronger hold than in town, and African farm workers try to arrange for their children to undergo initiation as part of their 'education'. On many farms no other form of education is available, though farmers are more and more making use of a system whereby, if the farmer builds a school and finds enough pupils, he may apply to the education department for a teacher.

This system became more popular with farmers since the announcement by the Minister of Bantu Education, in the Senate on 2 June 1959, that any farmer who 'wishes to make use of the schoolchildren under supervision of the teacher to assist with certain farm activities' can arrange this and that it will be fitted in to the curriculum for farm schools. In 1968 there were 2,696 farm schools in the Republic, excluding the Transkei, at which there were 210,689 children in the lower primary classes and 28,911 in the higher primary. There were 4,283 teachers of whom 3,700 were paid by the Department of Bantu Education.[16]

Social life for adults on a farm is simple and monotonous. Births, marriages, and deaths, a weekly beer party with labourers from neighbouring farms, and an occasional visit to the market town are its highlights. A few farmers, especially those living near a town, have tried to provide

[15] For a dramatic example see an excellent novel, *In A Province*, by Laurens van der Post.
[16] Minister of Bantu Education, *Hansard* No. 11 of 1968, col. 3889.

social amenities to compete with the glittering attractions of urban life.

Housing for African workers on farms is poor. The 'huts', or African quarters, are usually about half a mile from the white farmhouse. As a rule they are constructed of mud and do not effectively keep out wind and weather. The huts form a small hamlet or agricultural village of six or seven families, but the words 'hamlet' and 'village' should not mislead the reader into thinking in terms of English or Continental hamlets; hamlets are close to villages and not isolated and remote, as the 'huts' on a South African farm are; and they have a village pub as a social centre, an institution almost wholly lacking in South Africa generally and certainly never found hear the huts.

As a general rule farmers treat their African workers in a patriarchal and kindly fashion. Physical ill-treatment has become an exception; labour is scarce, and farmers who get a bad name are avoided by Africans seeking work. Contracts are verbal, usually for six months or a year, or 'from harvest to harvest', and should a farmer fail to keep his bargain he would be pretty sure to incur a shortage of labour. The unit of employment in the case of married men is the family, and the employer stipulates for the labour of the wife and children when required. This is traditional, and is also a fruitful source of dispute.

While the lot of the African working on white farms is, on the whole, not positively unhappy, it has some decidedly disturbing features. The diet is almost exclusively starchy and lacks protective food values; housing is poor and unhygienic, and it is only because of a favourable climate and plenty of space that there is not more disease. Social amenities and educational facilities are almost entirely lacking; pass laws and cash debts to the farmer tend to tie the worker to the farm. On the other hand, African labour is untrained and inefficient, and there is no incentive to improve efficiency and output, because wage rates make little distinction between efficient and inefficient labour and because cash wages are too low. Farmers have no real knowledge of what their labour is costing them because there is no effective method of accurately evaluating payment in kind; this militates against efficient farm management and the best use of labour.

There are various reasons for the inefficient use of African labour and for the poverty and low wages of the labourer. The belief persists that low-paid labour is necessarily cheap labour. Judged by its productivity, African farm labour is dear, but it is difficult to persuade farmers of this. The white farmer has always regarded the African as an inefficient labourer who cannot be paid a higher wage; he does not trouble to train him effectively, because he has a deep-rooted belief that the African can do what he is told, but will never 'think for himself'. What he requires from the African is absolute obedience to instructions rather than initiative. He pays accordingly, and the African acquires experience in carrying out instructions, but never becomes trained as an agricultural worker. There is little wonder that young Africans between the ages of 20 and 30 who are looking for work prefer not to go on the farms; and that Africans of that age, born and bred on a farm, prefer to go to towns to seek the opportunities they miss on the farms.

Africans on the Mines and in Industries

Every week five or more special trains arrive at Johannesburg with hundreds of Africans going to work on the mines. Some of them have been there before; many of them are coming for the first time from the simple, pastoral life of the Reserves to the rush and noise of a big city, and to a strange, machine-dominated existence in a highly organized industry. The train journey is the first unfamiliar experience; thereafter come the harsh compounds with their brick buildings and concrete bunks, the mass-produced, balanced diet, the shattering experience of being rushed to the bowels of the earth in a cage to work at a dangerous job. Despite the considerable lengths to which the mines go in acclimatizing new workers and adjusting them to their new environment, it is a big change from the small village community, where a man has a recognized place in the life of the community and where he is surrounded by familiar and kindly objects, to the anonymous vastness of a mining compound where he has a number instead of a name and where he hears the roar of mining machinery instead of the lowing of cattle on the hills.

By the end of 1965 the value of minerals mined in South Africa was R18,500 million. Of this amount, gold accounted for about half.[17] The output of all minerals in 1965 itself was R1,152 million, of which gold accounted for more than half. The gross value of the production of all privately owned factories is about R3,500 million per annum. This production of wealth from mines and factories was, and continues to be, made possible by African labour.

There are on an average about 555,000 Africans and 65,000 whites employed in mining.[18] Of the 386,000 Africans employed in gold-mining, only one-third come from South Africa: the rest are from territories that lie outside her political control—Lesotho, Botswana, Swaziland, Rhodesia, Malawi, and Portuguese East Africa. Of all Africans employed in labour districts in the Republic (that is chiefly in mining and industrial undertakings) no fewer than 36 per cent are from outside South Africa. South African mining and industrial development is, thus, to a great extent dependent on labour from outside her borders.[19]

There are three ways in which an African from the Republic can

[17] Only 12 per cent of gold extracted in 1965 came from mines that were more than forty years old; 70 per cent came from post-1946 mines.

[18] These figures are averages taken from the *Statistical Year Book*, 1966.

[19] Not only labour; nearly half (45 per cent) of mining dividends are paid to shareholders outside South Africa, chiefly in England.

become an employee on a mine. He may go to the mine and find work for himself; or he may go to the recruiting office nearest to his home and sign a contract for a fixed period under the Assisted Voluntary Scheme; or he may be recruited by the Mine Labour Organization (N.R.C.) which exists to recruit labour for the gold- and coal-mines from South Africa, Lesotho, Swaziland, and part of Botswana. Under the first system he can select his mine and need not bind himself for more than a month at a time. Under the second system he has his fare paid to the mine and can still select his mine, but he must contract to stay for a minimum of 180 shifts, or about six months. Under the third scheme his fare is paid and he must contract for a minimum of 180 shifts, but he is drafted to whatever mine needs labour at the moment. About two-thirds of the Africans from the Republic are employed under one of the first two schemes; Africans outside the borders go to the nearest agent of the other great recruiting corporation, Mine Labour Organizations (Wenela). In 1951 this organization took to flying its workers from central African aerodromes to Francistown in Botswana, whence they travel by train to Johannesburg. In 1968 it was operating four Dakotas and four Skymasters which carry about 88,000 workers each year.

Recruits are put through a stiff medical test at their place of recruitment and the percentage of failures is high, sometimes as much as 25 per cent, an indication of the extent of undernourishment in some of the Reserves. It is not unknown for the family of a potential recruit to 'fatten him up', at the expense of their own health, during the months preceding the examination. The recruit has a further medical examination when he reaches the mine and he is usually put on light surface jobs for some weeks before going on to the strenuous underground work. He must be medically examined every three months while employed on the mines. The diet on the mines is balanced and, unless they contract silicosis, Africans are usually in better physical condition when they leave the mines than when they arrived. Although the usual spell of work is 270 shifts, lasting about ten months, Africans from Portuguese East Africa stay for 313 shifts, or about twelve months. There is, thus, a constant coming and going to and from the mines and the main labour force is not permanent. Having worked his shifts, the African miner returns to his home for a rest. Many return to the mines for further spells; if they do so within a specified time they acquire certain rights in regard both to employment and wages.

The average cash wage of an African miner in 1968 was 60 cents a shift underground and 51 cents for surface work. On a 270 shift basis for underground work this would amount to about R162 for ten months, or R16·2 per month. In addition he receives free board and lodging, medical attention, and certain amenities, all of which the mines estimate would cost a miner between R30 and R40 a month to provide for himself. The average wage for an underground worker who is a member of the Mine Workers' Union[20] for a full month worked, including overtime and special allowances, is R356.

There is a deferred pay system, compulsory for Africans from Portuguese territory and voluntary for the rest, by which a portion of the wage is paid only when the African reaches home. Not a great many Africans living in South Africa make use of this, though they do remit money to their relatives at home; they prefer to spend their money in Johannesburg where they buy articles to take home—clothes, sewing-machines, musical instruments, blankets, etc. A certain amount of money is spent on visits to shebeens, on gambling, and on prostitution, but it is impossible to say what proportion of their wages this is. Africans may now legally patronize beerhalls and there is no longer any need for them to visit shebeens. Nevertheless, the practice still exists.

Africans on the gold-mines are housed in barracks, called compounds, which consist of brick buildings round a quadrangle. The sleeping quarters are fitted with concrete bunks or, in some of the newer compounds, army-type cots, and each room may hold sixteen to twenty bunks. There are about sixty such compounds on the Witwatersrand and about 30 in the Orange Free State, each housing anything between 1,000 and 5,000 Africans. Under the Bantu Labour Act of 1964, which consolidated previous legislation and governs the employment of Africans in mines, hospital accommodation at the rate of at least one bed to forty Africans must be provided by the employers. Most mines have good hospital and medical facilities; others provide enough to satisfy the minimum standards laid down. On the whole, mine employers are well aware of the importance of the physical health of their workers and the industry spends more than R5,000,000 a year on medical services. The Ernest Oppenheimer Hospital at Welkom, the centre of the Orange Free State gold-mining development, is the finest in Africa.

Rations include bread, coffee, sugar, mealie meal, beans and other vegetables, and kaffir beer, the daily ration containing 4,500 calories. The meat ration is 3 lb a week, but the quality is poor. Recreational facilities provided are cinemas, concerts, athletic sports equipment, and facilities for tribal dancing and music. Workers are usually housed according to tribe, and tribal competition occasionally leads to faction fights. Mine managers, however, lay stress on competition between miners, rather than between tribes, and this lessens the chances of tribal friction.

There is a white 'boss' in charge of each gang or working party of Africans who do the pick-and-shovel work; a small number are employed in drilling and drill-sharpening, though, with improved mining techniques, the need for drill-sharpening is declining. Skilled work is reserved for whites. The Mines and Works Amendment Act of 1926, the famous

[20] Africans may not belong to the Mine Workers' Union.

'Colour Bar' Act, prohibits Africans from obtaining certificates of competency to do certain skilled jobs, such as blasting and engine-driving, jobs that are done by Africans in Zambia and the Congo without endangering the lives of their fellow-workers. The Africans on the gold-mines are quite competent to do these jobs, and the mining industry would, naturally, prefer to make a much wider use of African labour, but the mine-owners are deterred from doing so by the fear that the white workers would strike, as they did in 1922, if they thought their jobs were threatened. But though by law African miners cannot be trained and paid for skilled jobs, the expansion of the gold-mining industry since 1950 has made it increasingly difficult to find skilled labour, and it is probable that Africans in fact perform skilled jobs with the tacit consent of all concerned. In 1964, by agreement between the government, the mine-owners, and the leaders of the white trade union, an experiment was started by which selected and trained African miners were employed under white supervision on certain specified jobs previously reserved for whites. Despite assurances that the position of white miners would be improved, the majority objected to the experiment and disowned the leaders. The situation was complicated by domestic dissension in the Mine Workers' Union, and the government, fearful of losing popularity with the white miners, hastily terminated what many people regarded as a hopeful experiment.

Mining is hard work, and dangerous; and though the death and accident rate is slowly decreasing and the mine-owners do all they can to reduce it, more than 600 Africans lose their lives in gold-mining every year through accidents and disease. The Pneumoconiosis Act of 1956, which consolidated earlier laws, bases compensation on earnings; white miners or their dependants receive either a pension and a lump sum, or a pension, while Africans or their dependants receive a lump-sum payment only, the maximum being R360. Compensation for accident is governed by the Bantu Labour Act, subject to the African's right to claim for compensation under the common law or under the Workmen's Compensation Act; but, once more, compensation is by lump sum, a system that operates unfairly for Africans.

The African miner is not regarded as a town-dweller, but rather as a tribesman temporarily living in barracks. Accordingly, the Department of Bantu Administration and Development is responsible for maintaining law and order. Bantu commissioners, not magistrates, try petty cases, such as disobedience to orders, infringement of mining regulations, desertion, drunkenness, and assault. As we shall see later, African trade unions are not legally recognized. There are unions in some of the industries, but the mine-owners will not tolerate the suggestion of an African trade union on the mines. It is a criminal offence for an African mine-worker to take part in a strike or to absent himself from work. It would, indeed, be difficult to organize a responsible trade union on the mines because, unlike white miners, African miners are not a cohesive body of workers. Tribal differences, the transitory character of their stay at the mines, lack of a common language, and illiteracy must militate against effective organization.[21]

The description given above of Africans in mining applies chiefly to the gold- and coal-mines of the Transvaal, where, mainly along the Witwatersrand, the largest mining concentrations are to be found. It may, however, apply, with a number of variations, to African workers in other mines and in industries. About 12,000 Africans are employed in diamond-mining. Over 475,000 are in industrial employment and about half of them live in industrial compounds; 43 per cent of the industrial compounds are in the Transvaal, 44 per cent in Natal, and most of the rest in the Cape Province. These compounds are smaller and more dispersed than the mining compounds; the food and accommodation are, on an average, not as good as on the mines, and there are fewer social amenities. On the other hand, industrial wages for Africans are higher than mining wages; in many industries these wages are statutory, being fixed by the Wage Board or by an industrial council. While Africans on the gold-mines are, with negligible exceptions, migrants, those in industry have tended to become permanent. On a few mining compounds there are married quarters for some of the surface workers; but mining policy is to employ migrant labour. On the new Free State mines, at Odendaalsrus and elsewhere, the quarters are a great improvement on the Rand compounds and the mine-owners were anxious to extend considerably the provision of married quarters: but government policy made this impossible.

The effects of mineral development on the economy of southern Africa—South Africa and all her neighbours—has been immense. Mining has resulted in railway development, in the expansion of agriculture, and in the establishment of primary and secondary industries. South Africa is not a wealthy country. Contrary to popular opinion she is poor; and without mineral development she would have been immeasurably poorer. While the economic effects of this development have been great, the social effects on all races have been equally great. On Africans it has been shattering—it destroyed their tribal economy and irreparably damaged their tribal customs and loyalties. This is particularly true of the industrial worker. On the miner, the effect of contact with Western civilization is violent and demoralizing, and he may return to this tribal home having lost his natural dignity and simplicity and acquired disease and a veneer of Western civilization. But many do go back to a tribal home. The permanent industrial worker has lost for good his former way of life. He and his family have to readjust themselves painfully to a new environment that is harsh and unsympathetic.

[21] The success of African trade unions on the copper-mines of Zambia suggests that if the mine-owners would allow them to organize, African gold-miners would soon overcome these difficulties.

This readjustment was not made easier by government policy. It was noted above that African industrial workers tended to become permanent urbanites. By 1968, however, the policy of apartheid was being applied in such a way as to turn all African workers in white areas into migrants. In the Western Cape, Africans in large numbers were being endorsed out, back to their supposed 'homeland', and could thereafter only be employed as contact labour for twelve months at a time. A permit to re-employ can be obtained but the status of the worker has ceased to be that of permanent employ. In Johannesburg, where the greatest concentration of urban Africans is, the Deputy Minister of Bantu Administration and Development, early in 1968, told the Bantu Urban Council that Africans must never consider themselves as permanent urbanites. Moreover, a directive from the Minister's department to local authorities in February 1968 abolished the right of urban Africans to own the houses they had themselves built. These measures have not diminished the number of Africans who are, in all but name, permanent city dwellers. That number steadily increases. But apartheid further undermines the security that detribalized Africans are painfully struggling to acquire for themselves and their families.

3

THE PEOPLE (*continued*)

THE WHITES

THE white population of South Africa in 1968 was about 3,563,000, of whom roughly 80 per cent lived in urban areas. During the first three decades of this century it would have been true to say that the majority of the rural population was Afrikaans-speaking and of the urban population English-speaking. After the 1930's, however, the Afrikaner moved to the towns, a social and political fact, as we shall see later, of great importance.

The word Afrikaner requires some amplification. Until the first decade of this century it meant a white South African whose mother tongue was Afrikaans, but though the usage remained common in the rural areas of South Africa, the word has acquired a political and emotional significance associated with the rise of Afrikaner nationalism. Although Smuts and Malan grew up in the same Afrikaans-speaking rural village and would have been called Afrikaner boys, before his death most Nationalist Party speakers would have denied the title to Smuts, their political opponent, and granted it to Malan, their political leader. This appropriation of the term Afrikaner by the Nationalist Party was at first resented by those Afrikaans-speaking South Africans who did not belong to that party; but they came to regard their exclusion with equanimity and to think of themselves as *Suid-Afrikaners*, i.e. South Africans. Though Afrikaner was a useful emotive word while nationalism was struggling to assert itself, some Nationalist writers had begun to wonder whether its use was not too exclusive after 1948 when nationalism had triumphed. A word that excludes Smuts and Hofmeyr solely on the grounds of politics, and a Coloured poet, honoured by the Afrikaans Academy for his Afrikaans poetry, solely on the grounds of colour, might well be regarded as too exclusive, and its use in this book will, it is hoped, be clear from the particular context in which it is employed.

About 53 per cent of white South Africans use Afrikaans as their home language and 41 per cent English.[1] Probably 70 per cent are, to a greater or lesser extent, bilingual, the degree of bilingualism ranging from what is ironically called 'a working knowledge', through the ability to read and to understand the other language, to the fluent use of either. At first many more Afrikaners were bilingual than were English-speaking South

---

[1] *Statistical Year Book 1966.* The term 'South African' is usually applied to white citizens, but legally all the inhabitants are South African citizens.

Africans, but by 1948 the position had begun to change in two ways: more English-speaking people were seeing to it that their children became bilingual, and fewer Afrikaners were attaining that proficiency in English that was common in previous generations. The rapid development of the Afrikaans language and literature after 1930 and the urbanization of the Afrikaner were responsible for this. With the increasing use of Afrikaans in commerce, there was less incentive for the Afrikaner to learn English, and more incentive for the English-speaking South African to learn Afrikaans.

Both languages are official, and all public documents must be in both languages. Members of the public use either language in official correspondence and in addressing an official. The rule in parliament is that either language may be used and that no interpretation is provided. *Hansard*, however, appears in both languages.

On the committees of voluntary societies and of sporting bodies there are frequently members who cannot understand Afrikaans and for whose benefit the proceedings must be in English, but the exercise of tact and good will has usually overcome any awkwardness. Afrikaners tend to dissociate themselves from organizations that are predominantly English-speaking, while in some cases, as in youth movements and committees for adult education, parallel organizations have developed, one in English and the other in Afrikaans. Afrikaans cultural organizations urge their members to use Afrikaans only, and to patronize those businesses that cater for Afrikaners. Afrikaners were wont to complain, and sometimes still do, that in the large cities they have frequently to use English because the shop assistants, the railway booking clerk, the bank clerk, and others with whom they have to do business can speak little if any Afrikaans. There was justice in this complaint, but by 1968 the civil service was overwhelmingly staffed by Afrikaans-speaking personnel and the great majority of business houses were only too anxious to please Afrikaans speaking customers. English-speaking South Africans now complain that the boot is on the other foot.

The fight for the full recognition of Afrikaans was an uphill one. It was directed not so much against English-speaking people as towards preventing the Afrikaner from becoming anglicized. The English language, with an established international position, was, and to a certain though very much lesser extent still is, the language of trade and commerce, of the professions, of amusement and recreation, and of urban society. The urge to learn English, and the temptation to regard it as the only cultured language, were strong, and there was at one time a tendency among Afrikaners with pretensions to a more 'polite' way of living to look down on Afrikaans as a 'patois' and as 'the *taal*', something of which to be slightly ashamed. Apart from English, the written and 'polite' language was Dutch, and it was the language of the pulpit in the Dutch Reformed churches. But Dutch was, in reality, merely the husk covering the living and growing spoken language, Afrikaans.

After the Boer War of 1899–1902 a large number of English teachers and civil servants came to South Africa, and particularly to the ex-republics of the Transvaal and Orange Free State, and they greatly strengthened the tendency to regard English as the language of educated people. Afrikaners still speak about the generation that had its schooling in the first decade of the twentieth century as the 'lost generation', meaning that they had become anglicized.[2] Text-books were almost all in English, and English was the medium of instruction in practically all schools. Dutch, not Afrikaans, was the second official language, though only a small percentage of the population spoke the Dutch of Holland. Indeed, had the struggle been one between English and Dutch, the English language would probably have won. But the living and growing language of Afrikaans was waiting to push through the crust of Dutch. This happened during the second decade of the twentieth century, and it happened with all the force of a popular movement. Afrikaners began to write in Afrikaans and found an immediate and enthusiastic response. The movement was closely linked with the rise of the Nationalist Party under General Hertzog, and Afrikaans never lost the strong political associations that accompanied its revival. A favourite text at that time was: 'The language of the conqueror in the mouth of the conquered is the language of a slave.'

From 1912 the Afrikaans movement gathered force. Afrikaans newspapers were established; the Bible was translated into Afrikaans; the new generation of Dutch Reformed ministers was trained in it; text-books were printed in Afrikaans and it became the second medium of instruction in schools and universities. Dutch remained only to be studied as a modern language, and in universities as an adjunct to Afrikaans. A body of literature grew up in prose, in poetry, and in drama, much of it preoccupied with past history, particularly with the Boer War. But by the 1950's it was getting past that stage, and the best Afrikaans writers no longer found it necessary to belong to a particular political party or to deal exclusively with the rise of the Afrikaner and his fight against British Imperialism. So far there had been very little satirical writing, which is possibly a sign that Afrikaans writers still took themselves and their work a little too seriously. Further, in their determination to keep the language 'pure' and elegant while expanding its vocabulary, academic writers robbed it of some of its vigour and created a gulf between the spoken and the written language.

Such things are, no doubt, a passing phase. During the sixties a number of young Afrikaans writers reacted against the hidebound conservatism of the older generation and began to write novels and poetry in a more

---

[2] Other Afrikaners of that generation suffered a violent reaction, from which they appear never to have recovered, *against* all things English.

modern idiom and dealing with the kind of problem that occupies present-day writers in other countries. These writers are, collectively, known as the *Sestigers*, and the two best known are Étienne le Roux and André Brink. Their break with isolationism evoked a powerful counter reaction from those who believed that Afrikaner strength lay in the very isolationism that was being rejected. So fierce did this struggle within the ranks of Afrikaner nationalism become that, at one time, it threatened the unity of the Nationalist Party itself. This will be discussed in chapter 7.

The Afrikaans movement, coming when it did, had profound social and political effects on South African life. After the Boer War the Afrikaner was, spiritually and socially, in very low water. The Afrikaans movement rehabilitated him and restored his self-confidence. It brought him into the life of the country on equal terms with English-speaking South Africans, who for him represented England, the victorious aggressor. Wise statesmanship on the part of Great Britain assisted the process by granting self-government and, ultimately, the independence of dominion status; but it is hardly surprising that Afrikaners cling to the belief that, next to Divine Providence, their survival and revival was due to their own efforts. Nor is it entirely surprising that Afrikaner nationalism has not yet shed its somewhat strident tones or learned that it need no longer be constantly on the defensive.

By no means all Afrikaners joined the nationalist movement of the second decade of this century. In fact, the Nationalist Party was a breakaway by General Hertzog from the main body of Afrikaners, who were led by Generals Botha and Smuts. Their policy was 'conciliation'—to reconcile English and Afrikaner and to build a united nation. Hertzog's argument was that a united nation could only be built on a basis of complete equality, and that the first task therefore was to rehabilitate the Afrikaner. This could not be done by continually appeasing English susceptibilities, but only by insisting on language rights, on a separate flag, on South Africa's right to an independent existence, and if necessary to secede from the British Empire. In 1933, when Hertzog had succeeded in securing these aims, he once more joined with Smuts. But by then nationalism had become a force that generated its own power, and it went on without him.

A phenomenon that has puzzled observant visitors to South Africa is that the bitterest enmity exists, not between Afrikaner and English, but between Afrikaner and Afrikaner. Afrikaner politicians and editors reserve their sharpest darts for their fellow-Afrikaners. The cause of this bitterness is possibly to be found in the difference of attitude towards England and the part she has played in South African history. At least one-third of the Afrikaner population, following the Botha–Smuts–Hertzog tradition, desires co-operation with English-speaking South Africans and sees in such co-operation the only prospect of a united nation. Many nationalist Afrikaners would probably, if left to themselves, agree; but for more than half a century the Nationalist Party has asserted Afrikaner rights in order to survive and grow. For political success such assertion has to be emphatic and even violent, and it frequently has the appearance of denying similar rights to other groups. From there it is an easy step to regard any suggestion of full co-operation with other groups as treason to Afrikanderdom. It is all the more easy for Afrikaner nationalists to do this since, historically, Britain and British ideas seemed to succeed because Afrikaners were not united. To weaken or even to threaten Afrikaner unity has become the unforgivable sin in nationalist Afrikaner eyes.

The Afrikaner who has grown up in a large town is, as a rule, indistinguishable in outward appearance from his English speaking fellow-citizen. If he is an educated professional or business man, he speaks English perfectly correctly, though with more or less of an accent. If he is an artisan or an unskilled worker, his accent, grammar, and vocabulary will deviate noticeably. In his amusements, his recreation, his occupation, and his general way of life there is little difference between him and his English-speaking fellow-countryman.

There is a fairly marked difference between the Afrikaner farmer and the town-dweller, either English- or Afrikaans-speaking. About 82 per cent of European farmers are Afrikaans-speaking. The word *boer* in Afrikaans is still commonly used to describe a farmer. By profession he is a *boer*.[3] By descent an Afrikaner farmer may be a Boer, with a capital letter, hence he is sometimes referred to tautologically as a Boer farmer.

The Afrikaner farmer is, traditionally, a kindly and leisurely man with a sense of humour that sucks the last ounce out of a situation. He is slow to anger; he has rugged common sense born of generations of struggle against the forces of Nature; he works hard and is not a 'planter' or 'plantation owner'; he does not easily part with hard cash and he is convinced that townsmen are 'clever' ('slim' is what he would call it) and bent on defrauding him. He has many of the qualities and characteristics of the pioneer Trekkers, modified by the material progress of Western civilization; he is individualist in outlook and leisurely in habit; he has natural good manners and dignity. He will not tolerate equality with non-whites, but among those of his own colour he is no respecter of persons. He treats his labourers in a kindly and tolerant fashion and regards their many shortcomings as divinely ordained. The vagaries of the climate and his Calvinist religion have made him something of a fatalist.

Though there are many exceptions, the majority of Afrikaans farmers are not progressive. A long tradition of large farms easily acquired, the presence of a relatively abundant supply of 'cheap' labour and a contempt for 'experts' have induced bad economic habits and retarded scientific farming. Climatic conditions and out-of-date farming methods keep costs of production high, so that South African agricultural produce cannot

[3] In Afrikaans the word is pronounced like the German *buhr*, and *not* 'boor'.

compete successfully in the world market. The internal market is weak because 70 per cent of the population is too poor to be able to buy. Since the farming vote represents the most powerful single interest in parliament, all governments have found it expedient to subsidize agriculture. This is done by numerous control boards that guarantee high prices, by preferential duties and railway rates, and by subsidizing export. The expense to the country is enormous, in actual money, in inflated cost of living, in malnutrition, and in the continued production of subsidized crops on uneconomic soil.

The Director of Economic Services in the Department of Agricultural Economics and Marketing said in 1966[4] that weaknesses and short-comings in the agricultural industry that had been present for a long time were thrown into relief by the drought. He listed these as: overstocking and injudicious use of pasturage; crop production in marginal areas; inadequate and inefficient production of fodder; failure to apply soil conservation measures; the tendency towards a greater number of farming units that are farmed intensively but are too small to provide an adequate livelihood in modern conditions; and over capitalization of farming as a result of injudicious buying of land and other capital goods.

It is interesting to note that after 1950 urban Afrikaners began to complain about the favours shown to farmers, most of whom were Afrikaners. The fantastically high prices for wool in 1951 brought these complaints to a head. Letters to the Afrikaans Press, though careful to congratulate the wool farmers on their good fortune, complained that they were using their windfalls to evade supertax by buying up land at exaggerated prices. The result of this was not only loss of revenue to the State, but it meant that farms went out of production and that the price of land was artificially inflated, thus deterring younger men from being able to acquire their own farms. Another interesting though less readily noticed result is that reported by Dr. C. Neethling, head of the Department of Economics and Markets. According to *Die Burger* of 23 June 1959, Dr. Neethling said that 5,419 farms in Natal and 2,074 in the Orange Free State that had been occupied by whites in 1945 were, by 1959, occupied only by non-whites. They were, of course, still owned by white people but they were being farmed on their behalf by non-whites. By 1968 the artificially high price of land and its attendant evils had not been checked. In a major speech in Durban, on 28 November 1967, the Leader of the Opposition, Sir de Villiers Graaff, said that white farmers were leaving the rural areas at the rate of 2,600 a year and that their places were being taken by tens of thousands of Africans. 'It is not', he said, 'a depopulation of the platteland but a re-population'.

The determination to evade income tax and supertax is so widespread that one may be tempted to regard it as a general human characteristic

[4] *Statistical Year Book 1966.*

to see nothing immoral in it. It certainly is a fairly general characteristic of the Afrikaner farmer and dates back to the eighteenth century, when 'good government' neither interfered nor taxed. At a Nationalist Party Congress in 1951 it was pointed out by one delegate that the only remedy lay in abolishing income tax and substituting a graduated land tax. It is improbable however that such an unpopular measure would be lightly undertaken by any South African government. There are some 87,000 white farmers, distributed over all rural constituencies, whose votes no government dare ignore. Meanwhile, agriculture in South Africa exhibits many of the characteristics of a gigantic system of outdoor relief for which the rest of the country pays in direct taxation and inflated cost of living.

English-speaking South Africans are, for the most part, town- and city-dwellers, active in commerce and industry, in skilled trades, in mining, and in the professions. Isolated pockets of English-speaking farmers occur in three provinces, and in Natal the majority of farmers are English-speaking. In the large cities most of the capital and wealth is in the hands of English-speaking South Africans, many, though by no means all of them, Jews. By 1960 so-called Afrikaans capital had increased, but even so, Afrikaner business-houses considered that they controlled only about 10 per cent of invested capital. Since 1960 it has become increasingly difficult to distinguish between 'Afrikaner' and any other kind of capital, and there have been spectacular mergers, particularly in mining, that are indicative of a change of attitude of Afrikaner and English-speaking big businessmen.

The contribution of English-speaking people to the development of South Africa is great. The Afrikaner of the nineteenth century opened up the country and settled it; but for many years his main contribution to the material wealth of South Africa was agricultural. English-speaking South Africans were responsible for mining and industrial development, for railway construction, for the establishment of towns and cities, for commerce and banking, for shipping and for harbour construction—in fact, for changing South Africa from a backward agricultural community into a semi-industrial modern state. In this process, moreover, the enterprise, hard work, and capital of the Jews played a considerable part. It was not, however, only in material matters that English-speaking South Africans developed the country. In primary and secondary education, in the establishment and endowment of universities, the building of libraries, the development of the theatre and encouragement of the arts, in the spread of learning, in social welfare, and, last but not least, in the establishment of parliamentary traditions and of the rule of law, English-speaking South Africans played a major part.[5]

[5] For an excellent account of the part played by English-speaking South Africans in building up the country, see John Bond, *They Were South Africans*.

The English-speaking South Africans must not be thought of as 'foreigners'. They were British men and women who had come to settle in South Africa and make it their home. Many of them and of their children married into Afrikaner families, and descendants of these mixed Afrikaner and British marriages no longer care to describe themselves as Afrikaners or as English-speaking South Africans, but prefer to regard themselves simply as South Africans, and to look back with pride at the contributions which both their Afrikaner and English-speaking ancestors made to the establishment of Western civilization in South Africa.

It would be easy to exaggerate the social and political effects of having two official languages. Any description of the two language groups is apt to leave the impression that they are mutually exclusive and antagonistic, whether openly or not. That is far from being the case. A great many people are, normally, unconscious of belonging to any special 'group'. In situations where they do become conscious of it, most people manage to avoid friction and embarrassment by the exercise of common sense, good manners, and tolerance. Economic and social circumstances are, to an increasing extent, making people bilingual. During the 1939–45 War Afrikaans- and English-speaking troops of all ranks found that they got on very well together; and unilingual English-speaking people discovered a new urge to learn Afrikaans, and to let their children learn Afrikaans, so as to lessen the points of friction between the two groups. During the war it was interesting and amusing to watch people switching with ease from one language to the other, and not infrequently mixing the languages, to the annoyance of purists.

On the other hand, it would be equally easy to go to the opposite extreme and to imagine that language differences do not matter in South Africa. They do. And the division along the line of language grew intensified after the Nationalists came to power and more and more identified language and culture with political interests. This was an outcome of the conviction, even after the struggle for the recognition of the Afrikaans language had been won, that to preserve it meant to insist on its use, often at the expense of English, to establish separate parallel organizations where Afrikaans could be used exclusively, to found cultural societies for the promotion of Afrikaans literature and culture, and to demand separate schools where Afrikaans was the only medium of instruction. This insistence was felt to be necessary, not only to establish the language but to ensure the emotional stability of the Afrikaner. But to a large extent he has cut himself off from contact with a wider culture and with international thought by the neglect or rejection of English. This isolation is not inevitable in the fact of a dual language, but the danger is that a vested interest, political and cultural, has grown up around Afrikaans. The cultural and linguistic struggle for its recognition paid good party-political dividends and Afrikaner politicians are loath to relinquish a weapon that has served them so well. But until they do, the Afrikaner himself will be the chief loser.

By 1961 there were some healthy signs that Afrikaans thinkers and writers are alive to the dangers of isolation from world thought. Though it is true that bilingualism is increasing, Afrikaans- and English-speaking teachers are gravely disturbed at the low standard of English being taught, particularly in the rural areas. Afrikaans-speaking students come up to the universities unable to express themselves grammatically in speech or writing. In 1959 there were celebrations in honour of what was called 'The Wonder of Afrikaans', a great deal was spoken about the almost miraculous survival of the language, and Afrikaners were exhorted not to lose their heritage. But more than one speaker warned against the other danger—that of losing contact with the world by neglecting the English language.

During 1967 the leaders of a body called the *Genootskap vir die Hand-hawing van Afrikaans* (Society for the maintenance of Afrikaans) were active in warning that Afrikaans was once more in danger of being sub-merged by the more powerful English language and exhorting all true Afrikaners, even at personal inconvenience, to assert their right to speak and be served in their own tongue. There were incidents at hotels, at one of which the owner stoutly asserted *his* right to speak English in his own hotel. Most Afrikaners regarded the warnings as unnecessary and the incidents as somewhat embarrassing breaches of taste; and several Nationalist Party leaders told their followers that the battle for Afrikaans had been won and that they could relax. Nevertheless, the explosive potential of the language question should not be underestimated. Countries with two official languages generate a strong brand of politically explosive material that can be touched off by small incidents.

THE COLOURED PEOPLE

One-tenth (or 1,860,000) of the population is officially classed as 'Mixed and other Coloureds' and is defined as consisting 'chiefly of Cape Coloureds, but includes also Cape Malays, Bushmen, Hottentots, and all persons of mixed race'.[6] 'Mixed race' means those who have some European blood in their veins, but are not of 'pure' European origin. Since the number of Hottentots and Bushmen is negligible, most people, when they refer to the 'Coloured People', are thinking of the racially mixed group nearly 88 per cent of whom live in the Cape Province, about 7 per cent in Transvaal, and the rest in Natal and the Orange Free State.

This mixed race has its origin in the seventeenth-century slave popula-tion. The first batch of slaves brought to the Cape consisted of Negroes from the West Coast, while the others came from East Africa, Madagascar,

[6] Union Government Special Report No. 234 of 1960.

Ceylon, India, and Malaya. In the earliest years of the settlement at the Cape unions, regular or irregular, were frequent between Europeans and slaves, chiefly those from the East. During the first twenty years (1652–72) 75 per cent of children born to slave mothers had European fathers.[7] In 1685 marriage and intercourse with slave women were prohibited, though marriage with half-breeds was still allowed. Since, however, there were far more European males than females at the Cape, this prohibition did not stop miscegenation. Although in all probability Europeans did not mix to any extent with Hottentots, whom they regarded with considerable contempt, the slaves and half-breeds did.

During the nineteenth century, and particularly after the liberation of slaves in 1834, colour consciousness grew. By then the new 'race' had been established, however, and it continued to increase as a separate group. A certain amount of miscegenation between Europeans and Coloured still took place, and from the last quarter of the nineteenth century there was a slight admixture of African blood.[8]

There is a great variety in physical features and in colour among the Coloured people. They vary from the typically Negroid types to those that are indistinguishable from Europeans. Many between these two extremes could be taken for southern Italians. Except for the use of words of Malay origin, they have lost all trace of any non-European language; they speak English or Afrikaans according to their own social environment or that of their employers, and, at the lower social levels, mix the languages in a kind of South African cockney, and have, too, a cockney sense of humour.

The cultural and recreational interests of the Coloured are those of the European. In art and in literature there have been a few competent painters and writers, but no one outstanding. There have been a number of top-rank ballet dancers, notably Johaar Mosaval of the Royal Covent Garden Ballet; and the Eoan Group's opera season is looked forward to eagerly by white and non-white Capetonians and, in recent years, by audiences in the major cities of the Republic. The annual Coon Carnival, a purely Coloured institution, takes place in Cape Town on the second day of the New Year and is extremely popular, especially among the Coloured working classes. For months beforehand songs are practised, costumes prepared, and plans made by the competing bands. On the second of January (traditionally known as *Tweede Nuwejaar*—second New Year— and universally accepted as a Coloured holiday) the 'Coons' march through Cape Town, watched by thousands of white and Coloured spectators, to the Green Point Common where singing competitions take place, It is a gay scene, full of life and vigour. Many of the songs are traditional Dutch songs with variations, that have for the most part died out among the

[7] See Sonnabend and Sofer, *South Africa's Stepchildren*, South African Affairs Pamphlets.
[8] *Union Year Book No. 24*, 1948.

whites. Others are composed for the occasion and show the influence of American popular music. There carnivals are frowned on by the more educated and cultured Coloured people as being degrading to Coloured dignity.

Coloured men are employed in occupations closed to Africans. The building industry in the western Cape Province employs more Coloured artisans than white, and in the printing industry there are a considerable number of Coloured men and women. In other skilled trades it is more difficult for the Coloured to obtain entry. In the numerous factories that have been established in the large urban areas of the Cape Province, Coloured men and women are employed as operatives. In the western Cape Province the bulk of farm labour consists of Coloured, and a great many are employed in domestic service, in hotels, and as office messengers. In many Cape towns the postmen are, traditionally, Coloured. There are Coloured doctors and teachers working among their own people, but for lack of openings there it is difficult for a Coloured man to make a living in any of the other professions such as the law, engineering, or architecture. Coloured women find employment as nurses among the Coloured, and in cities they are increasingly employed by white firms as shorthand typists, dressmakers, shop assistants, and waitresses.

Though, in the nature of things, it is impossible to say how many Coloured have succeeded in 'passing' over the colour line, that is, in being fully accepted as white, it has occurred to a considerable extent. It is tacitly accepted that some reputedly (and officially accepted) white families have 'coloured blood', though the imputation is at times merely malicious; and that when individual members of Coloured families have succeeded in passing for white they are loyally ignored by the other members. During the 1939-45 War there were cases of members of the same family serving in different units, one in a European regiment and the others in a Coloured battalion.

When so great a premium, social, political, and economic, is placed on a 'white' skin, it is inevitable that those Coloured whose appearance makes it possible should be tempted to 'pass'. There have been cases where, in entering children for a European school, either the father or the mother has kept in the background for fear of jeopardizing the children's chances of being accepted. And there have been a number of cases where children who have been admitted to white schools are reported to other parents or to the authorities as being Coloured. An investigation is instituted, involving more or less publicity, and almost invariably the children are forced to leave. The stigma attaching to this usually has a most unfortunate effect on the children, and in one case a boy committed suicide as a result of it.

The Nationalist Party had for many years expressed concern about miscegenation and about 'passing'. Already, in 1927 when the Nationalist-

Labour Pact was in power, an Act was passed prohibiting extra-marital relations between European and African. From 1948, when the Nationalist and Afrikaner Parties came to power, they immediately set about passing legislation to prohibit both illicit intercourse and marriage between European and Coloured. The Immorality Act of 1927 was amended to include Coloured, and a Prohibition of Mixed Marriages Act was passed which made marriage between white and non-white a crime and held marriage officers responsible for refusing to solemnize such marriages.

After the passing of the Immorality Amendment Act of 1950 the annual number of prosecutions increased to such an extent that, in the latter part of 1959, there were signs that public opinion was becoming disturbed. A number of letters on the subject appeared in the Afrikaans press, and while many of the letter-writers advocated increased penalties for transgressors, a few openly questioned the value of a law that caused so much social damage and failed so patently to achieve its object. Nevertheless, the Immorality Act continues in operation. There are about 900 prosecutions in an average year of which less than half are successful. Close on 50 per cent of those prosecuted are whites and there is a wide-spread belief that far more infringements of the Act occur than are brought to court. An anomaly arises when the accused, as frequently happens, apply for a separation of trials which then take place in different courts. In 1965 seven white men were acquitted for lack of sufficient evidence while the seven African women who had been accused with them were found guilty. Such cases are adjusted administratively by the grant of pardon.

The Act was strongly attacked from a number of quarters. Professor B. B. Keet of the Theological Seminary of the Dutch Reformed Church at Stellenbosch, twice raised the matter in *Die Kerkbode,* the official organ of the Church, arguing that it is impossible to approve of a law that makes an action immoral only when it occurs between people of different colours. Other critics pointed out that the application of the Act entails snooping, tale-bearing, and other disreputable methods of law enforcement. Police-men shine torches into stationary cars at night and enter private houses servants' quarters on suspicion. Since cases are difficult to prove, Coloured women had been induced to give evidence for the State and, as might be expected, have on occasion given perjured evidence. So bad had this become in a number of cases in which policemen themselves were accused that the magistrate trying these cases spoke strongly against the practice of relying on such evidence.

Apart from the unsavoury methods employed to gain convictions, and the malodorous publicity that accompanies cases tried under the Immorality Act, there are other hardships. In one case a European man and a Coloured woman had been living together for fifteen years and had three children. They were found guilty and sent to prison and the family was broken up. In another case, the parents were sentenced to imprisonment for four months, but the case received so much publicity that after four days they were released on instructions from the Minister of Justice. Meanwhile the three children had been uncared for and were living on such scraps of food as they could pick up or beg. Such cases, though not frequent, do occur, and it is only when blatant injustice legally perpetrated is brought to light that the Minister is able to exercise his powers of pardon.

The Mixed Marriages Act has produced few prosecutions. The number of marriages between white and non-white, previous to the Act, was infinitesimal. After the passing of the Act, no one who was obviously coloured would attempt to marry anyone who was obviously white. Such cases as come before the courts are, therefore, cases in which the marriage officer and both partners are genuinely convinced that there is no legal impediment. The police, probably on private and malicious information suspect one of the partners, and a prosecution takes place. Whether the prosecution succeeds or fails, the effect on the people involved is devastating: either the marriage is broken up or the couple emigrate to a country where more benign laws prevail. In 1967 Breyten Breytenbach, an Afrikaans poet living in Paris, wished to return to his native land with his young wife who is Indonesian. She was refused a visa and had they returned they would have rendered themselves liable to prosecution under the Mixed Marriages Act. Until the Act is repealed, therefore, they are exiles. The case attracted more than usual attention because Mr. Breytenbach had previously been awarded the much-coveted Hertzog Prize for Afrikaan poetry by the *Akademie*.

The passage of the Mixed Marriages Act was hotly opposed and has come under constant attack on moral and theological grounds. At a consultation of the World Council of Churches held at Cottesloe (near Johannesburg) in December 1960, at which representatives of the three most important Dutch Reformed churches were present, a resolution was adopted as follows: 'There are no Scriptural grounds for the prohibition of mixed marriages. The well-being of the community and pastoral responsibility require, however, that due consideration should be given to certain factors which make such marriages undesirable.' A few months earlier eleven Afrikaans church leaders published a book called *Delayed Action* in which the Act, among many others, was roundly condemned. It is a measure of Afrikaner prejudice on this matter that, though the critics stuck to their guns, they were repudiated by large majorities in their respective synods.

In an attempt to prevent 'passing', the Nationalist Government passed the Population Registration Act. This Act, which had more than one objective,[9] provides for the issue to everybody of an identity certificate

---

[9] In *Die Burger* of 21 February 1950, Dr. Malan, then Prime Minister, was quoted as saying that 'a national register is the basis of the whole policy of apartheid'.

showing his or her race—white, Coloured, African, or Asian. The Director of Census must compile a national register, based on the Census of 1951, in which citizens are classified according to race. Anyone may, on payment of the prescribed fee, object to his own or to anyone else's classification, and such objection is heard by a board appointed by the Minister of the Interior. An appeal from the decision of the board lies to the Supreme Court, but the expense and publicity involved are a strong deterrent to the exercise of this right.

According to the original Act of 1950 a white person is one who (a) is 'obviously white in appearance', or (b) is 'white by general repute and acceptance'. But if he is Coloured by general repute and acceptance, he will not be considered white even if he obviously is so! In the original Act descent was only of indirect importance as evidence; but an amending Act of 1967 made descent of primary importance as a test to be applied *before* the tests of appearance or general acceptance. This makes it still more difficult to succeed in an appeal against a classification where documentary evidence, such as birth or baptismal certificates, do not exist. Moreover, the Act opens the door wide to the common informer and to those who, from personal or other motives, wish to injure someone else.

Once the matter of race classification has been decided the holder of an identity card must show it on demand to any authorized person. Once race has been registered it is wellnigh impossible to 'pass' as a member of another group; but the Director of Census or the Secretary for the Interior may at any time re-open a case if he believes a wrong classification has been made. Those who are passing as white or have successfully appealed against classification are, therefore, never free of the haunting fear of being denounced.

By 1961, eleven years after the passing of the Act, the Population Registration Appeal Board had tried some 3,000 white—Coloured and 42,000 Coloured-Asian-African cases. By 1968 the number of cases had dropped to about 100 a year, but it was estimated in 1966 that 148,000 Coloured border-line cases had not applied for identity cards (thus risking prosecution) for fear they might be placed in a racial category that would jeopardize their employment, their ownership of property, their children's education.[10], and their social status generally. It may be imagined what mental suffering is entailed by this uncertainty in a country where freedom, security, economic and social welfare, and most of the things that make life worth living are dependent on a so-called 'race' classification from which there is no escape.

The political status of the Coloured people progressively deteriorated after 1909. In 1853, when the Cape Colony obtained representative government, there was no colour bar. European, Coloured, and African

[10] See Muriel Horrell, *A Survey of Race Relation, 1966*, p. 123.

males enjoyed the franchise on the same qualifications. These qualifications were subsequently raised in order to restrict the number of new non-European voters, but they were the same for all races. In 1909 the Cape franchise was entrenched in the South Africa Act but only Europeans were eligible for parliament. In 1930 the political influence of Coloured voters was diminished when European women were enfranchised by the Hertzog Government, and it is noteworthy, in view of subsequent legislation, that Malan, then a member of the Hertzog Cabinet, had earlier opposed votes for women unless Coloured women were included. In 1931, voting qualifications were abolished for European males but retained for Coloured and Africans, thus further weighting the scales in favour of the Europeans.

The Nationalist Party came to power in 1948 on a policy of apartheid, which included placing Coloured voters on a separate roll, and in 1951 it introduced a Bill to do this. The passing of the Bill, the storm it raised, and the constitutional crisis that followed, are more fully described in chapter 4. The Separate Representation of Voters Act, which eventually became law in 1956, had several consequences. In the first place, Coloured voters were no longer able to participate in a general election and were thus to a large extent debarred from expressing an opinion, through the ballot-box, on questions of national importance. Secondly, where formerly they could exercise the vote in all fifty-five Cape constituencies, they were now limited to electing four members. Their influence had been considerable in some twenty-five constituencies and decisive in about seven; since, before 1956, they usually voted for the United Party, these constituencies now became possible Nationalist seats. In the third place, as experience with the separate representation of African voters in the Cape had shown, however capable the whites elected by Coloured voters might be, they would not be able to effect much for their constituents because they were too few in number. In any case, as we shall see in the following chapter, representation of Coloured voters in parliament was abolished in 1968.

Another aspect of the Coloured question about which the Nationalist Party had long been concerned was residential segregation. In Cape Town and its suburbs, and in many other towns in the Cape Province, there are districts where Coloured and European live side by side. These are usually, though by no means always, the poorer quarters. Some local authorities tried to bring about separation by including a servitude in certain areas prohibiting the transfer of fixed property to non-whites. But, unless such a servitude existed, there was nothing to prevent a Coloured man from acquiring property wherever he liked. In 1950 parliament passed the Group Areas Act by which, after a fixed date, no transfer of property without a permit might take place between the different racial groups in demarcated areas. Almost every year after the Act was passed, the minister had to ask parliament for a large number of amendments giving him increased powers to coerce those local authorities that were unwilling to face the enormous expense and the odium of applying the policy.

In 1955 the Group Areas Development Act provided for the assessment of compensation in cases of forced sales and empowered the Group Areas Development Board to develop new areas for different racial groups and, if necessary, to do so without the consent of the local authority which must, nevertheless, foot the bill. Group Areas for Coloured have been proclaimed in other provinces but it is naturally in the Cape Province that the largest number of Coloured people have been affected, and more particularly in the Western Province where, until recently, white and Coloured have traditionally and by law been free to live where they could afford to. In all the small towns of the Western Province, such as Stellenbosch, Paarl, and Somerset West, in the larger towns such as Worcester and Port Elizabeth, and in the city of Cape Town and its suburbs, tens of thousands of Coloured people have been compelled to leave areas where they had settled for generations. In some few cases whites had to move too; but the overwhelming majority of those affected by this attempt to zone cities according to colour are non-whites. In the so-called District Six, for instance, near the centre of Cape Town, there are an estimated 61,000 Coloured and Malays, 800 whites, and 600 Asians. Yet District Six was proclaimed a white area in 1966 and, in due course, its non-white inhabitants will have to leave an area where Coloured people settled soon after the emancipation of slaves in 1834. It is an area, moreover, within walking distance of the employment most of the inhabitants find in the centre of Cape Town. Their new home will be about ten miles away.

As was to be expected from experience in the United States, forced sales of property usually entail a loss that compensation by government fails to make good. Such losses are most easily observable in the case of churches. By the end of 1967 the church buildings of more than fifty Coloured congregations had been affected by group areas proclamations and in most cases the congregations were undergoing financial crises so severe that an Afrikaans daily newspaper opened a fund to assist them. But financial loss and crisis are not the only social results of mass removals. Coloured and white ministers of religion have pointed out that when communities are moved from a settled area where churches, schools, halls, community centres, and social and welfare clubs exist, the dislocation and insecurity have devastating social effects. Gangsterism and crime increase and church and club membership declines.[11]

In February 1968 the Department of Planning, in a report tabled in parliament, gave the following information: at that date, 1,073 group areas had been proclaimed. Of these, 581 for whites, 297 for Coloured, 131 for Indians, 8 for Africans, 1 for Malays, and 4 for Chinese; and proposals for another 97 centres had been published. In only three urban areas with

[11] See letter by Dr. A. M. Hugo in *Die Burger*, 30 October 1967.

populations exceeding 20,000 had group areas not yet been demarcated. These figures give some idea of the extent and depth of the demographic surgery involved in implementing the Group Areas Act.

The City Council of Cape Town, where the largest concentration of Coloured people lives, has consistently opposed the Nationalist Government's policies on race separation; but they have fought a losing battle because both central and provincial governments have tightened their control over local authorities. Coloured people in the Cape Province still (1968) have a municipal franchise on the common roll, and Cape Town has a few Coloured city councillors; but the government has repeatedly stated its intention of creating separate Coloured municipalities and taking Coloured voters off the common municipal roll. In Cape Town there are a few Coloured traffic policemen and firemen, but, acting under the Industrial Conciliation Act of 1956, the Minister of Labour has reserved these jobs and, for the future, only whites may be appointed.

The City Hall and the suburban halls under the City Council's control were among the few places in South Africa where unsegregated mixed audiences watched plays and ballet, listened to music, or attended public meetings. Cape Town libraries, too, were unsegregated. These rights were gradually taken away. Following a number of cases in which the courts ruled that if separate public amenities are provided they must be substantially equal, the Separate Amenities Act of 1953 was passed empowering public bodies to provide facilities exclusively for one race or to provide separate but not necessarily equal facilities. This permissive legislation did not achieve its object and many local public bodies continued to provide unsegregated facilities. In 1955, accordingly, the Separate Amenities Ordinance was passed by the Cape Provincial Council empowering the Administrator, after consultation with a local authority, to direct it to provide separate amenities; if it fails to do this, the Administrator may instruct the Provincial Secretary to do so—at the expense of the local authority. Even this did not achieve its purpose of bringing local authorities to heel, and the government resorted to issuing proclamations under the Group Areas Act which extended the meaning of the word 'occupy' to cover not only land but places where refreshments are sold. It then became illegal for racially disqualified persons to attend such gatherings unless an exempting permit had been obtained from the Minister. Such permits normally stipulate that the audiences must be racially segregated and that separate lavatories and refreshment booths must be provided.

The Cape Peninsula is famed for its beaches, which South Africans of all colours have always enjoyed and to which thousands of visitors from the northern provinces come in summer to acquire a tan that makes them almost indistinguishable from the Coloured people. Here, too, apartheid was gradually enforced. The City Council was able to stall on the ground that it was necessary first to establish definite high- and low-tide marks. This difficulty was overcome by empowering the Minister of Lands to disregard high- and low-water marks. A notice in the *Government Gazette* of 3 July 1959 empowered the Minister of Lands to divide the beach or the sea as bathing places and added that a regulation by him may apply to 'the whole beach or a specified part of it, or to the whole sea or a specified part of it'.[12] With such sweeping powers given to the Minister of Lands, neither the City Council of Cape Town nor King Neptune would be able to prevent beach apartheid.

While a substantial minority of the Coloured people in the towns constitute what in England might be called a middle class—upper or lower—there is a great deal of poverty among the Coloured people at large. Inadequate housing, poor clothing, and malnutrition result in a high death-rate. The expectation of life of a Coloured male is forty years. as against fifty-nine for a white male. Tuberculosis is rife. Widespread drunkenness among Coloured people is both a cause and a result of poverty. There exists in the Cape Province a system known as the 'tot system' by which Coloured agricultural labourers are given a number of tots of wine during the working day as part of their wages. It has the weaknesses of the truck system of wages, and, moreover, it engenders and encourages the taste for strong drink. In the towns Coloured people may buy wine and brandy at canteens and bottle-stores; there is an ineffective legal limit of four bottles a day in any one bottle-store, and the brandy is cheap and harmful. The result is seen in week-end drunkenness and all its consequences. Many people, of all parties, are concerned at this state of affairs, as are many of the Coloured people themselves; but the wine farmers and the liquor trade are a powerful political pressure group and nothing is done to improve matters. The abolition of the tot system is an obvious first step which no political party feels itself strong enough to take.

Although the Coloured people are, on the whole, cheerful even to fecklessness, educated men and women among them feel frustrated and embittered because they realize most clearly the colour-bar limitations that prevent them and their children from attaining good positions. Intelligent and hardworking as many of them are, they know that this will not ensure them an entry into most professional ranks, or even into many skilled occupations. Socially, they are debarred from white cinemas; they must occupy separate stands at football matches; they are not admitted to white restaurants and cafés, and have few of their own. They form a community of their own and have their own social life; but ever present at the back of their minds is the realization that they are not full citizens in the land of their birth. They used to pride themselves on having the vote in common with whites. That right was removed in 1956, and in 1968 their right to

---

[12] Report in *Die Burger*.

vote for representatives in parliament, even on a separate roll, was abolished.

During 1965 more than 1,000 Coloured people emigrated to Canada and an unknown, though probably smaller, number went to Britain. At the end of June 1968 the Canadian government said that 1,076 Coloured people had gone to Canada in 1966, and 1,366 in 1967; and during the first six months of 1968 there were more than 600 applicants representing between 1,200 and 1,500 persons. These numbers are significant when it is borne in mind that those who leave are not people who cannot make a living in South Africa. On the contrary, they are professionally and technically trained men and women—doctors, teachers, mechanics, nurses. Moreover, South Africa is trying to attract immigrants with just those qualifications. But they must be white.

While the Coloured people resent the colour bars that operate against them, most of them have themselves strong prejudices against Africans. They had always cherished the fact that, unlike Africans, they were administered on the white side of the colour line. During the last war the Smuts Government set up a Coloured Advisory Council to advise the government. A proportion of Coloured people accepted this and were prepared to co-operate with the government; but the great majority of educated Coloured men and women would have nothing to do with it. They feared that the Council was an attempt to separate them, politically and administratively, from the whites. There were, they said, no 'Coloured' affairs. Their fears were realized when a Coloured Affairs Department and an elected Union Council for Coloured Affairs were created.

Coloured leadership is divided about whether or not to co-operate with whites and, more particularly, with the white government. At one extreme are a diminishing number of educated Coloured people who refuse to assist a white government to provide separate administrative and consultative machinery for Coloured people. The majority either cannot risk their jobs by openly opposing government or they believe that there is more to be gained, personally or for their people, by co-operation. In the early fifties, when the Bill to place Coloured voters on a separate roll was before parliament, there was a temporary and uneasy union of all Coloured groups; but once the deed had been done the old divisions reappeared. Indeed, the divisions were probably sharpened by the greater isolation into which Coloured people had been forced.

The Nationalist Party is divided on the place to be assigned to Coloured people. While agreeing that Coloured voters must vote on a separate electoral roll, some Cape Nationalists feel that they should be allowed to to elect Coloured representatives to parliament. Towards the end of 1960 this feeling led a number of Cape Nationalists openly to advocate this modification of the policy of apartheid. They were prompted, partly by a conviction that the Coloured people belonged on the white side of the colour line, and partly by a realization that, unless timely concessions were made, the Coloured leaders would make common cause with Africans. Dr. Verwoerd, supported by the Transvaal Nationalists, sternly vetoed these proposals and announced that he proposed to create a Coloured 'state'. The Cape Nationalists were brought to heel, and a number of Coloured leaders, more widely based than usual, announced plans for a united Coloured front to co-operate with other racial organizations in defence of their rights. This movement, with others of its kind, petered out.

The Cape Malays are a distinctive group of about 40,000 Mohammedans. Their ancestors came from the East, largely from Java, some as slaves but most as political exiles, and mixed with European and Coloured and other groups. Though, in due course, they adopted the language of the Europeans, they retained their religion and remained a distinctive group. For generations the Malays and their descendants were the skilled workers of the Cape— silversmiths, carpenters, coopers, cabinet-makers, and tailors; and Malay domestic servants helped to introduce many of what are now typical Cape dishes.

Although the Malays are classed, officially, as Coloured, their religion keeps them separate from the rest. Marriage between the two groups does take place, but Malay parents prefer their daughters to marry Malay rather than Coloured men. If a Malay marries a Coloured girl she becomes a Mohammedan. Their temperate habits and their business acumen ensure that they are, for the most part, economically better off than the rest of the coloured community.

The Cape Malays belong mostly to the Sunni sect of Mohammedanism and look to Mecca for their religious leadership. Though their home language is usually Afrikaans, the language of the mosque is Arabic, and all religious feasts and fasts are scrupulously observed. In spite of colour bars, the Malays are psychologically better adjusted to life than the Coloured. Their religion and their social status are respected by Europeans, and being Mohammedan, they have no desire to emulate the white Christians or to pass into their society.

THE ASIANS

When, in the 1860's, British settlers in Natal began to cultivate sugar they found that they could not get enough Zulu labour to work the plantations, and Asians were brought in as indentured labour. Many of these labourers stayed on after they had served their indentures, either as free labourers, or as independent small farmers, shopkeepers, and traders, or domestic servants. Soon their families and friends joined them to settle in a country which, colour bar or no, provided a better living then their native land. In 1911 the Indian Government put a stop to the recruiting of labour, and the South African Government, alarmed by Indian agitation for rights—an agitation led by Gandhi—prohibited free immigration. By then the Asian population had grown considerably and South Africa was faced with an Asian 'problem'.

At that time Gandhi was leading a passive resistance movement for Asian rights, and already various restrictions had been imposed on the Indians. They were not, and are not now, allowed to live in the Orange Free State. They might reside in the Transvaal, but were forbidden to own land, a prohibition which was legally overcome by the formation of land companies or by persuading a European to act as nominal owner. In Natal they were allowed to own fixed property, but their parliamentary franchise, secure while Natal was under the final control of the British Government, was abolished when it achieved responsible government. In the Cape they suffered fewest restrictions.

By 1924 the 'Indian Question' became acute, particularly in the Transvaal. Municipalities complained, with some justice, that Asians created slums by sub-letting and that the value of urban property fell when they settled there. Asian trading-stores in the Transvaal and Natal were prospering and this may have added to European discontent. To meet it, the Smuts Goverment introduced a Class Areas Bill for segregating Asians throughout the country. The agitation against the Bill, both in India and in South Africa, was furious, and when, in the middle of the controversy, the Smuts Government fell, the Bill was dropped. In 1926 the Hertzog Government introduced an even more severe measure, but, for a time, wiser counsels prevailed and a round-table conference with the Government of India produced the so-called Cape Town Agreement which provided for assisted repatriation and, for those who remained, better conditions.

It is a misnomer to talk about repatriation. Asians in South Africa know no other motherland. There are 561,000, of whom some 21,000 live in the Cape, 73,000 in the Transvaal, and the rest in Natal. It is, accordingly, in Natal that the problem is most acute. In the first place, there is the usual colour prejudice that sees the increase of the Asian population as a menace to European standards. There is a great deal of poverty among Asians, but a few are extremely prosperous and want, naturally, to invest their money in real estate. In the second place, their way of life and their outlook on business are different from those of the Europeans who are their principal competitors in trade. The Nationalist Party regards the Asians as unassimilable, and most Europeans would agree with that description.

In 1946 the Smuts Government tried to deal with the situation in Natal by an Act which pegged property deals with Asians, while, at the insistence of the liberal element in his party which disliked the Act, it gave them the right to elect three European members of parliament. The Asians boycotted the elections and campaigned vigorously, in South Africa and at U.N., against the 'Pegging Act'. The passive resistance campaign in Natal never reached serious dimensions, but it attracted a great deal of publicity.

When the Nationalist Party came to power in 1948 it repealed that part of the Act which gave parliamentary representation but retained the restrictions on land purchase. In 1950 parliament passed the Group Areas Act which is more fully described in Chapter 7. The way in which the Act was used in Durban and Johannesburg, and in small towns of Natal and the Transvaal, to deprive Asians of long-established rights and restrict their trading activities by forcing them out of areas which they have built up into trading centres, makes it seem credible that the primary purpose of the Group Areas Act was an attempt to make life so intolerable to Asians that they would be forced to leave the country.[14]

The Asians of South Africa are a fertile, hard-working, ingenious people, and are not likely for long to be content with a situation in which they are discriminated against. They will not voluntarily return to India or Pakistan, and the cost of 'repatriating' the entire population—a plan that was seriously suggested in Nationalist quarters—will be far greater than any government could bear. A preliminary conference, held at Cape Town in 1950, at which the governments of India and Pakistan were represented, failed to reach an agreement on an agenda for a round-table conference. Meanwhile trade relations between the Union and, as they then were, her two sister Commonwealth states of India and Pakistan came to a standstill.

The presence of Asians further complicated the South African race situation. In 1949 South Africa and the world were startled by the suddenness with which the country's most serious race riot flared up in Durban. Starting from a trivial incident, in which a young African was knocked over by an Indian trader, a race riot between Africans and Indians developed in a matter of hours, and Africans killed a great many Asians and pillaged and plundered the Indian quarter. All the evidence is to the effect that the riot was totally unpremeditated. There is, at the same time, considerable and reliable evidence suggesting that the Zulu in Natal had long resented the Asians for various reasons: Asian shops were said to exploit the Africans; Asians could get licences to own and drive buses conveying Africans, while Africans themselves could not do so;[15] and Asian men were accused of 'interfering' with African women. There is also evidence that the Zulu sensed the attitude of their white masters towards the Asians and thought that, if they attacked them, the whites would not really mind. Finally, it has been suggested that the riot was one of general discontent and that,

---

[14] For fuller details of this aspect of the Group Areas Act, see a pamphlet by Alan Paton, *The People Wept*, and the excellent annual *Survey of Race Relations* by Muriel Horrell (South African Institute of Race Relations).
[15] This was later altered.

in this case, Asians stood between whites and Africans. Whatever the truth of the matter, the riots were a warning of how inflammable race relations are in a country where the popular 'solution' to the problem of race friction is to separate, confine, and restrict the races and thus to diminish the chances of tackling the root causes of the friction—grinding poverty and overcrowding. The warning was not heeded, and further riots in 1959 were but a sample of what might be expected unless wiser councils prevailed. Within the first three months of 1960 major clashes between Africans and the police occurred at Cato Manor in Durban, at Windhoek, in South-West Africa, at Langa in Cape Town, and at Sharpeville, on the Rand. At Cato Manor the rioting was sparked off by a 'routine police raid' on a Sunday morning; at Windhoek, by the compulsory removal of Africans to a new African township; at Langa and Sharpeville, by a massed demonstration against passes organized by the Pan African Congress, a breakaway group from the African National Congress which opposed the demonstration. The total casualties in these four clashes were about 80 people killed (including 9 policemen) and many more wounded.

In 1961 a new department of state, the Department of Indian Affairs, was established. This step, in line with the general theory of apartheid, was as unpopular with Asians as the establishment of a separate Department of Coloured Affairs was with the Coloured. Like the Coloured, Asians maintained that there were no 'Indian' affairs, and they rightly feared that such administrative fragmentation would not serve their interests as South African citizens. The establishment of the new department was, of course, a logical consequence of apartheid and serves to demonstrate the divisive nature of that theory of race relations.

In 1964 the government set up the National Indian Council, subsequently called the South African Indian Council, to act as a link between the minister of Indian Affairs and the Asian population and to make recommendations to the Minister. Though it was at first difficult to find Asians who would accept government nomination to carry out an apartheid policy, Asian opposition to the Council died down as they adopted the view that it was better to maintain contact with the government, even on the basis of apartheid, than to boycott the Council. In 1968 the Council was turned into a statutory body by Act of Parliament. It was still to be composed of nominated members only; but the Minister, introducing the Bill, said the policy was to move on to an elected Council.

4

GOVERNMENT

THE Union of South Africa came into existence on 31 May 1910 by an Act passed by the British Parliament at the request of the four colonies that constituted the Union. This was the South Africa Act of 1909. Later, between 1920 and 1930 various resolutions of Imperial Conferences, which were meetings of Colonial and British prime ministers, were given legal effect by the Statute of Westminster (1931) and by the Status of the Union Act (1934). The first of these was an Act of the British Parliament, and its principal effect was to repeal the Colonial Laws Validity Act of 1865, as far as it concerned South Africa, by which colonial laws that were repugnant to British laws were, to the extent of the repugnancy, void. The Status of the Union Act was passed by the Union Parliament, and did no more than amend the South Africa Act so as to bring it into line with the position as established by the Statute of Westminster. Whatever limitations there may have been on the sovereignty of the Union of South Africa were removed by it. In consequence, South Africa became an independent sovereign state, and the British Queen was also Queen of South Africa, being represented by a Governor-General, who, on behalf of the Queen, acted as a constitutional monarch on the advice of her South African ministers. In April 1961 an Act was passed by the Union Parliament altering the constitution from a monarchical to a republican one, and on 31 May the Republic of South Africa came into being.

Unlike the federations of Canada and Australia, where the provincial and state parliaments have certain sovereign powers, South Africa became a union, and sovereignty rested with the central parliament. Being sovereign, Parliament might alter its own constitution (the South Africa Act); but that Act itself specified that three of its clauses might be altered only by a two-thirds majority of both Houses, sitting jointly. These clauses were, firstly, a clause dealing with the recognition of English and Dutch[1] as official languages: secondly, a clause dealing with any alterations to the franchise that might diminish the voting powers of persons in the Cape Province by reason of their race or colour only; and, lastly, a clause empowering parliament to amend the Act by normal bicameral procedure

---

[1] At the time of the Union Dutch (not Afrikaans) was one of the two official languages. In 1926 the South Africa Act was altered and Dutch was made to include Afrikaans. Technically, therefore, the Union has three official languages.

except in the case of the two other clauses and of this clause itself. These were the so-called 'entrenched clauses'.

Until 1951 it was generally assumed that the entrenched clauses retained their validity, despite the altered status of the Union. In fact, when in 1931 the Statue of Westminister was being discussed in the Union Parliament, Smuts raised this point. Hertzog was then Prime Minister, and he and his colleagues declared that the entrenched clauses were unaffected. These clauses were, they said, a matter of national honour and good faith. In 1936, when African voters in the Cape Province were taken off the common roll and given separate representation, the two-thirds procedure was followed. In 1951 Malan's Nationalist Government introduced a Bill to take Coloured voters in the Cape off the common roll. On that occasion, however, the two-thirds procedure was discarded. The United Party and Labour Party Opposition challenged this, and the Speaker ruled that, in effect, the entrenched clauses had ceased to be valid.

This ruling raised a constitutional issue of the first magnitude. Some constitutional lawyers supported the Speaker's ruling, while others vigorously disputed it. Most South Africans were not concerned about the strictly legal aspect of the matter, but a large section regarded the entrenched clauses as part of the solemn contract that established the Union. The validity of those clauses had been reaffirmed by leading statesmen in 1931, many of whom were, in 1951, members of the government that now denied that validity. It seemed, thus, as if the foundations of the constitution were being undermined. Mass protest meetings were organized against Malan's action, and more than 100,000 voters signed a petition against the Bill to remove Coloured voters from the common roll. Ex-Servicemen and women, seeing in the Bill a threat to democracy for which they had fought, organized protest meetings; and a commando of ex-Servicemen, led by the Battle of Britain pilot, 'Sailor' Malan, and an Afrikaner veteran of the Boer War, Commandant Dolf de la Rey, and joined by contingents from other provinces, converged on Cape Town, where a mass meeting of 50,000 people was held. Before the meeting 10,000 ex-Servicemen and women marched with torches through Cape Town, and, later, a deputation presented resolutions to the leaders of political parties at the Houses of Parliament. This mass demonstration was a protest, not against the removal of the Coloured voters from the common roll, but against the threat to the constitution. The government was not, however, deflected from its course, and the Bill was passed by both Houses of Parliament sitting separately and received the assent of the Governor-General.

When the Act had been promulgated, four Coloured voters applied to the courts to have it declared invalid. The application was dismissed by the Cape Provincial Division of the Supreme Court, the Court holding that it was bound by a previous decision of the Appeal Court in the case of

Ndlwana v. *Hofmeyr* in 1937. In that case the Appeal Court had held that, since the passing of the Statute of Westminster in 1931, the courts had no power to pronounce on the validity of Acts of Parliament. The Judge-president of the Cape Provincial Division expressed doubts as to the oorrectness of that decision but held, correctly, that it could be reversed only by the Appeal Court itself.

The case of the four Coloured voters went on appeal to the Appellate Division in February 1952, and, after a hearing lasting six days, the Appeal Court unanimously ruled that the Separate Representation of Voters Act was 'invalid, null and void and of no legal force and effect', since it had been passed bicamerally and not, as required by the South Africa Act, by a two-thirds majority of both Houses in joint session. The full text of this judgement is to be found in the *South African Law Reports*, 1952, May issue, and need not be discussed here. What is more important for our immediate purpose is to describe the political and constitutional implications of the judgement.

The immediate popular reaction was to regard the judgement as a political defeat for Malan's Government, and the Opposition parties called upon him to resign. When the Act was passed many people had felt that the constitution of the Union had been violated and they now felt a sense of relief that its integrity had been upheld by the highest Court. This feeling was tempered, however, by the knowledge that the Nationalist Party Government would not accept the situation and that the real crisis lay ahead.

The Nationalist Party argument was, in essence, that the judgement restricted the sovereignty of parliament and, therefore, of South Africa; that if the courts were allowed to 'test' legislation they would, virtually, be in the position of being able to thwart the popular will and that government policy would be at the mercy of the courts. Malan and the Nationalist Party leaders and Press maintained that the South Africa Act of 1909 was an Act of the British Parliament, that the two-thirds majority entrenchment was inserted under pressure from Britain, and that, in effect, Afrikaner Nationalism was once more engaged in a bitter 'fight for freedom'.

The reply of the Opposition parties was that the Appeal Court judgement called in question, not the sovereignty of parliament, but the procedure adopted by parliament to express its sovereign will; moreover they said that the South Africa Act was indeed passed by the British Parliament but that this had been at the express wish of the four pre-Union parliaments and that there is no historical foundation for believing that the language and franchise clauses were entrenched under pressure from Britain. Finally, to evade the decision of the Appeal Court would be to destroy the foundations on which the Union was built and to shake public confidence in the courts.

In April 1952 the government introduced a Bill to provide for a 'High

Court of Parliament' to consist of all members of parliament sitting together. According to this Bill, if the Appeal Court gave a decision which had the effect of declaring an Act of Parliament invalid, a minister might refer the matter to a judicial committee of the High Court of Parliament for review. This committee, whose members need have no legal training, would then recommend to the High Court of Parliament whether or not to set aside the judgement of the Appeal Court. This Act was to have had retrospective effect to 1931, the date when the Statute of Westminster was passed.

In a leading article on the Act, the Nationalist paper, *Die Burger*, of 25 April 1952 said that its object was to put beyond all doubt the sovereignty of parliament, including the right to place Coloured voters on a separate register. Once that had been done, it would be unnecessary for the new High Court to meet again. The article added that no one was enthusiastic about the new court and it was a pity that it had to be created, but there seemed to be no other way out of the difficulty. It was, therefore, evident that the object of the Act was to validate the Separate Representation of Voters Act before the next delimitation of parliamentary constituencies so as to ensure that at the next general election the Coloured voters would not be able to influence the elections in Cape constituencies.

The reaction to this move of Malan's Government was immediate. The United Party, the Labour Party, and the Torch Commando announced a united front against the government. Inside paraliament the United Party and Labour Party fought the bill vigorously and took the extreme step of breaking off all 'pairing' arrangements with the government and refusing to take part in the committee stage of the Bill on the grounds that they would have nothing to do with the details of a Bill to set up what they described as 'an obviously fake court'.

Outside parliament a widespread movement of protest was set on foot. Membership of the Torch Commando, which Malan described as a militarist organization under Communist influence, grew, and included a number of retired judges. In Natal a strong and growing movement was started to demand a new National Convention which would place the Constitution of the Union beyond all party-political interference.

Despite all protests, the High Court of Parliament Act was passed by parliament in 1952. It, too, was tested and declared invalid by the Appeal Court. Knowing that the prolonged constitutional crisis was bad for the country, and hoping that the Opposition would realize this and compromise, the government made two more attempts, in 1953 and 1954, to gain a majority of two-thirds in a joint session of both houses. The Opposition, however, refused to compromise and the government finally overcame its difficulties by passing two Acts, neither of which required a two-thirds majority. In 1955 the Appellate Division Quorum Act increased the size of the Appeal Court from 6 to 11 and laid down that in cases in which the validity of an Act of Parliament is called in question, all eleven judges must sit. In the second place, the Senate Act of 1955 altered the constitution of the Senate so as to give the government the power, by 'packing' the Senate, to create the necessary two-thirds majority of both houses in joint session. Having thus prepared the way, the Senate was enlarged, and in 1956 the requisite two-thirds majority was found to pass the Separate Representation of Voters Amendment Act and the South Africa Act Amendment Act. The first of these two enactments placed Coloured voters in the Cape Province on a separate electoral roll to elect four white members of parliament, and the second removed the entrenchment of voting rights from the South Africa Act.

The South Africa Act of 1909 had left the franchise laws in the four colonies as they were, and Africans with the requisite qualifications in the Cape Province thus voted on a common roll. In 1936 they were deprived of their common roll rights and were allowed to elect three white members, on a separate roll, to represent them in the House of Assembly, while Africans throughout the Union elected four white members of the Senate by indirect election. In 1959 Parliament abolished African representation, and in 1960, when the term of office of the existing members expired, Africans ceased to have any direct voice in the affairs of the country.

When South Africa became a republic in 1961 the constitutional framework remained that of a union with a sovereign central parliament consisting of a President, a Senate, and a House of Assembly. The President is elected for seven years in a joint sitting of the two houses, and his powers are those of a constitutional monarch. The two houses have equal legislative power except in financial matters, and all Bills must be passed by both houses; a deadlock is dissolved by joint session procedure.

The House of Assembly consists of 160 members, who must be white. Of these, 150 are elected by white voters throughout the four provinces and a handful of Coloured voters in Natal; 6 are elected by white voters in South-West Africa; and 4 by Coloured voters in the Cape Province.

In 1956 the Senate was enlarged in order to give the government the required two-thirds majority of both houses in joint session and so enable it to remove Coloured voters from the common roll. Few people regarded the newly constituted Senate with equanimity. It had been the subject of denunciation, irony, sarcasm, and special pleading, and to most people it was an uneasy reminder of an expensive and unworthy essay in South African constitutional history.[2] Even those who owed their membership of the Senate to the Senate Act had been known to scoff at its constitution, and it was with relief that the country learned, in the latter half of 1959, of the government's intention to reconstitute it. In 1960 this was done and

---

[2] So overflowing with senators was parliament that one Minister is reported to have said that when a stranger in the Lobby smiled at him, as if expecting to be recognized, he always said 'Good morning, Senator', so as to be on the safe side.

the Senate came to consist of 54 members, of whom 11 were appointed by the Governor-General-in-Council (after 1961, by the President-in-Council), including 1 to represent[3] the Coloured people and 2 from South-West Africa. In each province the M.P.s and M.P.C.s elect a number of senators, on the single transferable vote, proportional to the number of M.P.s and M.P.C.s in that province. In 1961 the numbers were: Transvaal, 14; Cape Province, 11; Orange Free State and Natal, 8 each. Finally, 2 senators are elected by the M.L.A.s and M.P.s for South-West Africa. All the opposition parties opposed the Bill to reconstitute the Senate, mainly on the grounds that it made no provision for representation of Africans and Asians, that the Senate would become merely a reflexion of the Assembly, and that the Bill disregarded the intention of the National Convention of 1908 to give equal representation to the provinces and to make the Senate an effective house of revision. Senators are elected or nominated for ten years but the government may dissolve the Senate within 120 days after a dissolution of the Assembly. The Assembly is elected for not more than five years.

All white citizens of 18 years and over are entitled to vote unless disqualified by reason of insanity or criminality. Immigrants may apply for citizenship after five years residence, the decision resting in the discretion of the Minister of the Interior who may, according to the Citizenship Act of 1949, take cognizance of secretly sworn information in coming to a decision.

Until 1956 Coloured males in the Cape Province who were 21, literate, and either occupied property worth R150 or earned R50 a year, could become voters on a common roll; and in Natal there were a small number of Coloured voters, registered before Union. The Separate Representation of Voters Act of 1956 placed Coloured voters in the Cape on a separate roll, to elect four white members. Voters in Natal were left on the roll but the Act provided that no new names should be added. In 1968 all Coloured voters were disfranchised and the Coloured Council was enlarged to consist of 40 elected and 20 nominated members. The term of office of the three existing M.P.s representing Coloured voters (one had died earlier) was extended for the life of the present parliament, that is until 1971. After that date the parliament of the Republic will represent whites only.

For the purpose of white elections, each province of the Republic is divided into constituencies of which there are 150 in all. Until 1951 provision was made for delimitation of constituencies after every five-yearly census. From 1951, the census became decennial, and so too the delimitations.[4] At the time of Union it was felt that the rural areas, with their

[3] The wording of the Act is that he is appointed mainly 'on the ground of his thorough acquaintance with the reasonable wants of the Coloured people of the Cape'. Strictly speaking he does not 'represent' the Coloured people.

[4] A delimitation was, however, made in 1957.

sparse population, would be outvoted by the more densely populated urban areas. Constituencies were, therefore, 'loaded'. That is to say that when the Delimitation Commission has decided on the quota for each province, i.e. the number of voters required to form a constituency, it may take sparsity or density of population into account to the extent of 15 per cent above and below the quota. In other words, an M.P. in a rural constituency may represent 26 per cent fewer voters than in an urban constituency. As long as the main political parties enjoyed roughly the same support in the rural areas, this system had no marked political effects. But since the strength of the Nationalist Party in the rural areas steadily increased at the expense of its main opponent, the United Party, the Nationalist Party achieved a distinct electoral advantage. In the general election of 1948 the Nationalist and Afrikaner parties polled 140,000 fewer votes than their combined opponents, but returned seventy-nine members against their opponents' seventy-one. In the 1958 elections, after making allowances for uncontested seats, the number of votes cast for the Nationalist and United parties was about equal, yet the Nationalists returned 103 members to the United Party's 53.

The size of a South African constituency may vary from under 9,000 to over 12,000 voters. In South-West Africa, however, it is much smaller. By the Act of 1950 which provided for representation in the Union Parliament from the territory, South-West Africa was entitled to return six members to the Union House of Assembly, while the total number of registered voters was about 24,000.

South African parliamentary institutions are modelled closely on those of Great Britain. The procedure in Parliament would, with minor exceptions, be familiar to anyone accustomed to the House of Commons in London. Cabinet responsibility; the control of the executive through finance; the election of the Speaker; procedure for public and private bills; question time—all these are features of the South African Parliament, as they are of all popular assemblies that derive from the Mother of Parliaments at Westminster. There are, however, a few marked differences. Party discipline exercised through the caucus is stricter in South Africa and leaves less room for individual deviation from the party line. A member may try to influence policy within the caucus where proceedings are secret; but once the caucus has decided the party cracks down heavily on dissentients.

Because of this stricter discipline, questions in the House are used almost entirely by government opponents to elicit information of a factual kind that might, when published, damage government prestige. The use of question time by a government supporter to criticize policy is unknown. So, too, is the useful device by which members from different parties in the House of Commons put a resolution on the order paper calling in question some aspect of government policy. South African ministers are thus exempt from the fear of public criticism from their own party members, and a useful check on the power of the executive is removed. It is clearly not in the public interest that some 70 per cent of the M.P.s should confine their criticism of government policy to the privacy of the caucus.

A third difference lies in the question whether ministers should resign their interests in public companies. Both in Britain and in South Africa this has traditionally been a matter for the prime minister's discretion. By a series of rules laid down by British prime ministers since the latter half of the nineteenth century, ministers resign all directorships of public companies as soon as they assume office. In South Africa it was for many years the custom that ministers resign from all companies except newspaper companies and mutual insurance societies. Since the latter have, in practice, become large-scale finance houses, Dr. Verwoerd laid it down that ministers might, in future, not hold directorships in them; and newspaper companies, having important printing and publishing subsidiaries, have in recent years come under attack in parliament by those who hold that ministers ought to be divorced from all business connexions. The Nationalist Party, however, is so closely connected with the Afrikaans press that it is unlikely to agree to a rule whereby ministers will be debarred from exercising control over so important a medium for propaganda as the party press.

PROVINCIAL GOVERNMENT

The four provinces of South Africa are controlled, subject to the approval of the central government, by administrators, provincial executives, and provincial councils. The administrator is appointed by the government and is assisted by an executive committee of four which is elected by the provincial council. The council is elected by parliamentary voters, and the number of constituencies is the same as for parliament, except that a council must have a minimum of twenty-five members.

Provincial councils have power to make ordinances governing primary and secondary education for white children (their most important function),[5] provincial roads, control of municipal and other local governing bodies, and general hospitals. They also have powers of taxing, but these are severely limited by the central government which prefers to pay subsidies to the provinces from general revenue.

Provincial borrowing for capital expenditure is strictly controlled by the central government, which also jealously guards all sources of revenue but tends to allow the provinces to levy the more irritating forms of taxation—amusement tax, licences, and wheel tax. The result is that the provinces are unable to raise more than about 40 per cent of the revenue they must spend if they are to carry out their functions. The balance is

[5] See, however, p. 199 below for the effect of the National Education Policy Act of 1967.

provided in the form of subsidies from the central government for educa-tion and hospitals. Apart from the financial unsoundness of bodies elected on purely party-political grounds being responsible for raising less than half only of the money they spend, an even more unsound result is that provincial councils being chronically short of revenue, tend to pass on to municipal councils certain functions involving expenditure that are properly provincial or national, and would be more efficiently run if they were conducted over wider areas.

To avoid overlapping and too great a divergence in provincial policies, an Inter-provincial Consultative Committee meets from time to time. This consists of representatives of the central government, including two ministers, the administrators, the directors of education, and the top provincial officials. This in itself is a recognition of the fact that the provincial system of South Africa is not an entirely satisfactory method of administration. Nor has the Consultative Committee succeeded in doing much more than iron out a few inequalities. There are a number of disadvantages in the provincial system as at present constituted. At the time of union it was hoped that the provincial councils would be elected on non-party political lines; but from the first the elections followed national party divisions. It can happen that a majority in a provincial council is not of the same party as that in power in parliament. This would not matter much if, as in a federal system, the provincial councils had sovereign powers in their domestic affairs and were not dependent on the good graces of the central government. As it is, the provincial councils are either pale reflections of the central parliament or are implacably opposed to its policies. In neither case are they able to follow really independent policies.

The provinces retain the boundaries they had as colonies before union. These boundaries are historical and anachronistic. Business organizations, national sporting bodies, and even the state-owned South African Rail-ways disregard them when establishing branches; to do otherwise would be uneconomic. Administratively it would be far more efficient to divide the country into nine or ten natural regions, and this could easily be done without doing violence to local susceptibilities. As it is, the provincial system has all the disadvantages, and few of the advantages, of both a unitary and a federal system. There are other cogent reasons for a con-stitutional change that would alter the provincial system, but these will be discussed in a later chapter.

The administration of South-West Africa differs slightly from that of the provinces. The territory received a new constitution in 1949 under which she is administered by an administrator, an executive committee, and a legislative assembly that has more power than the provincial councils. By agreement, the territory taxes herself and her tax system is not subject to the approval of the central government, as is the case with the provinces.

At the same time, the Union Government assumed responsibility for raising loans for the territory and for the railway system, thus relieving South-West Africa of considerable financial burdens.

LOCAL GOVERNMENT

At the last decennial census in 1960 there were 100 urban areas with populations (all races) exceeding 5,000, while 564 had smaller populations and the majority had less than 2,000. Large or small, they all have the same statutory form of local government. The smallest may be classed as public health area, local area, local board area, health committee, sub-urban area, quasi-urban area, or rural township; as some of these names indicate their main preoccupation is with health—sanitation, water supply, etc. Slightly larger areas may have a township board, village council, or village management board, depending on what province they are in. A village can aspire to achieve municipal status (still called borough in Natal) and will then be governed by a municipal council, usually called a town council or a city council. According to the South African Municipal Yearbook of 1966-7 there were 319 municipalities in South Africa, varying in population from Kentani, with 276 inhabitants, to Johannesburg with 1,128,452. From the stage of township upwards the boards or councils are always elected. In all provinces except the Transvaal there is a small ownership or occupation of property qualification for the municipal franchise. In the Free State and Transvaal, all non-whites are excluded; in Natal, Coloured have the vote on the same terms as whites, but not Africans or Asians. In the Cape, all races may qualifiy, but only a small number of Africans do because of the restrictions on their owning land in white areas; Coloured and Asians not only have the vote, but a number of Coloured councillors have been elected on to the Cape Town and Port Elizabeth city councils. In 1960 the government announced its intention of instituting separate 'town councils' for Coloured people who would then cease to be on the common roll or to be eligible to election to a common town council, and legislative effect was given to this by the Group Areas (Amendment) Act of 1962 which empowered the Minister of Community Development, in consultation with the Administrator of the province concerned, to establish consultative or management committees in any Coloured or Indian group area. By 1967, 34 consultative and 21 management committees had been established, each consisting of five or more Coloured persons (or Asians in the case of Asian areas) appointed by the Administrator of the province, though in one case the committee was filled partly by popular election. The committees are consultative but the intention is gradually to extend limited powers to them.

Various Acts of Parliament and provincial ordinances govern the constitution, functions, and powers of local authorities, whether of municipal status or not. It should be noted that in the Cape Province there is an additional unit of local government, the divisional council, which embraces several smaller units and has limited taxing powers.

The most important services which local authorities are empowered to provide—and in some cases must provide—are the environmental services: removal or rubbish, sewage, water supply, inspection of food, prevention of pollution of streams and the air, economic and sub-economic housing, and slum clearance. Then there are personal welfare services, which include libraries, parks, and art galleries, which can only be afforded by the larger municipalities. There are, too, personal health services such as vaccination and the isolation of cases of infectious diseases. There are protective services such as traffic control and fire brigades; and, finally, the services of convenience—streets, lighting, transport, electric power, swimming-baths. Two important functions of English local authorities, education and police, have in South Africa always been regarded as belonging to the provincial and central governments respectively.[6]

Most of these functions of local authorities are permissive and not compulsory. Thus, slums may be cleared, but the municipality is not compelled to do it. Theoretically the provincial authorities can compel a local authority to provide an efficient water supply and system of sanitation. In practice, these services are for the most part poor. It was estimated some years ago[7] that, among urban local authorities below the status of municipality, 58 per cent had no piped water supply, 15 per cent had no proper sanitary services, and 20 per cent had no system of refuse-disposal. The Social and Economic Planning Council considered that, while most of the municipalities provided fairly complete environmental services, these services were restricted and inferior when supplied to the non-white inhabitants. While, for example, most municipalities had reticulated water supplies for the European quarters, the non-white quarters were normally restricted to public taps. The Department of Public Health, in its annual reports, has drawn attention to the lack of proper sanitation for the non-white communities in urban areas. And in many of those towns where civic amenities are lacking in the non-white areas, the white areas are well supplied with services of a non-essential character.

In chapter 2 we saw that local authorities had fallen very far behind in the matter of housing for Africans, but that under pressure from the central government great progress was made after 1951. The same is true, to a slightly lesser extent, of white housing and slum clearance. So great and rapid has been the influx into urban areas that municipalities have been unable to cope effectively with the situation, particularly for the

---

[6] Except in Natal where the police (though not education) were formerly under the borough.

[7] *Social and Economic Planning Council Report No. 8*, U.G.40/1945. These conditions have, from observation, improved very considerably but it has not been possible to find comparable figures for a later date than 1945.

lower income groups who require sub-economic housing. The result is high rents that amount to about 25 per cent of a man's earnings.

The most important items of local revenue are from property rates, sanitary rates, municipal trading in electricity, gas, water, and transport, and fees, fines, and licences. The percentages that each of these items form of the total varies greatly from municipality to municipality. The figure for municipal trading is usually high (as much as 60 per cent of revenue) and financial experts have condemned this method of raising revenue as a form of concealed taxation. A surprising fact is that provincial and government subsidies amount to about 8 per cent of local revenue. In Britain, subsidies provide about 36 per cent of local revenue, and in most European countries the figure is much higher: the assumption in paying high subsidies to local authorities is, of course, that very few of them can be financially self-sufficient, and that the functions they are performing are, in reality, national rather than local and should be paid for out of national revenue. Many of the duties imposed on local authorities in South Africa under the Public Health Act, the Housing Act and the Natives (Urban Areas) Act among others, are in fact of a national character, and it is unreasonable to expect local authorities to find the necessary money from their own resources. To make matters worse, what subsidies are available are paid on a pro rata basis rather than by block grant, and this presses hard on the smaller municipalities. Furthermore, government property, such as public buildings and schools and hospitals, is exempt from rates. In Cape Town, for example, government property in 1967 was valued at R128,724,541 on which the City Council received no rates and the loss to the City was R1,930,868, which represents about 20 per cent of its revenue from rates.[8]

With negligible exceptions, every town and village in South Africa has its white and non-white populations. The pattern varies. In the Western Province of the Cape the white, Coloured, and African populations will be roughly in the proportions of 5 to 5 to 1. Further east and north the ratio between Coloured and African in urban areas gradually changes, the number of Coloured decreasing and the number of African increasing, until, in the Free State and Transvaal, the Coloured have almost disappeared and there are usually slightly more Africans than whites in any one centre. In Natal the pattern is different, and, in numbers though not in occupation, Asians largely take the place of the Coloured of the Cape. This is a very general picture, but what is important is that, just as the government and the provincial councils have to think in terms of different colour groups, so each local authority, large and small, has perforce to deal with the problems that arise from this multi-racial society. A large

---

[8] In 1956 the Borckenhagen Committee was appointed to investigate, among other matters, financial relations between local authorities, the provinces, and the government, but by 1968 its final report had not yet been issued.

number of local authorities have three groups to deal with, and the problem is aggravated by the suspicion and fear with which Asians and Coloured in general regard Africans. The different groups are at markedly different cultural and economic levels, and social customs and manners differ at each level; where the Asian is concerned, there is a strong religious difference as well.

It is at the stage of local government that many of the problems and difficulties of a multi-racial society are best seen. It is there that national policies impinge most directly on the individuals of all population groups, and that the various laws that constitute national policy, or reveal its absence, are given personal significance. The regulations drawn up under these laws by distant departments of state have here to be carried into the lives and homes of human beings in day-to-day administration. It is in the sphere of local government that the social effects of laws and regulations are felt. In order to give the reader a clear picture of local government from this point of view, we propose to describe in some detail a particular urban area. It is an area of medium size, and, to simplify the picture, one in which there is no Asian population and only about 2000 Coloured people. The town, which we shall call Middeldorp, and the figures are chiefly those taken from the South African Municipal Yearbook of 1966–7 Statistics that change from year to year are described in the past tense as being true at the time of writing (1968). Institutions and continuing conditions are discussed in the present tense. The officials mentioned are types rather than individuals.

In 1921 the white population of Middeldorp was 4,300. By 1936 it was 5,300; by 1946 it was 7,700; by 1958 it was 12,500; and by 1968 it had risen to 17,500. The African population in those years numbered 4,500, 7,500, 12,800, 25,000, and 31,000, most of them employed by whites. Thus, between 1921 and 1968 the white population had quadrupled and the African population had increased to more than seven times its original size. Such increases are typical of the urbanization during those years.

In 1968, then, Middeldorp was a thriving semi-industrial town, on one of the main railway lines and national roads. It had rateable property valued at about R29,000,000; its revenue and expenditure balanced at about R2,700,000 and it had a municipal debt of more than R4,000,000.

The town council of nine members was elected by the white voters. Councillors are all unpaid and devote a considrable amount of time to their voluntary job; each councillor serves on at least two, and usually three of four, committees of the council. One such committee is the Bantu Affairs committee, responsible for the African location, about two miles from the outskirts of the town. All municipal by-laws affecting Africans must be approved by the Minister of Bantu Administration and Development, and each municipality must keep a separate Bantu revenue account which is credited with money received from pass and registration fees, rents of stands (or small plots) on which the African's houses are built, rentals from trading sites, fines, and a portion of the money collected by the government under the Bantu Services Levy Act. Against this revenue, the account is debited with charges for municipal services, such as water, lighting, and sanitation, and with interest and redemption on money borrowed on behalf of the African location.

The revenue from the location is about R300,000, from which the town council has to provide services and amenities for 31,000 Africans, as compared with the R2,700,000 for 17,500 whites. Unlike most local authorities, Middeldorp does from time to time spend a few thousand more on the location than it receives from it; but local white opinion, as through-out the rest of South Africa, simply does not regard the African location as an integral part of urban society, and the outmoded system persists of making the poorest section of the community pay for its own municipal services, and get nothing more than it pays for. The town councillors of Middeldorp would certainly not be able to persuade ratepayers to spend good 'European' money on African locations. The total municipal revenue and expenditure of local authorities throughout South Africa in 1968 was about twenty-five times greater than the revenue and expenditure of the African locations controlled by them. Expenditure on African locations for the whole of South Africa was, in fact, slightly in excess of revenue, which means that a few of the largest municipalities are beginning to accept a measure of responsibility for their African citizens.

The difference between Middeldorp's R2,700,000 and its location's R300,000 is immediately apparent. The white town has water-borne sewage, electric light and power, 40 miles of paved streets and sidewalks, a fine town hall, a public library, parks, and public gardens, and plenty of playing-fields. In keeping with these are the things not paid for by the town council but made possible by the enterprise of Middeldorp's white citizens and the labour of its black: fine houses, large schools where education is free and compulsory, cinemas, shops, hotels, and churches. The African location has no water-borne sewage; electricity lights the streets inadequately and has just recently begun to be laid on to individual houses; there are only two miles of paved street and many miles of dusty roads full of potholes; there is a poorly-built community hall *cum* cinema; and—a recent addition'—there is a pleasant beer garden; there are no public parks or gardens and only a few rather straggling trees; the few recreation fields look like very poor relations of the beautiful fields in Middeldorp. Again, in keeping with these things are the small, over-crowded houses, far from weatherproof; a few dingy shops; a high school and four primary schools, all overcrowded and able to take only 60 per cent of the children of a schoolgoing age—the rest play in the streets while both their parents are at work. There are as many churches as in Middeldorp, but because of the simplicity of poverty, some of them are not as ugly as those of the white town.

It must not be thought that every African in the location is poorer than every white in Middeldorp. As one walks from the centre of Middeldorp towards the location, the quality and the size of the 'white' houses become progressively poorer; and there are a number of men in the location—a doctor, some of the schoolmasters, a few builders, and the top clerks at the Bantu affairs department—who have better incomes, houses, and furniture than the poorest of the whites. There is an African middle class, small as yet, whose standard of living is higher than that of the poor white section of Middeldorp. Nevertheless, the people of Middeldorp, rich or poor, all regard themselves as 'superior' to the African, poor or rich.

An official of the municipality, called the location manager,[9] is in charge of the administration of the location. His office is on the outskirts of the location, and he and his staff of white and African clerks issue passes and permits and administer the Natives (Urban Areas) Act and the various regulations under the Act that aim at controlling the movement of Africans into towns. They also administer poor relief, housing, and health regulations, all products of national or provincial legislation; and they collect the taxes and maintain, under the town council, the Bantu revenue account. The manager of Middeldorp urban location is an excellent official who understands the needs of the people he must rule and is sympathetic to their aspirations. Lack of funds, and the need to carry out national policy with which he, as an individual, may not necessarily agree, have not discouraged him as they have so many of his colleagues in other urban locations. A heavy responsibility rests on him, and he stands between his African wards and the white ratepayers as represented on the town council, the one clamouring for improved conditions and the other clamouring for 'economy'.

One of the most difficult tasks of the manager is to administer the regulations that attempt to control the entry of Africans into urban areas. Middeldorp is an urban area into which no African may enter to live without permission. He will, on entering Middeldorp, apply to the manager for a permit to seek work. If he finds it, a service contract with his employer must be registered with the manager; if he does not find work, he must leave within seven days. The permit to seek work and the service contract are passes that must be produced on demand by the police. With the small staff at his command, the manager finds it impossible to carry out these regulations adequately. There is no fence round locations; and in most locations it is impossible to trace Africans who fail to report. Criminals, who may be up against the police on other grounds, often manage to get a forged or a borrowed pass. The manager of Middel-

[9] The title of this official and the area he administers have not yet been stabilized. Sometimes the area is called a Bantu Township and he is known as the Superintendent.

dorp location has a comparatively easy task, because the population is not large and 'foreigners' can to some extent be traced. In Johannesburg or Cape Town with their enormous African townships, it is virtually impossible to do this, and any two officials in either area are likely to give widely different estimates of their population. But even in Middeldorp the task of administering the regulations has become formidable if not impossible.

Until 1961 it was illegal to sell any alcoholic liquor to Africans who were, however, allowed to have kaffir beer. This is a traditional African drink, brewed by African women from fermented kaffir-corn and containing a maximum of two per cent of alcohol. It is bound up with African social customs and has some nutritional and anti-scorbutic value. In Middeldorp the system of home brewing was allowed, and each family was permitted to have not more than four gallons on the premises at any one time; but like all restrictions on the individual, this regulation was difficult to administer and, in an attempt to do so, periodic beer raids were carried out by the police. Other municipalities followed the alternative policy allowed by law—municipal brewing and sale in municipal beer halls. The profit from these beer halls was large and was used for social, recreational, and welfare purposes in the locations. But the system was not popular among Africans, and it led to a good deal of illicit brewing and to the addition to the beer of highly intoxicating ingredients, apt to make the consumer fighting drunk.

The illicit sale of 'European' liquor, the establishment of shebeens, and the bribery and corruption that attended these, had reached such proportions by 1959 that the government set up a commission of inquiry. The evidence of the police on the amount of time involved and the impossibility of effective control, and of administrators on the ill-will that resulted from raids that failed to achieve their real purpose of stopping the illegal trade, was overwhelming and well-nigh unanimous. Despite objections from the churches and from temperance societies, parliament removed the restrictions in 1961, and made the sale of alcoholic liquor to Africans legal.

After 1950 the job of the manager became more and more difficult. In the first place, African discontent and ambition had, as elsewhere in Africa, increased, and Africans no longer asked only for a little more generosity, a few more crumbs from the white man's table, a little more second hand charity. Many of them began to clamour for rights as citizens. Secondly, the response to these more insistent and strident demands was, at the national level, increasing doses of apartheid and, to implement it, of measures to 'control' Africans. The location manager who had been at his job for a long time looked back nostalgically to the days when things were 'easier', when his relations with his wards were less troubled. By 1968, though he was in municipal employ, he and his council had to carry out laws and regulations which they had not made and of which they might disapprove, and they were no longer allowed that measure of discretion which might soften administratively the harshness of legislation. The Nationalist Government's policy has been to curb the continued growth of urban African population except as migrant labour; and to this end it passed a law by which no African is regarded as a permanent resident of an urban area such as Middeldorp unless he was born there, or has been in continuous employment there for ten years or has resided there continuously for fifteen years.[10] Not being a permanent resident, he may not have his wife and family with him, for they are presumed to be resident 'somewhere in the Reserves'. The location manager has, on every working day of his life, to deal with Africans who are unable to produce evidence that they have complied with all the regulations but who, nevertheless, are in fixed employment and want to have their families with them. He knows that many of them have come from smaller towns or from farms and have never had any contact with Reserves; he knows, too, that some of them are unable to produce evidence simply because a previous employer has left the town or has died or, in a more relaxed period, had omitted to register his service contract. He knows these things and he sympathizes with them. But he knows full well that he dare not be too lenient with such applicants.

Middeldorp is more fortunate in this respect than large urban centres. During 1965[11] the number of African men endorsed out of the nine largest centres was 66,303, and the number of African women was 19,833. During the same period 131,282 men and 14,475 women were admitted to those areas, but only as contract labour for a fixed period not exceeding 12 months. 'Endorsing out' is the term used to describe the stamping of a reference book to the effect that the holder has no legal right to be in that area and must leave forthwith. The presumption is that, to have been endorsed out, the African concerned must have been arrested and appeared in court. The whole process of arrest, trial, endorsement out, and possible punishment involves hundreds of thousands of Africans each year in loss of time, loss of employment, loss of rights as a worker, and in the break-up of family life. The expense to the courts in time and official energy is enormous and Middeldorp can count itself fortunate that much of this happens elsewhere—so fortunate that its white citizens normally refuse to believe that it happens at all.

One of the most hateful tasks that the location manager at Middeldorp has had to perform is to issue reference books to African women, made compulsory by an Act called the Natives (Abolition of passes and Co-ordination of Documents) Act of 1952. To them these are still passes, and much as the men have hated the pass system, both men and women have

[10] Native Laws Amendment Act, 1957.
[11] Figures given in parliament by the Minister of Bantu Administration and Development, 12 August 1966.

yet more deeply resented its application to women. This is partly because of the fact that they are liable to be searched, and yet more because summary arrest of a woman for pass offences leaves her home and children unprovided for. That Middeldorp escaped the demonstrations and riots that occurred elsewhere when the reference books were issued was due to the fact that the manager is sympathetic and applied the law with as little harshness as he could. This did not, however, lessen the resentment of Africans for all who were associated with reference books.

Then came the application of the Group Areas Act. Middeldorp had only 2000 Coloured inhabitants, but there was an area between the town and the location where Coloured, white, and Africans lived in fairly close proximity, so the Group Areas Board called upon the town council to make proposals for separating them. Dr. Dönges, then Minister of the Interior and in charge of the Group Areas Act, had said in parliament that the Act would be carried out with justice towards all sections; but it was rather much to expect of town councillors that they should recommend the removal of white voters when they could solve their problem by removing African and Coloured non-voters. Once more, the location manager was the man who had to carry out the policy.

Since legislation of this kind was bound to produce discontent, and since Africans no longer suffered in complete silence, it was only natural that it should produce 'agitators'. There have for many years been laws restricting freedom in order to restrain 'agitators', and since 1950 these laws have been tightened up, and new laws added, to such an extent in fact that individual liberty has come to depend largely on the good will and permission of government or of those to whom its authority has been delegated. By suitable definition of such words as 'undesirable', an African may be banished from Middeldorp even if he was born there: and, to prevent vexatious legal delays, he is prohibited by law from applying to the courts for an interdict until he has been moved to some place perhaps a thousand miles away from his home town.[12] It is the central government rather than the local authority that normally uses these powers, but it is hardly surprising that the location manager of Middeldorp, hard pressed as he so often was, sometimes yielded to the temptation to use this method of getting rid of 'trouble-makers'.

It is no wonder that the location manager sometimes sighed for the 'good old days', recalling the time when looks were not sullen; when Europeans from Middeldorp used to move in and out of the location freely to co-operate with Africans in running child welfare, social clubs,

---

[12] Natives (Prohibition of Interdicts) Act of 1956. It is impossible, in a book not solely devoted to that purpose, to deal with the extent to which civil rights have become privileges at official discretion. Readers who want further information are referred to Brookes & Macaulay, *Civil Liberty in South Africa*, and to the annual *Survey of Race Relations in South Africa*, by Muriel Horrell, South African Institute of Race Relations.

night schools, and other welfare activities. By 1961 the location was a prohibited area for whites and entry was by permit only. Moreover, the government's dislike of 'mixed' committees prevented any organization drawing public funds from functioning on the practical basis of co-operation between black and white. Subsequent legislation narrowed the area in which white and non-white could meet socially or for a common social purpose; and even where there was no legal bar to association, 'mixed' meetings invariably invited the attention of the Security Branch of the police, and this in itself is a deterrent.

Like all other locations, Middeldorp had a Native Advisory Board of six African members, three elected by the African inhabitants and three nominated by the manager who was chariman of the board. The functions of the board were purely advisory; all regulations affecting the location had to be laid before the board before being sent to the provincial Administrator or the Minister of Bantu Administration and Development for approval; and the board might suggest amendments or new regulations. The manager of Middeldorp has been the kind of man who can get the most out of his board, and he used it in a friendly way to keep in touch with the people. But, like most other people in his position, he found that the system of advisory boards was a failure and that few Africans were interested in them.

Part of the trouble with such boards is that they have no executive power or financial authority. But the real truth of the matter is that Africans and whites are, whatever the theories may be, inhabitants of the same town, and no system of local self-government that does not recognize this fundamental fact is likely to have any permanent value. The Urban Bantu Councils Act of 1961 allows a local authority, and in certain circumstances makes it compulsory. to establish urban Bantu councils instead of Native advisory boards. The Act introduces several new principles. The members are elected ethnically, that is, by members of the different tribes that may be living in the location; and the appointed members are to be selected from among the representatives of officially recognized tribal chiefs. The principle of ethnic grouping is contrary to the advice of most local authorities and had little prospect of being maintained in urban areas where society had become intertribal. In the second place, limited civil and criminal jurisdiction, similar to that exercised by African chiefs and headmen in tribal reserves, is conferred on an approved nominee of the council. Finally, the Minister may, in consultation with the council and the Minister of Justice, establish a home guard to maintain law and order in a particular urban area.

The task of the location manager in Middeldorp will not be made easier by this attempt to revive and strengthen tribalism in urban areas. Not only will he have to deal with artificially revived tribal jealousies but he will have to dip into his all too meagre Native revenue account to finance the home guard and the unwanted tribal courts. Seven years after the passage of the Act only four local authorities had established Urban Bantu Councils.

Such, then, is Middeldorp. It is a fairly representative town, full of kindly, friendly people, black and white. It has its quota of saints and sinners. Its town councillors are mostly business men, though an occasional professional man or woman may be elected. They do their work without pay. From time to time there is talk of bribery; and councillors have been known to become wealthy by buying land at the right time and place. Though all of them are under social pressure to see to it that the wealthier parts of the town have the best streets, they do not always yield to this pressure. It was only from the 1940's that party politics played a part in council elections. When King George VI and the Royal Family visited South Africa in 1947, the Mayor of Middeldorp was a Nationalist who acted with traditional Afrikaner courtesy and hospitality, though the party to which he belonged had not favoured a royal visit.[13]

As a social organism Middeldorp is typical too. The organism is divided into black and white by two miles of land. In both halves social divisions based on wealth and occupation are evident; but the working class in the town does not combine with the working class in the location. The location exists almost entirely to serve the needs of the white half. A few teachers, ministers of religion, African clerks, small shopkeepers or hawkers—perhaps 200 all told—serve their own African fellow-citizens, and the rest are all employed by the whites in the town as domestic servants, unskilled labourers, messengers, and office-cleaners. The white knows the African as a servant; the African knows the white as a master. The African sees the white at home; the white hardly knows what the African's home looks like, and does not realize that he has pressing social and domestic problems. He does not even know his surname.

There are in Middeldorp, as elsewhere, points of contact between the two groups apart from the master–servant relationship. White men and women can be found who give freely of their time and thought to co-operating with Africans to run welfare societies, Scouts and Guides, and night schools, though their activities have been curtailed by various apartheid laws. There is a Joint European-Bantu Council on which intelligent Africans and Europeans meet to discuss race relations and African welfare in the location. The Christian churches initiate and support much of this kind of work. But these things do not touch the mass of the white or the African population.

It is a curious organism in which each half lives its own social life, but in which the two halves are intimately connected by economic ties. By day the

[13] There is a story told that at one such reception—it was not at Middeldorp—the official host, to make his position quite clear, told the Queen that he was a Nationalist. Her Majesty is said to have disarmed him by replying: 'O yes, I know all about that. You see, I come from Scotland.'

two halves coalesce; by night they separate. Each half is suspicious and afraid of the other because neither half knows the other as human beings. A social organism built on such lines cannot thrive. Justice and fair-dealing, common sense and human kindliness, do not die, but they cannot function freely in such an atmosphere.

There is another aspect of this urban duality. In Middeldorp and in all other urban areas a new, noisy, and immensely vigorous society is taking shape. It is a society in which African tribal customs and values are disappearing or being modified and European social customs and cultural values are acquiring new meaning; a society in which daily life is over-regulated and the effective discipline of public opinion is weak; a society in which normal life is impossible for many individuals unless they break the laws that seek to confine them. Most white South Africans know nothing of this pulsating life that is being lived close to them. A few whites have African friends; but for the most part the very laws that control Africans debar whites from participating in this exciting development. Urban society has a fundamental unity by which all citizens should share responsibilities and privileges. Middeldorp—and South Africa—cannot escape the penalties of disregarding that unity by depriving more than half its citizens of the responsibilities and privileges.

Middeldorp is in little a slightly simplified version of the whole of South Africa. The problems of a multi-racial society are not easy to solve. Whites in South Africa have the ultimate responsibility because they have the political power, and, faced with the problems, they have not succeeded in evolving a workable policy. They have failed because they have ignored the fundamental human needs of those whom they govern. The social organism that is Middeldorp will always be weak and liable to disruption until the white inhabitants learn to regard Africans as fellow-citizens who can, themselves, take a pride in belonging to Middeldorp.

This leads to one final observation: for years the white inhabitants of Middeldorp shuffled off their civic responsibilities on the ground that the African inhabitants of Middeldorp were migrants for whom it was a waste of good ratepayers' money to provide decent housing and social amenities. For years the citizens insisted through their town council, that the major responsibility for migrant Africans rests with the central government. They invited and welcomed control by the central government because they never regarded Africans as fellow-citizens. Once the central government had come into control the black half of Middeldorp it was a short step to control of the white half; and Middeldorp has found that the local liberty on which it prided itself has been sapped. Middeldorp town council has become the rubber stamp of the central government. The white citizens will regain their own liberty only when they have learnt to regard all who live and work in Middeldorp as citizens.

5

ADMINISTRATION

THE public service of South Africa trebled itself between 1930 and 1960, and has since then steadily increased. In 1960 the number of whites regularly employed by the central and provincial administrations was one in six of employable whites between the ages of 16 and 60. By 1968 the figure was probably one in five. In 1968 it was estimated[1] that the number of whites employed in official agencies at central, provincial, and local level was close on 400,000 whites and that if those employed on government-controlled industrial enterprises are added the number is as high as 500,000, which represents 26 per cent of the electorate. The significance of these figures is that a high proportion of the voting population is dependent on public employment and is precluded from taking public part in party politics. The public service and the political parties are under constant temptation to exploit this situation at elections. Before the General Election of 1966, for instance, large wage and salary increases were made in the public service despite the warning that this would contribute substantially towards inflation and the rising cost of living.

Another consequence of this large and increasing public service is that it has become impossible to fill the numerous posts on the establishment with properly qualified men and women, and the service is forced to lower the standard of education for new entrants. The obvious remedy would be to make greater use of non-whites, but white public opinion is still firmly opposed to the employment of non-whites in any but menial grades. Non-whites are, for instance, freely employed as postmen, but in the existing social climate it would be impossible to employ them as clerks inside the post offices. In effect South Africa is trying to run her public service by drawing on 20 per cent of the population only. This failure to throw careers open to talents, irrespective of race, places an intolerable burden on the white population and results in a public service progressively unable to cope with the needs of an expanding society.

The public service is divided into 29 departments[2] of state under eighteen ministers (including the prime minister) and six deputy ministers. Ministers and deputy ministers are responsible to parliament and the

---

[1] E. G. Malherbe in *The Nemesis of Docility*, 1968 Presidential address to the South African Institute of Race Relations.
[2] The number fluctuates as the departments are re-grouped in the light of experience or for political reasons.

organization of departments is much the same as in Britain—secretaries, under-secretaries, boards, commissions—and it is unnecessary to describe them in detail. A few major differences may, however, be noted. The air, land, and sea forces are directly under one Ministry of Defence. The police force is normally controlled by the Department of Justice and not by the Department of the Interior, which would be the equivalent of the British Home Office.[3] The Minister of Education[4] controls university and technical education, but not primary and secondary education, which are provincial matters.[5] It should be noted, too, that African primary and secondary education was formerly a provincial matter, while university education fell under the Minister of Education; but in 1953 African primary and secondary education was taken over by the (then) Department of Native Affairs, and in 1958 it came under the newly created Department of Bantu Education with its own minister. The Extension of University Education Act of 1959 placed African university education also under this department.

Entrance into the public service, the questions of authorized establishment of departments, discipline, administration and interpretation of public service regulations, promotions and new appointments, reorganization of departments, and other public service matters are under the control of the Public Service Commission. This consists of three officials appointed by the State President. The Commission makes recommendations on all these matters and reports annually direct to parliament. No increase in establishment may be made without the approval of the Commission, and the expenditure involved is subject to Treasury approval. No recommendation of the Commission regarding an individual appointment may be altered or rejected by the government except with the sanction of the President. Such an alteration, approved by the President, is reported to parliament by the Commission.

In theory the whole public service is outside politics, and appointments and promotions are made without reference to party political affiliations or to personal relationships. In practice this is not invariably so. South Africa is—in terms of white population—a small country where many people are related. In the two republics, before the Boer War, it was considered only pious for someone in office to 'assist' relatives and friends. This tradition has not entirely died out. It is not long since a politician was asked at a public meeting whether he had helped to get his aged father a particularly lucrative job. His reply was: 'Naturally. What son wouldn't?' Nevertheless, there has not been a great deal of nepotism in the public

[3] In 1966 the then Minister of Justice, Mr. B. J. Vorster, became prime minister and in the cabinet re-shuffle he retained the department of police, explaining that this was a temporary measure. In 1968 Mr. Vorster relinquished the police portfolio.

[4] The full name of the department was, until 1968, Education, Arts, and Science, but in that year it was altered to the Department of National Education.

[5] But see pp. 198–9.

service, though the idea of 'rewarding' a faithful political follower dies hard, not only in South Africa.

Appointment, and particularly promotion, of public servants goes on without regard to party political affiliations until a fundamental difference in policy manifests itself, when it breaks down. During the 1939–45 War there was a difference of this nature between the United Party under Smuts and the Nationalist Party under Malan. The Nationalist Party was totally opposed to South Africa's participation in the war, and Smuts could not take the risk involved in promoting known Nationalists to key positions. When, in 1948, the Nationalists came to power they reversed several of these war-time promotions, notably that of the General Manager of Railways, and recompensed public servants who had been interned and had, therefore, missed promotion. Another such fundamental cleavage occurred when the Nationalists came to power in 1948 on a policy of apartheid.[6] When the position of Secretary for Native Affairs fell vacant the government overrode the recommendation of the Public Service Commission and appointed someone known to be in sympathy with government policy.

The Nationalist Party Government has expressed itself very clearly on the need for fully bilingual personnel in the public service and is unlikely to promote people who do not wholly sympathize with that policy or are not reasonably bilingual. But this alone can hardly be called party political interference in the public service since bilingualism is a nationally accepted policy. Much, however, depends on the practical interpretation of the word bilingualism and on whether the policy is applied sensibly. After 1948 English-speaking boys and girls were reluctant to join the service, partly because commerce and industry offered more attractive opportunities, but also because they and their parents believed they would have small hope of promotion against Afrikaans-speaking competitors. Whatever the cause, the fact remains that the lower levels of the public service were being staffed by young men and women whose knowledge of written and spoken English was minimal, and in the absence of serious competition it is they who would in due course receive promotion to the higher ranks of the service.

The belief that the Nationalist Party favours Afrikaans-speaking public servants probably arose from the government's policy of applying periodic bilingual tests in the service, those who failed being given a definite period in which to become proficient. Most of the failures were senior English-speaking officials who did not have the time or the opportunity to become proficient in Afrikaans and whose promotion was therefore delayed. All this gave rise to the saying that to be bilingual means to be able to speak Afrikaans. It is difficult to establish the actual facts, apart from individual cases of hardship; but whatever the facts, the results have

[6] See chapter 7.

been unfortunate. The field from which the public service is drawn is already limited by racial policies that exclude four-fifths of the population from making that service a career; its further limitation, on what are in effect party-political grounds, continues to have a disastrous effect. By 1968 there were ominous signs that there were not enough efficient public servants for effective administration and that the remedy was being sought in greater numbers rather than in better quality.

Until 1952 it was possible to say that there had been only a few flagrant cases of partisan appointment to the judiciary, by both major political parties, and that such appointments had not been so outstandingly successful as to encourage the belief that partisan appointments were in the public interest. After 1952, however, there were a number of appointments to the bench in which it was generally believed that factors other than legal eminence were predominant. This is the considered and publicly expressed view of the Bar Council. By tradition only Q.C.s[7] are appointed to the bench, and the exceedingly brief time that was, in several cases, allowed to elapse before a newly appointed Q.C. was offered a judgeship caused serious misgivings to those who value the high reputation that the South African judiciary enjoyed in the past. Moreover, public disquiet was not allayed by the considerable number of junior judges who were, after 1952, appointed to senior positions over the heads of those with many more years of judicial experience.

There are two departments that require description in some detail because of their importance in a multi-racial society. They are the departments of Bantu Administration and Development and of Justice.

DEPARTMENT OF BANTU ADMINISTRATION AND DEVELOPMENT

The Department of Bantu Administration and Development is in many ways an *imperium in imperio*, a government within a government. By custom, from convenience, and by policy, administrative and legislative matters affecting Africans have, over many years, been taken away from the department normally concerned with such matters and placed under the control of what was known, until October 1958, as the Department of Native Affairs. At that date the department was split in two: the Department of Bantu Administration and Development, and the Department of Bantu Education. We shall here deal only with the former of these two and leave the latter for discussion in chapter 8.

The Department of Bantu Administration and Development is responsible for the control and administration of all the Reserves, with a population of about 4,250,000. In the Reserves it administers justice through Bantu

[7] The term Q.C. was altered when South Africa became a republic to S.A., or Senior Advocate, but existing holders of the title were allowed to retain the initials.

Commissioners' courts and through government recognized chiefs; it collects taxes and administers Native Trust Funds; it is responsible for soil conservation and for fostering industries; it administers social welfare Acts; and it controls the recruitment of labour to work outside the Reserves. After the passing of the Bantu Authorities Act of 1951 an important function of the department was to set up and control the tribal, district, regional, and territorial authorities envisaged by that Act. Parliament had in the past delegated to the Governor-General-in-Council (in practice, the Minister) wide powers to legislate for the Reserves by proclamation. The department, thus, both legislates and administers; in fact, it performs in the Reserves the work of parliament and of a dozen departments of state. Outside the Reserves, in the white areas, the department has a general responsibility for African welfare and administration, in collaboration with local authorities. Until the early 1950's this responsibility was discharged by supervising the local authorities rather than by active participation in urban affairs. But a number of new Acts, and amendments to existing legislation, brought the department so thoroughly into urban affairs that local authorities found themselves unable to take any decisive step without prior approval of the Department of Bantu Administration and Development. To a large extent local authorities lost the power of independent action affecting their African populations.

In the past, in so far as it applied to tribal areas, this system had certain advantages. It removed from party-political debate, though not from parliamentary control through the minister, the details of African administration and placed them in the hands of sympathetic officials; it enabled African customary law to be applied by men who understood it and, in general, it made possible the application of special techniques in the government of people, many of whom were still largely tribal and primitive. The system has its dangers, however, the greatest of which is to be found in the wide powers which the minister is given. By the Native Administration Act of 1927 (and amendments) the Governor-General was regarded as supreme chief over all Africans, and the minister, acting on his behalf, exercises all the powers that a despotic chief was assumed to have among the Zulu. These powers are exercised by proclamation which cannot be called in question before any court of law. The minister and his officials may compel tribes, or portions of tribes, to remove from one area to another; he may prohibit an individual from leaving his usual place of residence without permission, or he may order him to leave one area and stay in another; he may cause the arrest, and detention in gaol, on no specific charge, of any African who he has reason to fear may disturb the peace. All these powers to banish have been freely exercised. For example, eighty-seven Africans, including a number of chiefs, were served with removal orders between 1948 and 1961, and in October 1959 an African trade union organizer, Mrs. Mafekeng, was summarily served with a banishment order from Paarl, where she had lived for thirty-two years. Clashes between the police and non-whites occurred on the day she was to have been removed; but she eluded the police and escaped to Basutoland.

Such autocratic powers, uncontrolled by the courts, are dangerous when employed in simple law enforcement and day-to-day administration. They become far more dangerous when employed in the task of persuading people that a particular *form* of government (as distinct from day-to-day administration) is what they really want. They are then used, not to administer and enforce necessary laws, but to silence critics, to banish those who do not accept the official policy, and to encourage waverers to support policies of whose excellence they are not convinced. After 1952 it was precisely in this way that autocratic powers were used to enforce the theory of apartheid in the Reserves.

The whole theory of Native Reserves and their viability in a modern economy was critically examined in chapter 2 where it was pointed out that the Tomlinson Commission had postulated individual, instead of tribal, tenure of land and intensive industrial development within the Reserves, with the aid of white enterprise, if the Reserves were to become an effective homeland for the African population. It was pointed out, too, that in rejecting these postulates the government had destroyed the props on which its policy might have been built. What was left of the policy was its skeleton: to restore the power of the chiefs, to bolster up tribalism and tribal authority, and to attempt to resuscitate it even in the urban areas. After 1952 it became a major task of the Department of Bantu Administration and Development to persuade Africans in the Reserves to accept this policy by agreeing to the establishment of district, tribal, regional, and territorial authorities as provided in the Bantu Authorities Act of 1951. So that the normal work of the department should not suffer, a whole new section was created, under a senior Native commissioner, to attend to this special job, and it was given resources of propaganda in the shape of a well-produced monthly journal and a staff of information officers whose function was twofold: to give information to chiefs and headmen and tribesmen, and to report confidential information back to headquarters.

There is no need to describe in detail the functions that the various Bantu authorities were being asked to assume. They are the normal functions of local government and administration, under the control of the department, that are to be found in any colonial system in Africa and that were, in fact, already in operation in most of the Reserves. It is, however, necessary to try to find out why there was (and in 1968 still was) so much opposition to a system that, superficially at any rate, was not new and that offered chiefs and headmen a restoration of powers they had gradually lost. It is probably true, as the government asserts, that there would have been less opposition in the Reserves had it not been for the implacable opposition of African organizations in urban areas. All that this proves, however, is that African townsmen will have nothing to do with a policy that denies them citizenship in one part of South Africa on the grounds that they may, at some future date, achieve it in another; and that Africans (including chiefs) in the Reserves are in closer contact with urban African opinion than was supposed, and are susceptible to influences coming from the urban areas. The constant flow of labour between the Reserves and the urban areas would ensure this.

Agreeing to the establishment of tribal authorities involves acceptance of the Nationalist policy of making the Reserves the only permanent home for Africans. This policy has been rejected as impracticable and undesirable by most Africans and by a large number of whites, and it is little wonder that chiefs and tribesmen continue to be hesitant about accepting it however attractive it may be made to appear by a steady stream of propaganda. The argument is advanced that no man can develop properly unless he has a home base and unless he is proud of his tribal traditions and his mother tongue, even though that may be a minor dialect spoken by a few thousand people. Great emphasis is laid on tribal differences and tribal, as distinct from African, nationalism. If, after a great deal of persuasion, a tribal authority is accepted, effective use is made of this by a ceremonious installation of the chief at which compliments and presents and staffs of office are exchanged, cattle slaughtered for a feast, and much kaffir beer drunk, all photographically recorded for the Press and for the official journal of the Department of Bantu Administration and Development.

Persuasion has not stopped at promises of future benefits. The department has invoked its autocratic powers in order to isolate the Reserves from undue outside influences. Chiefs who showed clearly that they were not to be persuaded have been refused official recognition or else quietly banished; schoolmasters who openly opposed the policy find themselves redundant; whites, travelling on their lawful occasions through the Reserves, are not allowed to leave the main road without permission; the entry into the Reserves of urban African 'agitators' is carefully controlled; and, as happened in a few cases, when the police are called into a tribal area to deal with a minor revolt, the Press is kept out. In the process of establishing tribal or district areas a good deal of ethnological reshuffling had to be done to ensure that the right subjects had the right chief. One way and another, some of the tribesmen had got mixed up and this had to be put right even if it meant moving Africans from one place, in which they had been content to live, to some other; or even if it meant appointing a chief whom many of his subjects failed to recognize as such. It was in such cases that the police had to be called in.

Persuasion and moral suasion had their effect. Replying to a question in parliament, in June 1968, the Minister of Bantu Administration and Development said that 5 territorial, 47 regional, and 429 tribal authorities had been established under the Bantu Authorities Act and that 547 chiefs and headmen were recognized of whom 375 received salaries. In answer to a further part of the same question the Minister was unable to say how many chiefs and headmen had been deposed since 1960. No separate record was kept of those who had been deposed and it would be necessary to consult more than 900 files to obtain this information.[8]

While it is unnecessary to describe the functions of chiefs and Bantu authorities in the Reserves generally an exception must be made in the case of the Transkei where the policy of separate development has been carried furthest. The Transkei, with Umtata as its capital, lies in the east of the Cape Province. It is 16,554 square miles in extent with an estimated population of 1,500,000 of whom 10,000 are Coloured and 14,000 white.[9] The African population, though tribally divided, is Xhosa-speaking, the largest linguistic group in the Republic, and it is estimated that, outside the Transkei, there are a further 1,000,000 Xhosa. While most other Reserves are scattered and fragmented, the Transkei is an unbroken area except for a number of so-called 'white spots', that is, towns where whites own land and control local government according to laws prevailing elsewhere in South Africa.

As early as 1894 the Cape colonial parliament introduced a policy of establishing local, district, and regional councils in which the chiefs had, as such, little part—a policy deliberately aimed, in fact, at destroying the power of the chiefs and of introducing local government on an elected basis. This policy, generally known as the Transkeian system, constituted South Africa's most original contribution to the science of governing Africans. In the Transkei there were twenty-six district councils, each composed of six members, four elected and two nominated, with the magistrate (a white man) as chairman. Three African representatives from each district council, one nominated and two elected, formed the basis of the Transkeian Territories General Council. The Chief Magistrate of the Transkei was chairman; twenty-six magistrates were *ex officio* members; and the chiefs of Western and Eastern Pondoland and of Tembuland were *ex officio* members, constituting the only survival from tribalism in the General Council.

The General Council (usually called the Bunga) dealt with an annual revenue of about R400,000 derived from quitrent and from a hut tax of R1. Its functions were to make roads and dipping-tanks, to maintain agricultural institutions, and to support education. It made grants to the district councils, which had no revenue of their own. The Bunga was an advisory body and might discuss any subject it liked, whether of national or of local interest. Resolutions on national affairs were transmitted to the Governor-General though they were seldom acted on; but its decisions on

[8] *Hansard* (1968) column 6745.
[9] See Gwendolen M. Carter, *South Africa's Transkei*.

local affairs were usually carried out. Its great difficulty, as was the case in urban locations, was lack of funds owing to the poverty of the inhabitants of the Reserves.

As a method of training Africans in local self-government the Transkeian system had a fundamental weakness: the district councils had no original taxing powers and were, thus, dependent for their small budgets on grants from the General Council, which was itself lamentably short of funds for the work it was expected to do. Britain found, in her African colonies, that tribal treasuries are an essential feature of indirect rule; and, though the Transkeian system was not technically indirect rule, since it was not based on tribal institutions, the same principle holds good.

In April 1955 the Transkeian Territories General Council decided to accept the Bantu Authorities Act and was subsequently proclaimed a Bantu Territorial Authority. The new Authority was distinguished from the old Council in three ways: it had original taxing powers; no white magistrates were members, a chief taking the chair instead of the Chief Magistrate; and its members were no longer indirectly elected but their appointment was strictly controlled by the Department of Bantu Administration and Development. Chiefs throughout the Reserves hold office at the pleasure of the minister, so that control over the composition of the Authority was a simple matter. In 1961 the Transkei Territorial Authority set up a Recess Committee to discuss with government the proposal that the Transkei should become self-governing. The proceedings were conducted in the greatest secrecy, even to the extent of a police guard on the room where the members of the Committee, sworn to secrecy, met. What emerged was a draft constitution which was subsequently embodied in the Transkei Constitution Act of 1963.

This Act purported to make the Transkei a self-governing territory within the Republic. It provides for a Legislative Assembly of 64 chiefs, appointed and paid by government, and 45 members elected by adult suffrage of registered Xhosa voters in and out of the Transkei. Non-African residents of the Transkei have no vote. The Assembly elects a chief minister and five ministers to constitute the cabinet and is empowered, subject to the approval of the State President (in practice the Minister of Bantu Administration) to deal with education, social welfare, health, roads, agriculture, water supply, and a limited administration of justice in inferior courts. The Assembly is specifically excluded from dealing with military matters, manufacture of arms and ammunition, external affairs, posts, telegraphs, and radio, railways and national roads, currency and banking, customs and excise, and the amendment of the constitution itself. The territory was granted its own flag and national anthem, and Xhosa was recognized as an official language.

The Transkei Constitution Act was vigorously opposed both in parliament and by Africans themselves. White critics ranged from those who feared that if the so-called Bantustan policy were to succeed it would jeopardize the safety of the whole country, to those who regarded it as an ill-conceived attempt to persuade the world that Nationalist Party race policies had a positive as well as a restrictive side. African opposition maintained that the self-government offered was a sham; that the government had kept a tight hold on all real political power while burdening the poverty-stricken Transkei with the maintenance of non-profit making social services; that in exchange for the semblance of power Africans had been deprived of representation in the only place where it could be effective, that is, in parliament.

Having failed to prevent the Act from passing, African opponents did not follow the popular pattern of boycotting the elections. Instead, they effectively demonstrated their strength by winning 34 of the 45 elected seats. Nevertheless, Chief Kaiser Matanzima, who led those who favoured government policy, had the support of a majority of the nominated chiefs and became chief minister.

While it is too early (in 1968) to pass final judgement on this experiment in decolonization, an interim assessment may be attempted. The normal procedure in preparing an African colony for self-government includes the gradual take-over of the public service and the devolution of increasing powers on to the colonial legislature. Moreover, during the period of preparation the governing power does everything possible to ensure that the colony will become an economically viable state. In none of these things has progress since 1963 been such as to encourage the belief that the ultimate objective of the government is genuine self-government of the Transkei. White officials are indeed training their African successors, often in a most professional manner. But, bearing in mind that the Transkei has had a longer experience of Western government, and has a far higher proportion of school and university trained citizens, than any other comparable area in Africa, the process has been slow. There are, for instance, a number of trained African lawyers in the Transkei, yet it was only in 1968 that, for the first time, it was announced that two African magistrates were to be appointed to try minor cases in which no white man was involved.

Nor has the process of devolving increased powers on to the Legislative Assembly been any more encouraging. Effective power is firmly in the hands of the government of the Republic which has shown no sign that it is preparing to relinquish it. Emergency regulations, promulgated in 1961, were still in force in the Transkei in 1968. Moreover, legislation since 1961 gave increasingly arbitrary powers to the government to arrest without warrant, imprison without trial, ban, and banish. These laws apply to the whole of the Republic.

It is in the matter of economic viability that there has been least progress and it is here that the gravest doubts about the government's policy exist. The Transkei has remained a rural slum whose chief export is low-paid labour. Nothing has been done to alter that. On the contrary, the position of the Transkei has been worsened by government measures to control the influx of labour from the Transkei and refuse permission to the families of migrant labourers to live with their breadwinner in the place where he works, outside the Transkei. These measures are designed to retain in the Transkei, or return to it, the absent breadwinner's wife and children who then become an additional burden on the overtaxed resources of an economically poor territory. The so-called border industries whose reputed object is to provide work for tribal Africans nearer to their homes in the Reserves, have in practice proved of far greater benefit to white employers than to black labour.

It seems probable that the Transkei is not a genuine experiment in decolonization. It is not a colony; and what colonial appearance it may wear is an artificial creation. Least of all is it a colony in which colonial subjects are being given greater rights in preparation for independence. All the restrictions on blacks in favour of whites that dominate Republican legislation apply in the Transkei. In Umtata where the Legislative Council meets, even the Chief Minister may not sit down to a meal or a cup of tea in a restaurant reserved for whites. Xhosa members of the Assembly and Xhosa officials are likely to draw unflattering comparisons with Lesotho and Botswana where race discrimination has been abolished. Xhosa men and women at work in the Republic and there subject to the disabilities attached to a black skin are unlikely to be comforted by the thought that their country, so they are told, is self-governing.

It was necessary to deal at some length with the Transkei and we now return to the remaining Reserves. The Ciskei followed the Transkei in accepting the Bantu Authorities Act and has a territorial authority and nine regional authorities. After much hesitation and delay the Zulu paramount chief accepted the Act, but it is uncertain to what extent tribal chiefs under him have done so. It may be assumed that if there had been a widespread acceptance by the Zulu people a territorial authority, such as in the Ciskei, would have been established. By 1968 this was not the case.

There are Reserves in the Transvaal and Natal where tribalism still has a fairly firm hold, though there are signs that there, too, it is weakening. The Nationalist policy might conceivably work in such areas for a time; but it is doubtful whether it would, in the long run, be possible to maintain a system that is so contrary to Western economy. Chiefs, headmen, and councillors are notoriously the most conservative element in tribal life, and a system of government based on them has no room for the growing class of progressive, educated Africans. And no system that ignores this class can hope to prevail.

There are superficial similarities between this policy of reviving and bolstering up tribal authority and the policy of indirect rule which Lord

Lugard and Sir Donald Cameron made famous in other parts of Africa. But there are two vital differences—the motive of the policies, and the social and economic circumstances in which they are applied. When indirect rule was beginning to be introduced in Nigeria, in Tanganyika and Northern Rhodesia, tribal life in those areas was still vigorous. It had not suffered the violent disruption that had occurred in South Africa as a result of European settlement and of the discovery of diamonds and gold. It was, therefore, still possible in those colonies to find enough land for all, to recognize and develop, rather than to revive, tribal authorities, and to make them an integral part of local government.

In South Africa conditions are radically different. Tribal life has been largely disrupted, or is being disrupted, and there is not enough land available on which to base tribalism. Moreover, the motive in the British colonies was to find a system of administration which would train Africans in local government and—most important—would lead them gradually to take part in central government. In South Africa the declared policy of the Nationalist Party is that Africans shall never play any part in central government. Even, therefore, if indirect rule as a system of local government were possible in South Africa, it is a truncated form of that policy from which one of the main motives has been removed. Under indirect rule in British colonies tribalism was made to serve a temporary transitional purpose. Under the Nationalist Party policy it becomes an end in itself. This, alone, would condemn it to failure.

Under indirect rule a Department of Native Affairs must, if the policy is successfully applied, play a diminishing part; in South Africa, the Department of Bantu Administration and Development has to carry an ever-increasing burden of responsibility. And the more it takes on, the more difficult does it become to divest itself of paternal authority. In the early days of the 1959 parliamentary session the Prime Minister, Dr. H. F. Verwoerd, made an important speech on policy which was widely acclaimed in the Nationalist Press as a 'new vision', the details of which were subsequently sketched in by the then Minister of Bantu Administration and Development, Mr. D. de Wet Nel. The gist of the argument was that such progress had been made in the Reserves that the time had arrived when increasing doses of self-government could be administered to Bantu authorities and the Union Government could consider successive steps of 'creative withdrawal'. Parallels from British colonial history were freely, if somewhat mistakenly, drawn; Africans in their homeland Reserves would learn to manage their own affairs, to tax themselves, to make their own laws; they should no longer be spoonfed by the Europeans. Since the Europeans had a moral responsibility to help Africans develop their homeland, a Bantu Development Corporation would be set up, as, indeed, it subsequently was with R1,000,000 to encourage Bantu industries —most of any further capital required would, it was thought, come from the Africans themselves. Bantu self-government had already advanced so far that it was no longer necessary for Africans to be represented in the Union Parliament, and such representation would, therefore, cease in 1960. In order to maintain close contact with African opinion in the Reserves, however, the Union Government would appoint five or more commissioners-general to represent it there, and these commissioners-general were compared to the resident commissioner in a British territory. Finally, if at some future date the Africans in the Reserves reached a sufficiently high standard of self-government, there was no reason why they should not, ultimately, become semi-independent states and form a sort of commonwealth with the Union.

This 'new vision' speech of Dr. Verwoerd was an overture to the Promotion of Bantu Self-Government Act later in 1959, and that in turn foreshadowed the Transkei Constitution Act which we have already discussed. Close examination of the administration and development of the Reserves and of the stubborn facts of economic life in South Africa leads to one of two conclusions: either the new policy adumbrated by Dr. Verwoerd is a fantasy or those who advocate it are setting about things in a manner least calculated to achieve their object. In effect, the government is proposing to create 'colonies' so that it can withdraw from them. But what sort of colonies? And what preparations are there for withdrawal? Bantu self-government turns out to be, in practice, the restoration of a decaying and outworn tribalism in which the elective principle is noticeably absent[10] and the main characteristic is authoritarianism exercised by the white government. 'Taxing themselves' is the name given to tribal levies which, if not voluntarily offered after official encouragement, may be compulsorily instituted by the minister. To those who know the poverty and economic backwardness of the Reserves, the R1,000,000 to develop industries, and the idea that additional capital would come from African 'investment', hardly merit comment. As for representation in the Union Parliament, the policy neglects the fact that more than half the African population no longer lives in the Reserves. In short, it is hard to avoid the further conclusion that the real object of the new policy was to disguise the fact that there was to be no departure from the traditional policy of regarding the Reserves as reservoirs of labour. Dressing up the old policy would, it was hoped, make a favourable impression on world opinion and satisfy those white South Africans who were seeking a moral basis for apartheid. It was no disadvantage that streamlining the policy would make the Reserves less of a burden on South African revenue. In any case, reservoirs of labour is what the Reserves have remained.

One result of the attempt to restore the power of tribal chiefs has been

[10] Except, as we have seen, in the Transkei where there is adult franchise. Even there, nominated chiefs outnumber the elected members in the Legislative Assembly.

as unexpected by the protagonists of apartheid as it was unwelcome to all who hope for a reasonable adjustment of race relations. Chiefs who are recognized as such by their tribal followers have several choices: they may accept the government's policy of Bantu Authorities willingly or unwillingly, with or without the approval of their followers; or they may reject it. If they accept the policy their actions are so closely controlled by the Department of Bantu Administration and Development that they become in effect, tools of the Administration, and their influence over their followers is bound to wane. If they reject the government's advances and refuse to become tools, they are supplanted by nominated chiefs whom the tribe does not recognize. In any event, tribal discipline—the very quality that the Bantu Authorities Act hoped to preserve—is bound to slacken, and the Act defeats its own purpose. Though evidence is hard to pin down, it seems as if something of this nature is taking place, particularly among the Zulu, where a noticeable deterioration in tribal discipline and cohesion appears to have set in. The attempt to revive tribal institutions in modern conditions may, therefore, have the unwelcome result of speeding the decay to those institutions before more suitable substitutes have had time to take root. That is what has happened in urban areas, with tragic results.

The policy on which the Bantu Authorities Act rests proved costly to enforce. In Zeerust and Sekukuniland, in Thembuland and Pondoland, the police and the Defence Force had to be called in to enforce the Act, and conditions akin to a reign of terror were established. In Pondoland a state of emergency was declared in 1960, and according to the Minister of Justice, 4,769 Africans and 2 whites were arrested. Every effort was made to prevent the Press and the world at large from knowing what was taking place, but it has been established beyond any reasonable doubt that nominated chiefs had to be protected against the anger of the majority of their tribesmen. Those chiefs who had accepted the Act and were prepared to co-operate with the government went in fear of their lives and established bodyguards supported by special police. In the 1961 session of the Transkei Territorial Authority a resolution was passed asking the government for arms and ammunition to protect the chiefs against their followers. In 1966 seven members of the Legislative Assembly were detained, under emergency regulations, and two of them were subsequently convicted of attempted incitement to murder the Chief Minister and were sentenced to seven years imprisonment. By 1968 peace and public order had been restored, but a surface tranquillity cannot wholly disguise the instability and insecurity that result from what is, fundamentally, a disruptive policy enforced by the extensive use of arbitrary powers. So far from restoring tribal loyalties, the Bantu Authorities Act disrupted many of the tribes to which it was applied.

JUSTICE

The other department that must be briefly described is that of justice, and, with it, the judicial system. South Africa has an independent judiciary. Judges are appointed by the President-in-Council and may be removed from office only on an address from both Houses of Parliament praying for such removal on the ground of misbehaviour or incapacity. This has never yet happened. The Supreme Court of South Africa consists of an Appellate Division, presided over by the Chief Justice, and six provincial divisions, each presided over by a Judge-President. The Appeal Court has no original jurisdiction; it is purely a court of criminal and civil appeal from the provincial divisions. The provincial divisions have criminal and civil jurisdiction and have appellate jurisdiction from the lower courts.

Throughout the country, and not only in the Reserves, there are native commissioners' courts to try civil cases between Africans and Africans, and in trying such cases the native commissioners' courts are given a discretion to apply Native law and custom. The Supreme Court in each province retains its inherent jurisdiction to hear cases between Africans only, but discourages the institution of such actions unless the issues are intricate or the subject-matter is of substantial value because costs are much lower in the native commissioners' courts. There are three Native Appeal Courts and a Native Divorce Court. Appeal from Native Appeal Courts to the Appellate Division of the Supreme Court is in the discretion of the courts themselves or of the Minister of Justice, who may want a Supreme Court ruling for future guidance. Appeal from the Native Divorce Court to the Supreme Court is an absolute right.

Each provincial division of the Supreme Court has an attorney-general who, unlike the Attorney-General in England, is not a politician. He is responsible for directing prosecutions, subject to the ultimate control of the Minister of Justice. There are also a State Attorney and a number of deputy state attorneys who are full-time salaried men performing much the same functions as those performed by the Treasury Solicitor in Great Britain.

The magistrate in South Africa is a paid official and, in addition to his judicial functions, performs a host of administrative duties. He is, except in Pretoria, the senior representative of the government in his district. There are 277 magisterial districts, and in most of them the magistrate's office acts on behalf of all state departments. Registration of births, deaths, and marriages; collection of revenue; payment of fees and licences; the issuing of permits; administration of old-age pensions and of poor relief— all these, and many more, are the responsibility of the resident magistrate and his office.

Judicially, the magistrate has jurisdiction to try all criminal cases except murder, rape, or treason, but his punitive powers are limited to fines of

R200, imprisonment for six months, and a maximum of ten strokes, unless the attorney-general remits the case to him with increased jurisdiction. Because of his limited punitive powers, more serious cases are investigated by him only by way of a preparatory examination. The magistrates also try civil cases where the sums involved are below a certain limit. They may not try cases involving disputes about a will, or divorce suits, or cases involving the mental capacity of a person. In an effort to relieve the over-burdened Supreme Court, regional courts were set up in 1952 with increased jurisdiction of R600, three years' imprisonment, and a maximum of ten strokes; subject to these limits of punishment, regional courts may now hear rape cases. The same magistrate may sit in both the magistrate's court and the regional court, but usually only experienced magistrates sit in the regional courts.

The jury system is used in South Africa in criminal trials only and not in civil cases. Further, the accused may choose whether he prefers to be tried by a jury or by a judge, with or without assessors, except that in certain classes of cases the minister may direct that the trial should not be heard by a jury; and the Minister of Justice may direct that a case, or certain classes of cases, be tried by a judge and two assessors. The judge normally sits with two assessors though he is not obliged to do so. This law, giving the accused the option, was introduced because of a number of flagrantly wrong verdicts by juries where black and white were concerned in a case. Juries are composed of Europeans only, and jury service is obligatory for white males who are qualified, and a right to be specifically applied for by white women; but men and women may not sit together. (Women have not yet exercised their rights in this matter.) The jury is composed of nine, and a seven-to-two majority decision is required for conviction or acquittal.

The death sentence must be passed for murder unless there are extenuating circumstances, when the court has a discretion; it may be passed for treason, rape, aggravated cases of robbery where grievous bodily harm has been inflicted or threatened. and for aggravated cases of housebreaking where the housebreaker carries a dangerous weapon or threatens or commits assault. In 1962 the so-called Sabotage Act was passed empowering the courts, in their discretion, to inflict the death sentence for sabotage, a term that was rather widely defined. Crime statistics shew a steady increase in the proportion of the total population prosecuted, sentenced, admitted to prison, or sentenced to death. Between 1947 and 1958 an average of 90 people were sentenced to death each year and an average of 50 executed. In the year ending June 1966 the number had risen to 139 sentenced to death and 70 executed. Corporal punishment, which in 1951 became obligatory in certain cases, rose from 4,406 cases in 1950 to 18,542 in 1958, and thereafter declined slightly to, in 1964, 16,887, the large majority of these being Africans and Coloured, though the number of whites and Asians who received corporal punishment rose steeply too.

A special criminal court of two or three judges, without a jury, may be set up by the minister to try cases of treason. There have been a number of famous treason trials in South African history, but the one that has attracted most international attention began in December 1956 and ended in March 1961. Commencing on the night of 4 December 1956 and continuing into 5 December 156 men and women, from all racial groups and from different parts of the country, were arrested on charges of high treason and sent to the Fort in Johannesburg. The accused included doctors, lawyers, journalists, clergymen, and teachers, and the basis of the charge was incitement and preparation for the overthrow of the existing state by revolutionary methods involving violence. The arrests were carried out in a dramatic manner clearly intended to create the impression that a dangerous conspiracy had been uncovered by an alert government and that the accused were desperate men and women. To those who had personal knowledge of many of the accused the charge seemed, as events were to prove, quite unfounded. The preparatory examination before a magistrate opened on 19 December and, a few days later, all the accused were released on bail.

The preparatory examination (including various delays) lasted till January 1958, and during the last adjournment in 1957 the Crown announced that the charges against 65 of the accused and against a printing establishment had been withdrawn. The remaining 91 were committed for trial before a special court of three judges. This trial began on 1 August 1958 and was marked by frequent adjournments on exceptions and on applications by the defence to have the indictment quashed. Eventually the Crown withdrew the charges against 61 of the accused (though they might be re-indicted) and altered the indictment against the remaining 30 so that charges under the Suppression of Communism Act were withdrawn and only the charge of high treason remained.

The case against the thirty began in August 1959 and by March 1960 the Crown had completed its evidence. Further delays were caused by the fact that, following on the shooting at Sharpeville, the government declared a state of emergency, and the accused, once more in prison after having been out on bail, believed that their witnesses might be prosecuted for subversion under the emergency regulations; they refused to accept the assurances of the then Minister of Justice, F. C. Erasmus, that this would not happen. The defence evidence was completed in October 1960 and, some seven months later, the Crown began argument. The trial dragged on with interruptions till March 1961 when the Court, having told the defence that there was no further need for argument, found the accused not guilty.

Immediately after the arrest a public fund was opened, under the auspices of the Archbishop of Cape Town and a number of public men and women, to provide for the adequate defence of the accused and for the support of their dependants. The Treason Trial Defence Fund had the support of such well-known people as Eleanor Roosevelt, Daphne du Maurier, T. S. Eliot, Christopher Fry, Alan Paton, Henry Moore, Graham Sutherland, and John Gunther. It collected and paid out, on legal defence and for the welfare of the accused and their families, about R260,000. The trial was widely recognized as a purely political one. For more than four years it disrupted the lives of men and women; many of the accused lost their jobs and all of them suffered hardships, psychological and physical as well as financial. That they were found not guilty of treason was small comfort for people who should never have been brought to trial.

A number of treason trialists subsequently left the country because they were harried by the security police and feared banning which might prevent them from earning a living. Thus Prof. Z. K. Matthews[11], a noted African, joined the staff of the World Council of Churches in Geneva and, in 1967, became Botswana's representative at U.N. Others, such as the late Chief Luthuli, remained in the country and were banned from leaving a restricted area—banned without trial or public explanation by the Minister of Justice. Mrs. Helen Joseph, also without trial, was placed under house arrest for five years, an order that was renewed for a further five years in 1967. In these ways the government, having failed to obtain convictions in duly constituted courts, resorted to legislation that enabled the Minister to by-pass the judiciary.

An important question that remains to be discussed is whether the machinery of justice works smoothly in a multi-racial society, and whether justice not only is done, but appears to be done. Leaving aside for the moment the fact that there are a number of laws that discriminate between white and non-white, we may inquire whether the non-white gets 'a square deal' in the courts, and from the police before he comes to court. These discriminatory laws will be discussed in chapter 6; but it is necessary to say here that at least 50 per cent of the offences which bring Africans to the courts are statutory offences, which, if committed by a white, would not be 'crimes'. These are offences against the pass laws, the masters and servants laws, municipal and location regulations, curfew regulations, and against the various Acts that control African movement and labour. For such offences by Africans the police have powers of summary arrest. A police official may stop any African male and demand to see his pass; failure to produce it is an offence rendering the African liable to arrest.

This point has to be stressed, because it is the exercise of these powers that constitutes an important element in the fear and hatred that most

[11] Prof. Matthews died in 1968.

Africans feel for the police. When something like half a million Africans a year are arrested for offences under laws that apply solely or principally to Africans, it would be surprising if the African community felt anything but antagonism to the police, black or white, and did not regard their appearance, not as a source of protection but as an omen of evil. This relationship between Africans and the police is a bad basis on which to build a system for maintaining the peace. In the police force itself it breeds the attitude that regards all Africans as potential criminals who will perjure themselves if necessary. European policemen share the colour prejudices of the community in which they grow up, and their experiences in carrying out the law among Africans do nothing to alter these prejudices. In 1959 the police were instructed not to arrest Africans for statutory offences where they could reasonably expect that the African will obey a summons to appear in court. If these instructions were consistently carried out there would be a great easing of tension; but the laws and regulations themselves are bad, and until they are repealed it is doubtful if there will be any real improvement. In any case, it will take many years of altered conditions and attitudes before Africans will be persuaded into regarding the police as anything but sworn enemies.

There is considerable evidence of ill-treatment by the police of non-white witnesses and of prisoners awaiting trial. Cases of this kind come before the courts from time to time, and both non-whites and white lawyers allege that only a fraction of the actual cases ever become public. From time to time questions are asked in parliament and figures become available. Thus, in June 1961 the Minister of Justice said that in the previous 28 months 347 members of the police force had been found guilty by the courts of assault and 52 had been found guilty departmentally. In reply to a subsequent question he said that between 1956 and 1958 69 white policemen were found guilty of assault on whites and 475 of assault on non-whites. In August 1966 the Minister of Police said that during 1965-6, 1,367 cases of assault by policemen were reported and 234 were convicted. It must be remembered that accusations against the police of excessive violence are difficult to prove and that non-whites are often afraid to give evidence.

The behaviour of the police in making arrests and quelling disturbances is not above criticism. Considerably more force than appears necessary is often used, and policemen are quick to use their revolvers when their own safety seems threatened or in trying to prevent escape. In 1965 the police shot at 172 suspected persons and killed 70. Furthermore, the indiscriminate use of fierce dogs can be a public danger as was seen in 1966 when the police, with a dog, entered a club in Johannesburg where non-whites were dancing. They were searching for a wanted man, and as the magistrate subsequently found, were not justified in using a dog. The result of doing so was that the dancers panicked and, in stampeding through a narrow exit, ten were killed and eleven seriously injured.

In fairness to the police force it must be added that its task in a multiracial society is no easy one. The laws of the country are such that they tend to destroy any incentive on the part of non-whites to observe the law. White policemen grow up with a prejudice against, and a fear of, non-whites. These are no bases on which to build a system of keeping the peace by mutual trust. The non-white population has little faith in the impartiality of the police, and without that faith the task of the police force becomes increasingly impossible to perform. The roots of this undoubtedly serious evil lie deep in the social structure of South Africa.

There is no sign that the relationship between the police and the public, of whatever colour, is improving; on the contrary, the conditions that make for mutual trust between police and public are deteriorating. Since 1948 many new laws have been passed that have two main objectives: to enforce apartheid at all levels and to provide for the security of the state. Most of this legislation gives police officials the right to enter premises without a warrant if they suspect that a law is being broken or is likely to be broken. A policeman may enter a house or a room, by force if necessary, where he suspects that the Immorality Act is being infringed. The police may raid offices and private homes, and the Security Branch (in plain clothes) may attend any meeting, even in a private home, on the plea that someone who has been banned under the Suppression of Communism Act may be present or that the security of the State may be endangered by such a meeting; and in most cases it is the police themselves who are the sole judges of whether the supposed threat is sufficiently serious to warrant police action. Members of the Security Branch regularly attend 'mixed' gatherings such as those held by the Liberal Party, the Civil Rights League, and similar organizations. Since these meetings are normally attended and addressed by highly 'respectable' citizens—city councillors, barristers, ex-judges—the reason for such constant attention by the Security Branch is probably to frighten would-be protesters against government policy. In 1959 the students at Witwatersrand University discovered that the Security Branch had persuaded a woman undergraduate to accept money for confidential reports on student activities. She happened not to be blonde, but the country at large was entertained for some weeks by the hilarity with which students greeted and treated this discovery. Though it is perhaps better that young people should ridicule such things than be cowed by them, it is of course no laughing matter. There is plenty of circumstantial evidence that, in subsequent years, the Security Branch had (and in 1968 continued to have) informers inside the universities that kept it in touch with the opinions and behaviour of outspoken students and members of staff. What makes this system all the more serious is that the informers appear to be unable to distinguish forthright criticism of apartheid and attempts to mitigate its worst effects on individuals from 'dangerous left wing views'. Whether this is due to ignorance or is an attempt to satisfy their masters, the results are equally disastrous—not for the informers, for they are protected, but for their victims who find themselves banned without recourse to the courts, and by the universities that find themselves deprived of the services of academic staff by the actions of the Minister of Justice.

Such wide and arbitrary powers would be dangerous in the hands of the most upright and highly trained police force. Unfortunately, however, the police force in South Africa finds it extremely difficult to obtain recruits and is often compelled to accept the second best, and in some cases it has accepted young men of doubtful suitability who have themselves had criminal convictions. Early in 1959 a policeman in the Transvaal was charged with assault, and the Press was unable to publish his name because, by law, the names of persons involved in criminal charges who are under eighteen may not be published. When, during the course of 1959, there was a spate of cases in which policemen were the accused, and the Minister of Justice was asked in parliament whether all those found guilty were discharged from the force, he replied that disciplinary action was taken but that they were not always discharged. As he explained, 'We try to rehabilitate them'. It is not surprising that when men of weak character are given wide powers they succumb to the temptation to abuse them. Nor is it surprising that, even though only a small percentage of the police force is at fault, public distrust tends to spread to the whole force. In any society such distrust would be dangerous. It is doubly dangerous in a society rendered unstable by the ease with which racial passions can be aroused.

Until 1967 it had been a weakness of the South African system of police administration that it fell under the Minister of Justice, either as a single or a separate department. Though the police force and the Department of Justice are both concerned with law enforcement, their functions are different and it is unsatisfactory to have one minister answering for, and having to defend, both departments in parliament. The impression left on public mind is that the police and the magistrate and the judges are all one. Even more unfortunate is the impression left on the police mind that their actions in catching criminals or obtaining convictions will, unless provenly criminal, be defended in parliament by the very minister whose business it is to see that justice is done and that policemen do not exceed their powers. When the former Minister of Justice, Prisons, and Police, Mr. B. J. Vorster, became prime minister, he retained the portfolio of police because, he said, it was in the interests of security that he should do so. The two departments were therefore separated, and in 1968 a ministry of police, separate from that of justice, was created.

When an African accused appears before the magistrate he suffers, with few exceptions, from serious disadvantages. The magistrate is, as we have seen, an extremely busy adminstrative officer; faced with a long roll of statutory offences, he cannot waste time. English and Afrikaans are the official languages, and the African accused may be familiar with neither; worse still, he may have a smattering of one, and an interpreter will be deemed unnecessary. If the African is not yet an experienced town-dweller, and has but recently come from tribal life, the procedure of the court will be utterly foreign to him. The tribal court, to which he is accustomed, is a leisurely affair in which anyone may take part; hearsay eivdence is admitted and importance is attached to evidence of character. In the European court the African habit of illustrating remarks by similes would contravene the rules of evidence. He does not understand the rule by which he must plead guilty or not guilty before the trial commences. When he pleads guilty he may mean merely that he has heard what the prosecutor has to say, Finally, if it is a case of his unsupported word against that of a white witness, his master, or the policeman, it is improba-able that his word will be taken. Since the African is too poor to engage legal defence, and since the idea of prisoners' aid is in its infancy in South Africa, the accused has little chance of conducting a successful defence. The prosecutor is either a police sergeant who is out to secure a conviction, or the public prosecutor who knows all the ins and outs of procedure and whose questions only too often bewilder an African witness.

The punishment for statutory offences is usually no greater than it would be for a white offender. Compared to their relative incomes, how-ever, it is far greater. A fine of R4 may represent a day's pay to a white man; to an African farm labourer it may be a month's pay, and to an urban African it may be a week's cash wage. In most cases, therefore, he accepts the alternative of imprisonment for a week or a fortnight, either in gaol or at a government road camp.

Offences against masters and servants laws, or against property such as sheep and cattle, are much more severely punished. A South African small town is surrounded by farms. The magistrate is on friendly terms with white townsmen and farmers, largely in his capacity as representative of the central government. An unpopular magistrate may be transferred on petition, and an unpopular magistrate is often one who is too lenient in his sentences on African labourers, or who takes the word of the African before that of his master. The magistrate is under constant social pressure to uphold 'white prestige'. This explains why the sentence imposed by the magistrate is so frequently reduced by a judge on review: sometimes the review is accompanied by caustic remarks on the severity of the sentence or the palpable unfairness of the trial.

A trial before the Supreme Court is almost invariably conducted with scrupulous fairness, and the bench in South Africa has a deservedly high reputation in this respect. Judges are hampered by popular colour prejudice when a white stands accused of a crime against a non-white and elects to be tried by jury; but even with this occasional handicap the judges are scrupulously careful to see that the African accused or aggrieved party is not prejudiced in his case. In any serious case before the Supreme Court such miscarriages of justice as may occur are not related to colour. In the matter of sentences, however, there is still a considerable difference made between white and non-white. Sentences passed on whites for assaulting Africans are always lighter than those passed on Africans for comparable assaults on whites.[12]

In explaining, though by no means defending, the discrimination that justice makes between white and non-white—and particularly the African—there are a number of things to be said. To most whites Africans appear to be a source of potential physical danger, particularly when they think of them—as they do—in the mass, as 'the Africans'. Therefore, when an African commits a crime of violence against a white, and more especially against a white woman, white public opinion feels that 'an example should be made'. South Africa has, fortunately, been spared lynch law; and, though it may be a harsh saying, it is no small thing that unequal laws are administered by due legal process, and that the rule of law—though it is bad law—is maintained.[13] When judges and magistrates come across cases of ill-treatment of prisoners awaiting trial, they are outspoken in their condemnation and severe in their sentences. The trouble is that a great many such cases never come before the courts.

Many whites are aware of the situation and openly condemn unequal justice. Newspaper editors draw attention to flagrant cases of unequal punishment. And the judges themselves, and many magistrates, try to mitigate some of the harshest laws. But most whites still regard Africans as not far removed from barbarism, as people who understand severe punishment only and to whom a light sentence is no deterrent, and as people to whom a sentence in gaol is neither a hardship nor a disgrace. Those who know Africans intimately realize that these assumptions are almost fantastically inaccurate; but most whites do not know Africans as human beings.

The history of the United States of America shows that there are powerful social and economic forces in a multi-racial society that militate against the impartial administration of justice. Even in the homogeneous societies of Europe it is only since the latter half of the nineteenth century that

[12] Cases may be found almost daily in the Press and could be quoted if that would serve any purpose. Quoting brutal cases, however, tends to give a distorted view of the situation unless all the circumstances are known.

[13] As will be seen in a subsequent chapter, respect for the rule of law has suffered, not in the courts, but in the legislature itself.

harsh laws and sentences against socially inferior classes have come to be regarded as unjust. In South Africa, social distinctions are intensified by differences in colour. Those who have political power use it to entrench their social and economic position. In such circumstances, justice is polluted at its source and cannot flow in a clear stream.

6

THE COLOUR BAR

IT is impossible to spend even a few days in South Africa without realizing the distinctions that are made between white and non-white. On railway stations and on trains and buses, at airports, post offices, and all public buildings, in banks, at race-courses and sports grounds, on the beaches, and in graveyards, there are separate 'facilities' for white and non-white, and the notices 'Whites Only' and 'Non-Whites' are ubiquitous. Restaurants, hotels, tea-shops, cinemas, and theatres make the same distinction but it is unnecessary to put up notices to that effect. The social, economic, and political life of South Africa is based on these distinctions and it is well to find out what lies behind them, what their real extent is, what their purpose is, and whether they fulfil that purpose.

The distinction made between white and non-white is usually referred to by the comprehensive name of the 'colour bar', and for purposes of closer identification an adjective is added: thus we have industrial colour bars, political colour bars, social colour bars, colour bar in sport, and so on. Much social discrimination is the result of custom rather than of legislation or regulation. The great social gulf between the first white settlers and the aboriginals with whom they came into contact acted as a deterrent to social mixing; and though in the early days the deterrent was not strong enough to prevent miscegenation, it gradually became the social custom to frown on Europeans who defied the conventions to the extent of intermarriage. The whites were heavily outnumbered and had a strong incentive to keep together against the danger of having their more progressive civilization swamped by the numerically superior group. Though the gulf has grown narrower it is still wide enough to account for the dislike, amounting to physical aversion, that most people of European descent feel for intermarriage. The very narrowing of the gulf powerfully reinforces colour prejudice on the part of the whites who, being outnumbered by the non-whites, fear that if social distinctions disappear political distinctions could no longer be maintained.

The fear of miscegenation is the strongest motive of colour prejudice, and a great deal of social discrimination is justified popularly on the grounds of its potential danger to the 'purity of the race': it may lead to mixed marriages. 'How would you like your sister to marry a Native?' is the popular, if illogical, expression of this prejudice. Lincoln's reply, that because he wanted justice for a Negro woman it did not mean that he wanted to marry her, has little effect on this deeply rooted anxiety. This is probably why prejudice is strongest against social activities where physical contact is close. Whites and non-whites go to the same race meetings, but to different enclosures; they do not play football together, or swim in the same public baths, or (normally) bathe from the same beaches; they buy goods at the same shops but do not go to the same restaurants and hotels. Since many small towns in the Cape Province cannot support more than one cinema, white and Coloured people customarily attend the same performance but sit in separate blocks of seats. This practice has now been forbidden by law unless an annually renewable permit has been granted to the proprietor. In the rest of the country non-white are not admitted to white cinemas and there are no separate non-white cinemas. In many African townships cinema shows are given in community halls.

Non-whites will watch the same rugby, soccer, or cricket match, though from different stands;[1] but they do not go to the same boxing matches which take place at night and in a hall. Boxing between white and non-white is unheard of and since January 1960 it has been illegal for white boxers in training to use non-white sparring partners. Films shewing boxing matches between white and non-white are censored. Nevertheless, white and non-white boxers have gone to Bulawayo to take part in competitions in which there was no colour bar, and white soccer teams have gone to Lesotho to play against a black team. Direct competition between white and non-white in any form of athletic sport is not allowed and this was one of the principal reasons why South Africa was refused admission to the Olympic Games. Finally, even among many 'advanced' whites who deplore much of this discrimination, mixed dancing is regarded as undesirable.

White South Africans do not, however, object to non-white servants who perform the most intimate domestic duties for them. The vast majority of white children in South Africa have always been looked after by non-white nursemaids. African or Coloured servants waken their employers with early morning tea or coffee; they prepare their food for them; make their beds for them; wait on them at table; do their laundry for them. This is, of course, only an apparent inconsistency. Domestically, the non-white is a servant and the white a master. In a public restaurant or at cinema, the relationship would be different; white and non-white would pay the same and would, in fact, be equal.

Social colour prejudice as it exists in South Africa is known in other parts of the world. The Southern States of America provide one example, and other parts of Africa provide further examples. In Britain there is colour prejudice. There is, of course, a great difference between Africans

---

[1] Except in Bloemfontein where the town council erected a giant stadium and, despite opposition from white sporting bodies, decreed that non-white spectators would not be admitted.

whom the people in Britain meet and the mass of Africans in South Africa. The former are mostly educated men and women who are studying overseas, and they have adapted themselves to European ways and manners and the ordinary educated Englishman associates with them easily, even if, at times, a little self-consciously. In South Africa, too, there are many whites who meet educated Africans on terms of equality. But there is this difference, that while English people meet the few educated Africans and so fail to understand why South Africans are colour-conscious, South Africans see the small class of educated Africans against a background of ignorance and semi-barbarism, and they are afraid to distinguish between them lest the small trickle of friendly association becomes a swollen river of social amalgamation.

Until 1948 social colour bars were, generally speaking, conventional. Political and economic discrimination, on the other hand, is for the most part the result of legislation. We saw in chapter 4 that only whites are eligible to sit in parliament or in the provincial councils, and that while whites enjoy universal suffrage from the age of 18, it is only in the Cape Province that Coloured males, from the age of 21 and with certain property and educational qualifications, were until 1968 directly represented, and then by whites elected on separate electoral rolls. From 1936 Africans in the Cape Province with the desired qualifications elected white representatives on a separate roll; but that representation was abolished in 1960. In Natal a negligible number of Coloured voters were enrolled both for parliamentary and provincial elections. The Separate Representation of Voters Act, 1956, however, provided that no new Coloured names would be added to the roll. In municipal government, again, it is only in the Cape Province that non-whites might qualify to vote, and there was no legal bar to their election to a town or city council. The government, however, announced in 1960 that, as soon as the Group Areas Act had been put into effect, there would be separate municipal councils for Coloured people who would then be taken off the common municipal roll. By 1968 this had not yet happened.

Other chapters in this book describe the administrative differentiation between white and non-white, and the increasing discrimination involved in the policy of apartheid. Such Acts of Parliament as the Group Areas Act, the Population Registration Act, the Immorality Act, the Mixed Marriages Act, the Extension of University Education Act, and the Industrial Conciliation Act, all discriminate between different 'racial' groups in South Africa. While some of the provisions of these Acts entail serious economic hardship, their main purpose is to achieve as much social separation as possible, even at the expense of economic efficiency. There are, however, laws specifically designed to prevent non-whites from working at whatever jobs they like or where they like. The Industrial Conciliation Act, for example, empowers the Minister of

Labour to reserve jobs for different racial groups, and a debate in parliament in 1959 made it clear that one of its objects was to safeguard the position of white workers in times of unemployment.

By the Land Act of 1913, Africans were prohibited from acquiring land except in the Reserves. The courts decided that the Act did not apply to the Cape Province, but the Natives Trust and Land Act of 1936 removed that exception. It is, of course, equally true that whites may not own land in the Native Reserves, but, since the land open to white occupation is about 87 per cent of the area of the Republic, this is not a serious restriction on them. Until 1950, Coloured and Asians could own land anywhere in the Cape Province except in a Native Reserve; but the Group Areas Act of 1950 put a stop to that. The right of Asians to hold land in Natal and the Transvaal has always been severely restricted.

The laws that restrict freedom of movement of Africans are popularly known as the 'pass laws'. A law of this kind was introduced into the Cape Colony by the British Government in the early nineteenth century, with the object of controlling roving Hottentots. It was subsequently abolished at the Cape, but the system was extensively used by the Boer Trekkers in the new states they founded, and it was carried over into Union. The Natives (Abolition of Passes and Co-ordination of Documents) Act of 1952 abolished the pass laws in the technical sense in which they were used in the Transvaal and Free State. Nevertheless, an African needs a permit to enter an urban area where he is allowed to stay for seventy-two hours only without further permission; if he goes to an urban area to undertake employment (not to seek it) he must have the prior permission of the labour bureau in his home area; as soon as he takes up employment his service contract must be registered; and he must have a permit to be outside the location after curfew hours. All these permits and registrations are entered in the reference book which he must carry with him at all times; reference books became compulsory for African women in 1963. Passes in the popular sense were never required by Africans in the Cape Province, but since the issue of reference books all the regulations just mentioned apply to them as well as in the rest of the Republic. Whatever name the law may give to permits and documents and reference books, to Africans they are 'passes', that is papers connected with restriction of movement, carried by them only, and having to be produced on demand.[2] Any police official may at any time demand to see any one of these papers, and failure to produce it it an offence involving a fine or imprisonment. It has been said that the number of technical

[2] The official Bantu Education Journal for September 1959 carried a notice to the effect that the department had been at pains to coin vernacular equivalents of the words 'reference book', and employees of the department and pupils were encouraged to use these rather than the objectionable word 'pass'. This instruction has had slight effect on popular usage.

offences of which an African may be guilty is such that any police official can at any time arrest any African and be sure of obtaining a conviction.

There are few aspects of administration that Africans resent so bitterly as the pass laws and regulations. They consider passes as badges of inferiority; they resent the constant interference of the police; the fines imposed are out of all proportion to the offence or to the income of the offender; and the conviction stands as a 'previous conviction'. There can be few adult Africans living in white areas who have not, at some time or other, offended against the pass laws. In January 1960 the Minister of Justice, in reply to a question in parliament, gave details of the instructions issued to the police in regard to the treatment of Africans accused of minor offences (see p. 120 above). From these instructions it is clear that the policy is to make that treatment dependent on the possession of a reference book which, as the Minister said, would be regarded as a guarantee of the honesty and bona fides of the holder' who 'may consequently be treated with more consideration than those who do not possess reference books'. It is difficult to see how the new regulations, thus framed, can have anything more than a very minor effect in easing the situation. Africans continue to regard the reference book as a 'pass' that must be carried day and night and can be demanded at any time by a police official. Even the most law-abiding African citizen who has left his reference book at home, even if it is in the pocket of the jacket he has removed while he works, will still be liable to arrest on the charge that he has committed a minor offence. In reply to a question in parliament in August 1966 the Minister of Justice said that during the first six months of that year, in the nine principal cities alone, there were 48,288 prosecutions and 36,762 convictions of African men and women whose reference books were alleged to be out of order.

The reasons advanced for maintaining the pass laws are that they help to control the influx of Africans to overcrowded areas, that they prevent desertion from service, and that they enable the police to trace criminals. These arguments are hardly borne out by the facts. About 90 per cent of prosecutions under the pass laws occur on the Witwatersrand, an area notorious for crime, for over-crowded slums, and for desertion. Since passes are reasonably easy to forge, the African criminal makes quite sure that, if he is stopped, he will not be arrested because of the absence of a piece of paper. And the pass regulations do not effectively control the entry into crowded urban areas. In the white rural areas the pass system does, indeed, enable farmers to prevent African labourers from leaving their service. But, on the whole, the pass laws do not achieve their object. What they do achieve is an interference with the mobility of labour and an enormous number of prosecutions and imprisonments for technical offences. Since no African regards the pass laws as other than unjust, their administration has no moral support from the African public. To have laws to which 80 per cent of the population are bitterly opposed is unlikely to inculcate a regard for law.

A number of Acts on the Statute Book discriminate against the African as a worker, and the most famous of these has given its popular name to the whole system of discrimination. It is called the Colour Bar Act. The Mines and Works Act of 1911 empowered the government to regulate the issue of certificates of competency in skilled occupations in mining and engineering. The first attempt to apply it was in 1923, when government proposed to prevent Africans from obtaining certificates. The regulation was tested in the courts and declared *ultra vires*, but the white trade unions agitated until the Nationalist-Labour Government passed an amending Act in 1926. This was the Colour Bar Act, which makes it illegal for Africans to perform a large number of skilled mining jobs.

The object of the Colour Bar Act was to reserve skilled jobs in mining for whites, and it was confined to mining until 1956, when the Industrial Conciliation Act (and subsequent amendments) gave the Minister of Labour unfettered power to reserve any job or any class of job for members of any race. The first reservation decrees were declared invalid by the courts, but that loophole was stopped. The same object of reserving skilled jobs for whites is achieved by refusing to enrol Africans as apprentices, thus effectively preventing them from acquiring skill. White workers, having achieved certain standards of living and of skill, fear that an influx of Africans into the skilled trades would enable employers to reduce wages and so lower trade standards. The skilled trade unions will not admit Africans to membership, and it is only in some of the semi-skilled unions that mixed membership obtains. The Industrial Conciliation Act prohibits the establishment of further mixed unions and an amendment limits the activities of existing ones by compelling them to organize separate branches, hold separate meetings, and elect whites only to their executive committees.

The regulations between employers and their African workers are governed by various masters and servants laws and by the Native Labour Regulation Act. Under these laws it is a criminal offence for an African to refuse to obey an order or to break his contract. For Africans employed on more than daily or weekly contracts, this effectively limits their right to strike. African trade unions have no legal status, and, with the severe limitations on the right to withold labour, effective combination becomes difficult. The gold-mines prohibit African trade unions altogether. In secondary industries Africans perform a great deal of semi-skilled labour, and, though their trade unions do not have legal recognition, they have succeeded in gaining wage increases by strike action.

The trade union movement in South Africa has always been split on the issue of industrial colour bars. Though numbers fluctuate, there were in 1968 some 89 registered white unions with a membership of about 279,000;

there were 37 Coloured and Asian unions with a membership of close on 40,000; and there were 46 mixed unions with a combined membership of 166,000 ofwhom just over half were Coloured or Asian. These unions have two national organizations: the Confederation of Labour with 33 affiliated registered unions and a membership of 119,000 whites; and the Trade Union Council of South Africa (TUCSA) with 68 registered unions with a membership of 166,000 and 13 unregistered (African) unions with a membership of 6,500. Some 70 registered unions belong to neither national body. The South Africa Congress of Trade Unions was an attempt to combine all African workers and unions, but it has been almost completely disrupted by government action and its leaders are either under banning orders or have fled the country. The Confederation respresents conservative white labour which believes in all colour bars and particularly in the industral colour bar as a protection for white labour. TUCSA too wants to protect white workers but the majority of its members believe that the way to do that is to admit African members and to guide them in forming unions, and to insist on 'the rate for the job' to prevent undercutting of wages. Government has refused to grant legal status to African unions and, though it is not illegal to do so, government policy is against allowing unregistered African unions to join registered white or Coloured and Asian unions. Despite this official disapproval, TUCSA, at a meeting in April 1968, voted by a big majority to continue admitting African unions. This has caused a split in the Council and a few unions have disaffiliated. Furthermore, the Minister of Labour has expressed himself strongly against TUCSA's action and has threatened legislation against all mixed unions.

The original Industrial Conciliation Act of 1924 provides machinery, retained in the Act of 1956, for the establishment of industrial councils; but it specifically excludes 'pass-bearing Natives'. Since most industries employ whites and Africans, an industrial council may ask the Minister to fix African wages in that particular industry. The Wage Act of 1925 provides machinery for fixing wages of unskilled and unorganized labour, white or non-white; but, like the Industrial Conciliation Act, it does not apply to farm labour, to domestic servants, or to government employees. Moreover, since the Wage Board carries out its investigations separately in different trades and in different areas, progress is slow. In many cases the last minimum wage-levels were fixed before World War II, and though wages have been increased by a statutory cost-of-living allowance, this has been too small to cope with the actual increase in cost of living.

There are many Acts of Parliament that do not contain a colour bar, but do, in administration, discriminate between white and non-white. All social welfare legislation is administered on the assumption that it costs more to feed a white person than it does a Coloured, and more to feed a Coloured than it does an African. Mothers' pensions, old-age pensions, assistance for the blind, school-feeding are all graded in this way. Then, again, the Stock Theft Acts contain severe penalties irrespective of race, but in practice the punishment of the African—both absolutely and relative to his economic state—is many times more severe than that of the white. Moreover, an amendment to the Stock Theft Act discriminates against non-whites by empowering the Minister to proclaim areas in which every sale of stock must be accompanied by a document from the seller to the buyer; if the seller is white he may sign this document himself, but if he is non-white (other than a landowner) he must get a certificate from an employer, a policeman, a chief or headman, or some other person mentioned in the amendment.

The various forms and sources of colour discrimination may be summed up as follows:

(1) Long-standing convention or custom, deeply rooted in the habits of white and non-white, and not dependent on any legal sanction, lies behind all social segregation, including that of organized sport. There were signs that strict social segregation was beginning to break down, but after 1948 the Nationalist Government amended existing laws and made many new laws to prevent this from happening, and applied legal sanctions to what were formerly matters of convention. By 1968 social contact between the races had become much more difficult than in 1948.

(2) There are laws with no colour bar, the administration of which, because of their very nature, press more hardly on Africans than on whites. There are, for example, different pension scales for different races; inferior public services for non-whites; harsher sentences for assault or rape; fines that would not be seriously felt by a white man but press hardly on a non-white.

(3) Laws containing a specific colour bar have either a social or an economic purpose, or, more commonly, both. The Mixed Marriage Act has a social purpose; the Colour Bar Act has an economic purpose; the pass laws and the laws regulating African labour have both a social and an economic purpose.

(4) Finally, there are colour bar laws in which the political motive dominates but where economic and social reasons, frequently obscured, play an important role. Examples of this are the various Acts providing for the separate administration of Africans; the various franchise Acts that have placed Coloured and African voters on separate rolls with much reduced representation; and the South Africa Act itself—an Act to constitute the Union and passed by the British Parliament.

It is clear, then, that with small and significant exceptions which will be noticed presently, South African national life has come to be based on colour distinctions that are as strong and rigid as the class and social distinctions that were characteristic of Europe until the nineteenth century. The immediate and obvious effect of this is that, economically, the whole country and all its people are suffering from the reckless waste of man-power and of land. Muscles and skills that could be harnessed to increase the prosperity of the country are kept untrained and idle. The mass of the population is unable to produce enough or to earn enough for sufficient food and housing, and medical reports are unanimous in asserting the disastrous results in deficiency diseases and high mortality rates.

The political results of the colour bar are not so immediately apparent, though equally far-reaching. Parliament does not represent the people of South Africa, and most members of parliament are out of touch with the needs and wishes of non-whites, who constitute about 80 per cent of the population. It is possible that the majority of Africans have not yet advanced sufficiently from tribalism to be able to exercise the franchise usefully in a multi-racial society; but many Africans are fully capable of doing so. To cut them off from the opportunity of making their influence felt in the legislature is to weaken parliament by making it too narrowly representative. Moreover, the policy of apartheid expressly excludes Africans from ever having political influence in parliament. The effect of this is to induce an anti-white African nationalism that cannot but weaken the country in peace and in war. Failure to give non-whites an effective stake in the country and in sound government must, in the long run, lead to revolt.

Another result of the political colour bar is that, in order to retain political control, South Africa has resorted to policies and laws that have progressively disregarded the standards of justice and of Western civili-zation. This has been done on grounds of so-called 'self-preservation'. In 1936 the Hertzog-Smuts Government removed African voters in Cape Province from the common roll on which they had been registered since 1853; this was done by a law passed, as required by the South Africa Act, by a two-thirds majority of both houses in joint session. In 1956, parlia-ment deprived Coloured voters in the Cape of their common roll rights, but in passing the Bill, disregarded the two-thirds majority rule, thus denying the validity of the procedure entrenched in the constitution. That the object of this measure, and the method used to secure it, were to retain political control was not denied. The justification offered was that this was necessary for the preservation of the white people.

It is chiefly in urban areas that non-whites become acutely aware of social colour discrimination, though even there it is probably a minority who actively resent this. So deep-rooted is colour discrimination that most people, white and non-white, accept it unquestioningly as part of the natural order of things, and many non-whites who bitterly resent economic and administrative discrimination, accept the social *status quo*. There are, however, growing numbers of educated non-whites who have adopted Western civilization and who are ambitious for themselves and for their children. These people, the natural leaders of the non-whites, resent more or less bitterly a scheme of things in which they are made to feel inferior and are treated, at best with condescension and at worst with injustice. They have few rights in their native land and are made to feel that these are privileges that can be taken away from them. The result is a dissipation in rebelliousness and non-co-operation of what would otherwise be socially constructive energies.

The policy of social and political discrimination have adversely affected South Africa's Commonwealth and international relations, particularly since the end of the Second World War. At a time when world opinion was moving away from racialism and towards greater freedom for colonial dependencies, the Nationalist Party came to power in South Africa on a policy of apartheid which demanded an even more stringent application of colour bar legislation, at variance with modern world opinion. She was, as a result, regularly attacked at United Nations meetings and found herself in the position of prisoner at the bar of world opinion. At first she had friends who agreed with her that internal affairs should not be debated at U.N., but her friends have become markedly less enthusiastic, and for a time South Africa withdrew from sessions of the United Nations. Some of the accusations against her have been well founded, while others have been marked chiefly by exaggeration and lack of understanding of the difficulties of a multi-racial society. Her defence, particularly against the latter kind of charges, has usually taken the form either of saying, 'This is our private affair' or of the counter-accusation, 'You are no better than we are'.

The result of being out of step with world opinion has produced a sense of isolation, and in defending herself against world criticism South Africa has not escaped the danger of regarding isolation, not with concern, but with defiance—the more so when the criticism is uninformed and therefore regarded as malicious. Afrikaners in particular have to a large extent come to regard themselves as maligned and misunderstood, standing alone against an unsympathetic world. In May 1951, the then Prime Minister, Malan, said in a public speech that the continued criticism of South African policy by the British Press would drive South Africa to become a republic. He used an illuminating parallel. Just as the Voortrekkers, he said, had left the Cape Colony in 1838 because of the false accusations constantly made against the Afrikaners by the British, so the modern Afrikaner would have another Great Trek, a trek not to another country, but to an independent republic. The implication was that South Africa could protect herself against the blasts of international criticism by wrapping herself in a cloak of isolationism. The fiercer the storms, the more precious to the wearer does the cloak appear to be.

It was not only the government that found itself at odds with world opinion. The Dutch Reformed churches officially supported the policy of apartheid, while Calvinist and other Protestant churches in Holland and the United States of America, as well as elsewhere, expressed their disapproval.

By 1961 a growing minority of Dutch Reformed Church ministers were disturbed about this break in Christian unity; but most of them were closely allied with the Nationalist Party's interpretation of Afrikaner sentiment and were content to accuse disapproving outsiders of ignorance of the situation in South Africa. An editorial in *Pro Veritate*, which represents the minority, said that race policies had increasingly come to dominate every sphere of Afrikaner life and thence of white South Africa. This was particularly noticeable in the Afrikaans churches, said the editorial and, continued: 'The remedy for this sickness unto death lies, in the very first instances, in the Afrikaans churches wresting themselves free from the grip which the racial ideology is exercising on them.'[3]

Even the South African medical world felt the repercussions of this policy. In 1950 the South African Medical Association proposed to invite the British Medical Association to a joint meeting and was asked by the B.M.A. to ascertain from the government whether any difficulties would be placed in the way of delegates on racial grounds. The then Minister of the Interior, Dr. Dönges, refused to commit himself in advance to granting visas to members of the B.M.A., saying that each case would be judged on its merits. The B.M.A. would not accept an arrangement that might lay its members open to being refused admission on the grounds of colour: and the joint meeting was called off. The South African Medical Association and numerous other public bodies protested against the action of the government, but to no avail; and without government co-operation the meeting could not be held. In this way South Africa continues to be denied the opportunity and the privilege of being host to international conferences.

Repercussions of South Africa's apartheid policy have been felt in the world of sport. In 1959 government permission was granted for a West Indian cricket team to tour South Africa to play against non-whites only. Many Coloured and Asian enthusiasts were anxious to have such a tour, but so much pressure was brought to bear, both in the Union and in the West Indies, against conniving at an apartheid tour that it had to be dropped. Again, a few non-white associations have applied for international recognition on the grounds that, not only did they have more members than their white counterparts, but unlike the latter they had no colour bar. As a result of such application the South African Table Tennis Board (non-white but with no colour bar) has been internationally recognized as the controlling body in South Africa, with the interesting result that the white table tennis players have to obtain its permission before inviting teams from other countries.

Such permission was sought to bring a team of white Australian players to South Africa and the Board agreed on two conditions: there should be no colour bar among spectators, and two matches against non-whites should be arranged. The white South African players felt themselves unable

[3] *Pro Veritate*, 15 October 1967.

to accept these conditions and gave as their reason that they had been told by the Minister of the Interior that matches between white and non-white were not allowed. In strict fact, this excuse was not valid because there was no law forbidding such a match. That the excuse was used is indicative of the fear that many whites have of going counter to government policy as distinct from the law of the land.

There are other examples of the difficulties caused in international sport by South Africa's customs and policies. The Olympic Games Governing Council, the controlling board of international association football, and other bodies are under continuing pressure; so of course, are the white organizations in South Africa. Possibly the most serious situation, from the South African point of view, arises in rugby football. When South African teams (the Springboks) tour New Zealand they play against Maoris without losing caste; but in deference to South African customs the New Zealand Rugby Board has thus far excluded Maoris from teams sent to tour the Union. A New Zealand team, ironically enough known as the All Blacks, toured South Africa in 1960, and the South African Press gave much publicity to the protests in New Zealand against excluding Maoris. It is interesting to note that a number of Springboks who had played in New Zealand publicly expressed the view that Maori players would be welcome: whether the government would have granted the necessary visas is another matter. In any event it is probable that public opinion in New Zealand itself will in future be strong enough to refuse to allow the composition of its national team to be dictated by the colour prejudices of its opponents.

There is another respect in which South African colour bar policy is a hindrance to progress. As the state in Africa that has by far the most economically advanced population, it is natural that the Republic of South Africa should play a prominent part in the development of Africa south of the Sahara. She does, in fact, play a considerable part in promoting co-operation with other territories to tackle common problems such as locust destruction; and she desires to maintain good relations economically with the other territories. The populations of these territories are overwhelmingly African, and, except for Rhodesia and Kenya, include a mere handful of whites. The policies of European mother countries that governed these territories differed, but they had this in common: they all envisaged a time when Africans would share fully in the common task of government. That time arrived in the sixties and by 1968 almost all the former colonies had become independent states ruled by African majorities.[4] To this policy the Nationalist Party policy of apartheid is opposed, and in political matters the governments of the new states and the vast majority of their subjects are deeply suspicious of South Africa. This makes co-operation for solutions of Africa's natural problems difficult. It will be seen later that

[4] The exceptions are: one Spanish colony, the Portuguese colonies, and Rhodesia whose constitutional position is still obscure.

the South African government has gone some length to overcome this difficulty and to promote good relations with the new states.

It is difficult to estimate the real strength of colour bar institutions and to assess the forces that are working against them. The great majority of South Africans of all colours acquiesce in, and probably approve of some degree of social separation, the degree varying with the individual and his social sphere. The English-speaking churches have all declared themselves opposed to separation in matters of religion, and there is no colour bar at synodical and similar meetings. In practice, however, there are very few churches where all races habitually worship in common. Again, though the universities of Cape Town and Witwatersrand may no longer enrol non-white students without authority, the principle of academic equality is accepted by the overwhelming majority of staff and students at those two institutions; yet it is doubtful if the majority would favour full social equality outside the lecture rooms. A great many whites are opposed to the Nationalist Party's policy of apartheid, not because they favour social equality or miscegenation, but because they do not believe that such matters can, in the long run, be determined by legislation and regulation. They feel that popular sanction for social separation is so powerful that legislation is unnecessary and vexatious.

Nevertheless, there is some evidence of cracks in the apartheid edifice. The Anglicans have chosen an African bishop to a South African diocese; and the Prebyterians and Methodists have elected Africans as Moderator and President. In the Afrikaans churches a small number of prominent ministers have taken the lead in establishing the inter-denominational, inter-racial Christian Institute which campaigns vigorously against apartheid. Despite government policy and administrative pressure to prevent any form of contact between white and non-white, social and political contact increased after 1948 because men and women who had not shut their eyes to what was happening in the world, and particularly in Africa, came to realize the vital need for such contacts and established and maintained them, often against considerable official and unofficial opposition. Long-established bodies such as the South African Institute of Race Relations and the National Union of South African Students redoubled their efforts to maintain old contacts and encourage new ones. The Liberal and Progressive parties were founded with a non-racial membership to oppose Nationalist race policies, and they continued to do so until 1968 when they were prohibited by law from having a mixed membership. The Liberal Party then dissolved itself and the Progressive Party decided to continue on a segregated basis. The Black Sash, a body of women established to protest against what they regarded as the violation of the constitution in the removal of Coloured voters from the common roll, went on from that point to practical work in defence of civil liberty and its work inevitably brings it into contact with African women and their organizations. Multi-racial conferences, sponsored by men and women of standing in the different racial communities, have been held and widely attended. The leaders of the South African Bureau of Racial Affairs, which has white members only, continued to meet African and Coloured leaders in spite of ministerial disapproval; and students at Afrikaans universities have had Coloured and African speakers to address them and have themselves paid friendly visits to non-white university colleges.

In the matter of sport there was a slight relaxation from the rigid attitude of the late Dr. Verwoerd. During the 1965 Springbok tour of New Zealand two members of the South African Rugby Board told New Zealand reporters that they hoped the next invitation from South Africa to New Zealand would include Maoris. Many South Africans, including Nationalists, welcomed this, but Dr. Verwoerd's reaction was swift: no racially mixed team would be allowed to tour South Africa. Mr. B. J. Vorster succeeded Dr. Verwoerd as Prime Minister in 1966, and early in 1967 he re-iterated that no racially mixed sport would be allowed in South Africa but that if South Africa's 'traditional' opponents wished to include non-whites in their teams the government would not refuse to let them in. Moreover, since the Olympic Committee would not accept two separate teams from one country, white and non-white athletes would in future be allowed to leave South Africa as one contingent. But, Mr. Vorster repeated, they would not be allowed to compete in South Africa. Finally, Mr. Vorster said he had arranged for an invitation to hold the Canada Cup competition in South Africa even though non-white teams from abroad might compete. He drew a distinction between inter-state and inter-person competitions and said the latter would not be allowed. This was a reference to a South African Indian, Sewsunker Sewgolum, who had won golf tournaments overseas but had either been refused permission to compete in South African open championships or granted permission under humiliating conditions.[5]

Since Mr. Vorster spoke an unconditional invitation has been sent to the New Zealand Rugby Board; nothing more has been heard of the Canada Cup; and the admission of South Africa to the Olympic Games in Mexico City has not turned out as South African athletes had hoped. The I.O.C. at first decided in favour of inviting South Africa and then, under great pressure from other countries, reversed the decision.

Some concession to world opinion was required to enable white South Africans to continue competing in sport at an international level, as most South Africans, irrespective of colour, want to do. Similarly, concession on social apartheid was called for if the Republic was to be on friendly trade terms with the newly-independent African states. Even in Dr. Verwoerd's time black envoys from Lesotho were officially welcomed in Pretoria; and

---

[5] He was not permitted to practice on the 'white' courses or against white opponents, and he was not allowed to use the club rooms. See Note on p. 144.

early in 1967 visiting ministers from Malawi and Lesotho were treated as honoured guests, staying at the best hotels and accepting and extending hospitality at official banquets. No non-white South African would be admitted to a 'white' hotel except as a servant, and ordinary white and non-white South Africans would court prosecution if they attempted to sit down together to a meal in a public restaurant. Finally, at the beginning of 1968, the first secretary of the Malawi consulate arrived in Cape Town and he and his family were allowed to occupy a house in an area reserved for whites.

It is probably in the industrial and commercial spheres that the strongest forces against economic colour bars are to be found. The increasing demands of secondary industries and of commerce brought about the widespread employment of Africans and Coloured as operatives and in semi-skilled jobs; and the demand became more insistent for the progressive abolition of the colour bars which prevent non-whites from being trained and used in skilled work. All but the most extreme supporters of apartheid came to recognize that strict economic separation cannot be carried out: and even the extremists tacitly admit the country's dependence on the work of all races when they say that the whites must be prepared to make sacrifices for the ideal of race purity.

As we saw, it was on the mines that the Colour Bar Act was enforced. With rising costs and the growing shortage of skilled labour, mine-owners would like to use Africans in skilled jobs. Indeed, during 1965 and 1966 the all-white Mineworkers Union, afraid that marginal mines would close down, itself agreed to an experiment by which trained Africans, under white supervision, were to be employed on jobs normally reserved for whites. Government approval was obtained, but this cautious though hopeful experiment was terminated when a so-called 'rebel' group of white miners threatened to strike and government drew back in alarm.

White workers are understandably afraid of having their wages undercut or of losing their jobs, as might well happen unless the state and the owners were to guarantee full wages and full employment. Nevertheless, the shortage of skilled labour has become so acute that both government and white workers have shewn signs of relaxing job reservation by colour. In January 1968 the Trade Union Council of South Africa estimated that, by 1971, 80 per cent of the labour force would be non-white and that the number of non-whites had in recent years increased in 14 of the 22 sectors in manufacturing industry. In the state-owned South African Railways, too, the shortage of labour had by 1968 compelled the Minister of Transport to relax job reservation on the railways; and in January 1968 a number of Africans took the place of whites (who had gone to better jobs) at ISCOR, the state-controlled iron and steel works. This process by which African move in to take the place of whites who move out to better jobs, can only be halted at the expense of industrial progress.

Skilled trade unions are not, of course, the only obstacle to the removal of the industrial colour bar. They are backed by the force of public opinion which regards the colour bar as traditional and has not yet become fully aware of its effect on economic production. An illustration of the force of such public opinion is to be found in the fact that the Nationalist Party consistently accuses the United Party opposition of planning to abolish the colour bar in industry, and regards the accusation as effective political party propaganda. That the United Party regards it in the same light is shown by its strenuous denials that it is planning anything of the sort. Despite the denial, however, it is among those who normally support the United Party that there exists a growing body of opinion favourable to the gradual relaxation of industrial colour bars. That it should be gradual is essential, for to abolish them suddenly, and all at once, might have catastrophic economic results in unemployment and in lowered industrial standards.

Among the forces making for the relaxation of economic colour bars is the African worker. Coloured workers are found mostly in the Cape Province, where they are still admitted to a variety of skilled trades. The industrial colour bar does not, therefore, press as hardly on them as it does on Africans who constitute something like 78 per cent of the labour force in South Africa and are becoming increasingly aware of their importance to the economy of the country. Thus far their organization has been weak; but there are plenty of signs that it is improving. More and more the African industrial worker is losing touch with the Reserves. Where formerly he regarded his urban or mine cash wage as supplementary to his stake in the Reserves, he has become an industrial worker and nothing else. This increases the incentive to improve his skill and to obtain higher wages. This demand from below, coupled with the economic needs of industrial employers, constitutes the most serious threat to the industrial colour bar.[6]

Probably the best illustration of the newly felt power of African workers is the famous bus boycott that took place in Johannesburg and Pretoria in 1957. In its bare essentials, the story is that African workers decided to walk to and from their work rather than pay an increased bus fare that had been sanctioned by the Road Transportation Board. The government took an extremely serious view of this and regarded it as a challenge that must be met. The Minister of Transport appealed to employers not to be lenient with late-comers or tired workers, and more than once stated that he would break the boycott which was a political threat organized by the African National Congress. Police harassed the walking Africans by demanding to see their passes and, when they were given lifts by sympathetic whites (a common occurrence), by stopping the cars on the pretence of searching

[6] For an excellent account of the economic effects of the colour bar see Doxey, *The Industrial Colour Bar in South Africa.*

for wanted men or for permits. Despite every threat and discouragement, something like 45,000 Africans walked distances of 18 to 20 miles a day, and kept it up for ten weeks until the Chamber of Commerce and the Johannesburg City Council intervened. The African workers had won their fight and had done so without any organizational machinery except for *ad hoc* committees, chosen as need arose. Moreover, the boycott revealed a new phenomenon: Africans were no longer content to let whites, or Africans nominated by whites, negotiate on their behalf; negotiations had to be with their own boycott leaders or not at all.

It is in political affairs that colour distinctions attract most attention, in and out of South Africa. Those among the non-whites who are educated, who have discarded tribalism, or who live among whites are the people who demand representation in parliament. There are a great many whites who feel, in a somewhat confused way, that there is something wrong about denying the vote to such people. Among the most thoroughgoing supporters of apartheid, for example, the argument is as follows: you cannot, in common decency and in justice, allow people to work in your industries and then deny them a say in the government; but we cannot allow them to vote because they will swamp the white vote; therefore, there is only one just solution: complete territorial apartheid. This argument involves a recognition of the justice of the African's demand for the franchise.

The United Party Government under Smuts passed an Act in 1946 giving Asians the right to elect three white members to parliament on a separate roll. This was done in spite of opposition within the party, chiefly from the province of Natal itself, where most South African Asian live. The Asians refused to co-operate and failed to elect their members; and, in 1948, the Nationalist Party Government repealed the Act on the grounds that the Asians were an unassimilable element and should have no part in government. Nevertheless, the fact remains that a South African parliament had recognized the need to grant more non-white representation. Moreover, by 1961 both the Nationalist Party and the United Party had abandoned the theory that Asians were unassimilable and admitted the need for Asian representation in parliament.

The question may well be asked: why is it then that, despite the existence of a not entirely unsympathetic sentiment, the political status of the non-white continued to deteriorate? This deterioration was not solely the result of the Nationalist doctrine of apartheid; it began in the 'thirties when Coloured and African women were omitted from the Act that instituted universal suffrage for whites, and it continued in 1936 when African voters in the Cape Province were taken off the common roll. What apartheid did was to remove Coloured voters in the Cape from the common roll, to kill by slow degrees the small Coloured vote in Natal, to abolish the incipient Asian representation, and to abolish the Natives' representation of three members of the Assembly and four senators. On the face of it the record of neither major political party reveals much 'sympathetic sentiment'; nevertheless, the sentiment exists. What stultifies it is the overriding fear of being swamped by non-white voters. Whites have an uneasy feeling that they cannot for ever postpone giving political representation to non-whites, and they try desperately to put off the 'evil' day. Unable to rid themselves of the conviction that Africans, if given the vote, will automatically vote 'black' against 'white', they fail to realize that the longer they withhold the franchise the more likely are their fears to prove justified.

The purpose of political and economic colour bars in South Africa is to ensure that effective control remains with the whites. In that way, and in that way only, most whites believe, will the standards of Western civilization be maintained. It is a deep-rooted and genuine belief. But the truth of the matter is that the more effective the application of the colour bar, the less likely is it to achieve its long-term objective. Western civilization has never been maintained by denying rights, but only by extending them; and those responsible for the denial are increasingly compelled to acquiesce in the curtailment of their own rights and the undermining of the very foundations of the civilization they hope to uphold. The real battle in South Africa has always been, irrespective of colour, between those who accept this and those who reject it. While colour bars cannot in the long run be maintained, the attempt to do so results in hatred and rebelliousness, and in the increasing dependence on the dictator's weapons of violence and the abrogation of the rule of law. The effect of this on white and non-white cannot be measured in one generation.

Note: Later in 1968 the question of an M.C.C. tour to South Africa hinged on the inclusion of Mr. Basil D'Oliviera, a Coloured man from Cape Town who had become a professional cricketer in England. He was omitted from the team as first announced and there was considerable rejoicing in Nationalist Party circles that an embarrassing situation had been avoided. A few days later it was announced that he was to replace another player, and Mr. Vorster decided that the matter had now become one that was being exploited for political propaganda purposes and announced that Mr. D'Oliviera would not be granted a visa to enter South Africa. The M.C.C. then cancelled the tour.

January 1969

7

POLITICS, POLICIES, AND PARTIES

PARTY politics in South Africa, from the birth of Union on 31 May 1910 to the advent of the Republic exactly fifty-one years later, were dominated by two things: the stresses and strains of English–Afrikaans relationships, and the fact that the majority of the population was practically unrepresented in parliament. There were, and still are, other elements in the situation. For one thing, personal loyalties play a large part in South African politics; then there is a very great difference of outlook between the new, hustling, pioneering Transvaal and the older, more relaxed, settled Cape. In addition there is the economic factor, sometimes a decisive one; even a prolonged drought may affect the result of an election. But the two dominant factors remain, like submerged rocks that give everchanging shapes to the waves and currents. Properly understood, these two elements, constantly reacting on each other, will give a clearer idea of the shifts and turns in South African politics. Parliament has always reflected white public opinion, and in this respect resembled the parliament in England immediately after the Reform Act of 1832, when it was elected by landowners, urban employers, and the top layer of workers, while the mass of the population had to wait for later reform Acts to enfranchise them. Within the Union parliament, party alignments, defections, and realignments were the result of English–Afrikaans relationships, and of the attitude of both groups to the unrepresented millions on whose labour the wealth of the country rested. The change to a republican constitution in no way altered this.

The first Union Cabinet, in 1910, was formed by General Louis Botha after elections that had been fought provincially rather than nationally. In Natal, for the first and last time, all candidates stood as independents. In the other provinces the Unionist Party, led by Jameson from the Cape, was predominantly English, and returned 39 candidates. The Labour Party had 4 members; and the Afrikaner parties in the Transvaal, Free State, and the Cape had the support of many English-speaking people and elected 66 members. It was only after the first parliament had met, however, that political divisions began to sort themselves out, and Botha became leader of what was then called the South African Party.

Botha's policy was to conciliate English and Afrikaners, and it soon became clear that a great many Afrikaners in the Free State and Transvaal did not support it. Their leader was Hertzog, and by 1912 the differences between him and Botha had become so great that an open split occurred and Hertzog began to form the Nationalist Party. There was an upsurge of nationalism linked with the growth of the Afrikaans language and based on a 'South Africa First' (that is before the Empire) policy. The outbreak of war in 1914, and Botha's determination to stand by Britain, inflamed nationalist opinion still further. The Rebellion, though officially frowned on by the Nationalist Party, stirred Afrikaner memories and added many members to the party. In the general election of 1915, the Nationalists polled 77,000 votes to the South African Party's 95,000. Botha, with 54 seats, had the strongest party but did not command an absolute majority, and was forced to depend on the good will of the Unionist Party which had 40 seats. The Nationalists, with 27 seats, were a cohesive and growing party, and they became in effect the Opposition. In the same year in which Hertzog formed the Nationalist Party, a conference of African leaders, alarmed by the colour bar in the South Africa Act and by the evident tendencies of Union policies, met in Bloemfontein and established the African National Congress—a little-noticed portent of the shape of things to come.

Botha died in 1919 and Smuts became Prime Minister. During the war (1914–18) the government had failed to cope with rising costs of living or to exercise any reasonable control over commodities and food. This question became the main argument in the 1920 general election, but as always in South Africa, nationalist sentiment played a large part. It was because South Africa was tied to the Empire, said the Nationalists, that people were having economic difficulties. As a result of the election the Nationalist Party became the strongest party with 44 members; the Labour Party gained largely from the Unionists, who returned 25 members, while Labour had 21. Smuts's South African Party had 41, and he decided to carry on with the help of the Unionists and of 3 Independents, but it was a precarious and unstable situation. Even before the election there had been talk that the Unionists and South African Parties would unite. Smuts, knowing the importance of Afrikaner support, was anxious to avoid an out-and-out alliance with the Unionists. The part he had played as imperial statesman during the First World War had enabled the Nationalists to taunt him with being the 'handyman of the Empire'. Smuts himself was unmoved by taunts, but his party could not afford to alienate Afrikaner sympathy, so he made an attempt to bring about a reconciliation between the Nationalist and South African Parties. This failed, partly because by now the Nationalists were convinced that they would eventually gain the upper hand in South Africa, and partly because the two groups could not agree on the question of the right of secession from the Empire. So Smuts decided to combine with the Unionists. The two parties merged under his leadership, retaining the name of the South African Party, and another general election was held in 1921 at which the Nationalists got 45 seats and Labour lost 15 of its previous seats to the new South African Party, thus giving it a clear majority of 22.

During the next three years Smuts's Government was faced with problems that had been slowly mounting and whose growth had been accelerated but obscured by the war. The so-called 'Rand Revolution' of 1922 was the outcome of the greatest of these. Faced with rising costs and shortage of labour, and gold-mines proposed to use Africans in certain skilled work—in other words, partially to abolish the colour bar on the mines. The white miners at once struck, and within a few weeks strikes had turned into a rising directed by a Communist Council of Action which had as its principal slogan: 'Workers of the World, fight and unite for a White South Africa.' The Defence Force was called out and the rising was suppressed, but Smuts's Government was identified, both by the Nationalists and by the Labour Party, with the Chamber of Mines and with large-scale capitalism that was not interested in protecting the white race. From now on the 'Native Question' was firmly in the political arena. The influx of Africans to urban areas, to work in the new industries, was one very important aspect of this problem. It created difficulties for local authorities, and it helped to draw labour from the farms where Nationalist Party strength lay. Trade unions saw in the influx a threat to their standard of living, and the Smuts Government, whose support increasingly came from urban industrialists, seemed to both Nationalists and Labourites to be either unwilling or powerless to do anything about it. It was at this time, too, that white politicians began to take note of an organization of African workers formed in 1919 by Clements Kadalie, a native of Nyasaland and a remarkable man.[1] This was the Industrial and Commercial Workers' Union of Africa, commonly known as the I.C.U., and though it was short-lived it succeeded in giving South Africa a bad fright. The leaders of the Nationalist Party, Hertzog and Malan, thought it worth while to keep on friendly terms with the I.C.U. in the Cape Province, where Africans still had the vote on the common roll; and both Hertzog and Smuts handled Kadalie and his organization with caution but with equal determination not to allow it to get out of hand.

Thus it came about in 1924 that a predominantly English-speaking party, the Labour Party, and a predominantly Afrikaner party, the Nationalist, formed an election pact. The Nationalists undertook to respect Labour's attachment to Britain and not to speak about secession, while Nationalist fears were set at rest by the assurance that Labour did not aim at socialism. Their common ground was no positive policy, but dislike of Smuts and his supposed association with finance capital. At the general election the Nationalists had 63 seats, Labour 18, and the South African

[1] Kadalie was a vigorous, flamboyant orator who easily swayed his open-air audiences. He had considerable organizing abilities.

Party 53, with 1 Independent; and General Hertzog formed a cabinet which included two, and subsequently three, Labour ministers.

The Pact Government, as it was called, remained in power till 1933, having again achieved a majority at the 1929 elections. During its terms of office there were two Imperial Conferences, those in 1926 and 1930, at which Hertzog represented South Africa. The decisions taken there were to have far-reaching effects on political alignments and on constitutional history. When Smuts came back from Europe in 1919 he had talked about the new and higher status that South Africa had achieved—dominion status. He was laughed to scorn by the Nationalists under Hertzog, and a popular Nationalist cartoon depicted a baboon (South Africa) tied to a pole (Great Britain) by a chain that was long enough to enable it to climb to the top of the pole—but still chained to Britain. At the Imperial Conference of 1926 Hertzog, mindful at once of his Afrikaans followers and of his pro-British Labour supporters, persuaded the Conference to put into writing the new relationship in the Commonwealth. With this document he returned to try and persuade the Afrikaners that South Africa had really achieved independent status. He succeeded up to a point, but already there were murmurs from the extreme right wing that Hertzog had given in to the Empire and had lost his republican ideals. When the next Conference, in 1930, agreed to give legislative effect to the Balfour Declaration on dominion status, as was done by the Statute of Westminster a year later, Hertzog declared himself satisfied with the constitutional position. From now on the breach between him and his more republican-minded followers widened.

The great economic depression of 1931 was directly responsible for the next shift in party alignments. When Britain went off the gold standard in 1931 the Pact Government in South Africa, in order to show its independence of Britain, refused to follow suit. The debates on the gold standard illustrate very well the point made at the beginning of this chapter—that the question of Afrikaans–English relationships, the miscalled 'racial' question, always dominated politics. The Nationalist Party stayed on gold because Britain had gone off it, and for a while economic considerations were entirely subordinated to nationalist sentiment. A flight of capital took place and the depression deepened. Then, at the end of 1932, Tielman Roos, an Appellate Division judge who had been a Nationalist Cabinet Minister, resigned from the bench and stumped the country in the interests of a national government that would deal with economic problems in an economic way and not on 'racial' grounds. The effect was instantaneous because Roos put into words what a great many people were feeling, and in 1933 Smuts and Hertzog formed a coalition government with Hertzog as Prime Minister, and received an overwhelming majority at the subsequent election.

Malan had not been enamoured of coalition, and was utterly opposed to a union of the two parties. Though he refused a cabinet position, he remained in the coalition for a short time and then withdrew with his supporters to form what was called the 'purified' Nationalist Party—purified, that is, of un-Afrikaner elements. On the other extreme wing, Colonel Stallard formed a Dominion Party as a sort of watchdog of the Empire. Hertzog and Smuts formed the United Party, with Hertzog as leader, and so the Afrikaner front was broken for the second time. As Hertzog had broken away from Botha in 1912, Malan broke away from Hertzog in 1934. Hertzog and Smuts had travelled by different roads to achieve reconciliation between English and Afrikaner; and in his long journey Hertzog had shed republicanism as an immediate practical policy. He still believed that a republic was the most suitable form of government for South Africa; but he also believed that it would only come when English-speaking South Africans were ready for it.

Fundamentally the new Cabinet was not a united one. Economic revival in mines, agriculture, and industry papered over the cracks, but the cracks were there. Although Hertzog had given up republicanism he was as determined as ever that South Africa should not be bound to Britain or feel herself in any way unfree. He was opposed to secession but he maintained South Africa's right to secede if she wished to. Hertzog and Smuts, both Afrikaners, differed in this respect: Hertzog always looked over his shoulder to see if the Afrikaners were following him; Smuts looked to see if the English-speaking South Africans were following him. So the Afrikaners distrusted Smuts, as the English did Hertzog. Five years after the United Party had been established it split wide open on the war issue. Hertzog proposed benevolent neutrality; Smuts was for full participation on the side of Britain and the Commonwealth. Smuts won by 80 votes to 67 and became Prime Minister of a Cabinet in which he included Labour and the Dominion Party.

The Nationalist Party was jubilant that Hertzog and his followers had stood firm on the question of 'fighting Britain's war'. There was much talk of a political reunion of Afrikaners who held similar views, but it was soon evident that while Hertzog and his lifelong friend and lieutenant, Havenga, were not prepared to go all the way with Smuts, they were equally unprepared to go all the way with Malan and the purified Nationalist Party. During the five years preceding the outbreak of war, Hertzogites and Malanites had attacked one another with all the fury reserved for family quarrels; and it was not easy to forget the hard words and accusations of disloyalty to ideals. Besides, Hertzog had genuinely arrived at the state where immediate republicanism no longer played a dominant role in his political thinking. He had become convinced that co-operation between the two white sections of the population was an essential prelude to a republic. His life's policy had been based on the assumption that such co-operation must be between equals and was only possible once the

Afrikaner people had been thoroughly rehabilitated. That stage, he felt, had been reached. Co-operation could now take place on a basis of equality, and he was no longer politically at home in a party that had begun to think in terms of domination by the Afrikaners.

The Nationalist Party, on the other hand, regarded an Afrikaner republic as nearer to achievement than ever before. They banked, some consciously and others without being aware of it, on a German victory, and entertained the illusion that Hitler's Germany would favour an Afrikaner republic. The rapid progress of the German armies made them feel that the dissolution of the Empire was at hand and that this was not the time for Hertzog's gradualism. They were, therefore, not inclined to appease English-speaking sentiment but proclaimed their belief in the republican ideal with Afrikaans as the first and English as the second, or subsidiary, language.

At the same time, both Malan and Hertzog felt the strong popular expectations among their followers—expectations that there would be a happy reunion of all 'true' Afrikaners. For a short while the two groups, Hertzogites and Malanites, were combined, rather than united, as parliamentary opposition under Hertzog. The new party was called the *Herenigde Nasionale of Volksparty*; but it was an uneasy alliance which had still to be cemented by a constitution and a programme of action. After months of discussion, complicated by intrigues against Hertzog's leadership on the part of the younger Nationalists, the two groups failed to agree. Both parties agreed on a republic as the desirable aim, but Hertzog insisted that it could come only in co-operation, on a basis of full equality, with English-speaking South Africans, and only by the 'broad will of the people'. The Malanites maintained that the Afrikaner would never get co-operation from the English-speaking South Africans and that a simple majority in parliament was sufficient authority to proclaim a republic. Once the republic was established the English would see that their advantage lay in co-operation.

Hertzog and Havenga resigned from the party and formed the Afrikaner Party, but the majority of Afrikaners remained with Malan in the *Herenigde Nasionale Party*, and Hertzog presently retired from active politics, leaving Havenga to lead the new party. No doubt the question of party leadership had entered into the situation. Had Hertzog rejoined the Nationalist Party it could only have been as leader, which would have ousted Malan whose reputation as an undeviating Afrikaner republican was unsullied and who had the firm support of the younger Nationalists. But the split, or rather, the failure to heal the split, went deeper than personalities. There is little doubt that the Nationalist leaders hoped for an immediate republic and regarded Hertzog as an embarrassment to their aims.

The general election during the war, in 1943, gave Smuts a sweeping majority. The Nationalists were uncompromising in their anti-war attitude and Malan had gone as far as to say that, if Germany won, it would be to South Africa's advantage to have a Nationalist government in power to conduct the peace negotiations—a government, that is, that would be *en rapport* with the German Government. Moreover, a draft republican constitution, not officially sanctioned but not officially repudiated, was made public. This constitution clearly envisaged a dominant Afrikaner republic from the civil benefits of which un-Afrikaans elements would be excluded. All this was too much for the bulk of the electorate who, wherever their ultimate sympathies might lie, felt that it was too late in 1943 to stop the war.

The post-war Smuts Government was faced with a multitude of problems that had been ignored while more pressing matters were afoot, or that, in the relaxed atmosphere of victory, were thought to be capable of solving themselves. Cost of living, acute housing shortage, scarcity of materials, rising expenditure, were none of them dealt with in an effective way, and discontent among government supporters was rife. The continued and accelerated flow to the towns, of Africans and of whites, aggravated the situation, and the 'Native question' once more became acute: there had been a strike on the gold-mines that was suppressed by shooting; Africans were demanding better wages and more rights, and the African National Congress was growing in numbers and in influence. Moreover, the Natives' Representative Council, a body set up in 1936, had grown tired of passing resolutions of which the government took no notice. The Council had become, as one of its members aptly said, a 'toy telephone'—an inevitable outcome, because if the Council really represented African opinion, it was bound to ask for rights which no government was prepared to grant.

Since the danger of conquest by Germany was over, government supporters and Nationalists alike felt they could afford the luxury of a change of government. The Nationalist Party cleverly exploited the weak spots in the United Party's armour, A somewhat half-hearted policy of immigration was pictured as a threat to jobs, an attempt to flood the country with unassimilable elements, and an aggravation of the housing shortage. Above all, the Nationalist Party accused the United Party of having no clear-cut Native policy, and thus of allowing the 'threat' to European civilization in South Africa to develop. They tried to persuade Havenga and his Afrikaner Party to join them in ousting Smuts, but at that stage Havenga would go no further than an election agreement and a coalition. Finally, the republican issue was put into cold storage and Malan announced that it was not a plank in his electorial platform; nevertheless, election propaganda played heavily on Afrikaner sentiment and on the damage Smuts had done to it by taking South Africa into the war on Britain's side.[2]

[2] This view continued to be held by Nationalists. A leading article in *Die Burger* of 3 September 1959 reflected on the outbreak of the Second World War and maintained that, by his actions, Smuts had shown that he cared more for Britain than for his own Afrikaner people.

The result of the general election in May 1948 was a victory for the Nationalist-Afrikaner Party coalition. There were 70 Nationalist and 9 Afrikaner Party members, as against a combined opposition of 65 United Party, 6 Labour, and 3 representatives of Africans—79 to 74. Malan formed a cabinet with Havenga as Deputy Prime Minister and Minister of Finance, and three years later the two parties coalesced to form *Die Nasionale Party* with Malan as leader. Thus, for the first time since the establishment of Union in 1910, a party was in power that drew its support almost exclusively from one of the two major white population groups. In opposition there were: the official Opposition, the United Party, which was more broadly based on English and Afrikaans support but whose main strength was urban and whose main weakness was a constant trimming of urban progressive sails in a vain attempt to recapture the rural conservative breeze; the small and dwindling Labour Party based on urban industrial labour and largely English-speaking; and three Natives' Representatives elected by African voters in the Cape Province. In 1949 the Government was strengthened by six M.P.s elected under the South-West Africa Affairs (Amendment) Act.

When Smuts died in 1950 the United Party chose Mr. J. G. N. Strauss as its new leader, and in the general election of 1953 it made a strong bid to unseat the Nationalists, and to this end had an agreement with the Labour Party and with the Torch Commando, at that time still a strong extra-parliamentary force. In spite of all opposition efforts, however, the Nationalist Party increased its parliamentary majority though it did not yet have a majority of votes. This defeat set in train movements within the United Party that reduced its parliamentary strength still further, though it is arguable that they increased its internal coherence.

In the first place, a number of people had always found the United Party unsatisfactory on race questions but had supported it on the ground that the great and immediate danger was Nationalist policy. These progressive-minded opponents of the Nationalist Party were now in the same dilemma as young Liberals in England during the first decade of this century: should they break away from the Party or remain and try to liberalize its policies? There were strong arguments for the latter course, and most followed that for the time being. A smaller number were moved by three principal considerations: in the interests of race harmony it was essential for some public demonstration that all white South Africans did not accept current policies; it was necessary to provide a political home for those young men and women who could no longer accept United Party policy; if the policy of white domination were ever to be challenged, it was a matter of urgency to have a non-racial political party (as distinct from society or association) from whose platform liberal views could be asserted. Accordingly, the Liberal Party was founded in 1953 and Mrs. Margaret Ballinger, M.P., who represented Africans in parliament, was persuaded to lead it. Without money and without a press (until it established a fortnightly called *Contact*)[3] the Liberal Party attracted to its ranks a small band of South Africans of all races who threw their energies and abilities into propagating liberalism. Most of them were newcomers to politics and to public life, but a few were well known (or became so) even beyond the confines of the Union: Mrs. Margaret Ballinger, M.P., Mr. Walter Stanford, M.P., Mr. Donald Molteno (a former M.P.), Senators Leslie Rubin and William Ballinger, Mr. Jordan Ngubane, Mr. Alan Paton, and Mr. Patrick Duncan were among the original members of the Liberal Party.[4] The Party fought a number of elections and lost all except those seats representing Africans; in white constituencies it was decisively defeated though not disgraced. After the abolition of African representation the Liberal Party ceased to have any voice in parliament though it remained an active and growing organization, with some measure of success in making South Africa aware of a possible alternative policy to that of white domination. In mid-1968 the Liberal Party, acting on a decision previously taken, dissolved itself when the Prohibition of Political Interference Act was passed. This Act made it illegal for members of one racial group to take an active part in the political affairs of another. In effect it made an inter-racial political party unlawful, and the party felt that, rather than conform to a law that negated the very essence of its beliefs, it would go out of existence.

A second defection from the United Party was the Federal Party whose main strength lay in Natal where there was a strong feeling that the United Party was unsound on the questions of republicanism and of provincial rights. When the Torch Commando disintegrated after the electoral defeat of 1953, many of its members in Natal combined to form the Federal Party. The Party had, by 1961, no parliamentary representation, but the possible advantages of a federal, as opposed to a unitary, state in South Africa began to attract people outside Natal, and the idea of federalism, rather than the Federal Party itself, became of increasing importance.

A third defection took place in 1954 when a group of six (subsequently increased to seven) right-wing conservative United Party M.P.s rebelled against the Party leadership and policies and founded the National Conservative Party. All these M.P.s subsequently either joined the Nationalist Party and so retained their seats, or were defeated at the next general

---

[3] A few years later *Contact* became an independent fortnightly with Mr. Patrick Duncan as editor. Patrick Duncan died in July 1967.

[4] Mr. Stanford and Mr. Molteno resigned from the Party in 1959 to join the Progressive Party. Senator Rubin resigned in the same year to take up an appointment in Ghana, and when the representation of Africans in Parliament was abolished, Mr. and Mrs. Ballinger lost their seats and no longer took an active part in politics though they remained staunch and active members of the Liberal Party.

election, and the event is of little significance except as showing the dominating part played by white-black and English-Afrikaans questions: the conservative rebels left the United Party because they found its race policy too liberal; but in many statements made at the time the main stress was on the fact that they, as Afrikaners, no longer felt at home in the United Party.

Malan retired from active political life in 1954 and there was a sharp struggle in the Nationalist Party over the question of his successor. It was common knowledge that Malan's choice was Havenga, leader of the former Afrikaner Party and an elder statesman who had served under Hertzog for many years; indeed, it was generally understood that when the two parties had merged in 1951, Havenga had been promised the premiership when Malan retired. Despite all Malan's considerable influence, the Transvaal Nationalists nominated a more extreme and uncompromising Afrikaner, J. G. Strydom, and succeeded in defeating Havenga.[5] Some years later, in 1958, a similar crisis occurred when a successor to Strydom had to be found. The two strong claimants were Dr. Dönges (a Cape and Malan man) and Dr. Verwoerd (a Transvaal and Strydom man), and before his death, Strydom, fearing that the rivalry might cause a split in the Party, urged the election of Mr. C. R. Swart, Minister of Justice,[6] who as leader of the Party in the Orange Free State and the most senior leader of the Party as a whole, might have been expected to hold a balance between Transvaal and Cape rivalries. The withdrawal of Dr. Verwoerd and Dr. Dönges would have had the additional advantage for the Party that its leader would then have been chosen unanimously. Nevertheless, the Transvaal Nationalists did not accept Strydom's death-bed advice, and when this became clear the Cape Nationalists decided to nominate Dr. Dönges. In the three-cornered fight that ensued Mr. Swart was eliminated on the first count, and on the second count Dr. Verwoerd defeated his Cape rival, thus becoming leader of the Party, and so Prime Minister. Once more the moderate candidate nominated by the previous leader was rejected by the Party in favour of a more extreme Afrikaner.

[5] It is important to note that the constitution of the Nationalist Party is federal and the provincial branches (and South-West Africa) have separate annual congresses. The federal committee very seldom meets and does not lay down policy. The leader of the Party is chosen by the Nationalist Party Caucus, that is by the M.P.s and Senators of the Party; as the Transvaal has the largest number of M.P.s and Senators, this gives the leader of the Party in that province a considerable advantage in any dispute over the leadership of the Party as a whole. Once the leader is chosen he is not subject to an annual re-election and it would require something like a revolt inside the Party Caucus to unseat him. Malan was leader of the Party, and therefore prime minister, because of his undisputed position in the Party. But after he retired the Transvaal Nationalists could be reasonably sure that their nominee would become leader.

[6] Mr. Swart was appointed Governor-General at the end of 1959, and was elected as the first President of the Republic of South Africa in May 1961, a post from which he retired in 1967. Dr. Dönges was elected to succeed him but suffered a stroke before he could assume office. He died early in 1968 and Mr. J. Fouche was subsequently elected President.

The Nationalist Party survived both these crises because the unity of Afrikaners was to most Nationalists still an overriding consideration.

The United Party did not escape leadership trouble. Mr. Strauss had had the difficult task of succeeding Smuts whose personality and reputation had enabled him to keep the Party together. After the 1953 election, dissatisfaction with the new leadership grew, and in 1956 the Party chose Sir de Villiers Graaff in place of Mr. Strauss. In the 1958 election the United Party decided to shed its somewhat embarrassing Labour Party association and to fight the election under its own steam; but even that step could not stem the tide of Afrikaner nationalism and the Nationalists were returned with an increased parliamentary majority of 103 to 53, while the Labour Party was eliminated.

The difficulties inside the United Party did not cease. The more progressive wing was increasingly unhappy about policies that seemed to them designed to catch the rural Afrikaner votes rather than deal with the rapidly developing problems of a multi-racial society. The conservative wing, on the other hand, led by Mr. Douglas Mitchell of Natal, was sensitive to Nationalist propaganda that accused the United Party of being controlled by its 'liberal' wing and of having one policy for the more progressive urban areas and another for the conservative rural constituencies. During the 1959 session of parliament it became evident that the progressives of the Party were growing more restive and the conservatives more impatient, and that a break would occur unless Sir de Villiers Graaff could hold the diverse elements together.

The break occurred at the Party Congress in Bloemfontein in August 1959. The Congress took one step which, in the prevailing South African circumstances, must be considered as progressive: it accepted as part of its policy the restoration of African representation in the Cape Province and its extension to other provinces, such representation to be by whites and on separate electoral rolls. But that was the limit of what the conservatives would swallow. Faced with an imminent provincial election, Mr. Mitchell and his followers appear to have gone out of their way to make it difficult for the progressives to remain in the party, and Sir de Villiers Graaff was unable to restrain the conservatives. The final straw was a resolution that if the United Party were returned to power it would honour the undertaking, given in 1936, to buy more land for Native Reserves, but that it would not support the Nationalist Government in buying more land now to be added to the Bantustans which Dr. Verwoerd had envisaged as becoming separate States. Immediately after the Congress a number of United Party M.P.s issued a statement that they could no longer remain in the Party and gave as their reasons the resolution on land purchase for Native Reserves and what they called the 'undertones' that had been in evidence at the Congress. All the resignations did not take place immediately, but within a short time the United Party had lost twelve

M.P.s and a few M.P.C.s who proceeded to establish themselves as a Progressive Group under the leadership of Dr. Jan Steytler, M.P. Mr. Harry Oppenheimer, who had retired from active political life after the death of his father, publicly resigned from the United Party on the ground that his sympathies were with the Progressives; and though he did not immediately join the Progressive Group, he did in effect add the prestige of his name to it. In November 1959 the Progressives held a national conference and established the Progressive Party.[7]

During 1959 the Nationalist Party, too, showed signs of internal stress, and Mr. J. Basson, M.P. for a South-West Africa constituency, was unable to support Dr. Verwoerd's Bantustan policy and was evicted from the Party's parliamentary caucus. The head committee of the Party in South-West Africa did not immediately support this decision and resolved to give him and the Party time to compose their differences. This they were unable to do, and in October 1959 Mr. Basson was put out of the Party on a majority, but not a unanimous, vote of the head committee.

Although a General Election was not constitutionally necessary until May 1963, Dr. Verwoerd decided to appeal to the electorate in October 1961. It was generally supposed that he took this step, partly to strengthen his own position in the Nationalist Party, and partly in the hope of attracting English-speaking voters dissatisfied with the United Party and alarmed by the increasingly strong attacks on South Africa from outside. The results of the election showed that he had achieved his first objective, but it is doubtful whether a significant number of non-Nationalists supported him. Shortly before the election a new party, formed by Mr. J. Basson and led by ex-Chief Justice Fagan, had come into being and made an electoral agreement with the United Party; it was called the National Union Party and its policy was slightly more conservative than that of the United Party. The leaders of the two parties hoped, by this alliance, to attract dissident Nationalists to their support, but there is no evidence that they succeeded in doing so.

The main interest in the General Election lay in the 22 urban constituencies in which the United Party was opposed by the Progressive Party, which advocated a qualified non-racial franchise. The Progressive Party returned only one candidate but polled 70,000 votes against the United Party, which thus lost votes to both the Nationalists and the Progressives. The parliamentary strength, therefore, of this first parliament elected under the Republic, was as follows: Nationalists, 105; United Party, 49; National Union Party, 1; Progressive Party, 1; and 4 representatives of Coloured voters who normally vote with the Opposition. Shortly after the election, Dr. Verwoerd, maintaining that he did indeed enjoy the support of a significant number of English-speaking voters, appointed Mr. A. E. Trollip and Mr. F. W. Waring to his cabinet, both of them

[7] The programme of the Progressive Party is discussed on p. 169.

English-speaking politicians who had at one time been United Party M.P.s.

The distribution of seats after the General Election of March 1966 was as follows: Nationalist Party, 126; United Party, 39; Progressive Party, 1;. The four white members representing male Coloured voters in the Cape Province had not been affected by the dissolution of parliament since they were elected for a fixed period of five years. There should have been an election for these seats in 1966, but the government feared that the Progressive Party would win all four seats as they had, in 1965, won the two provincial council seats, and the election was postponed until October 1967 and then for another year. Before the second year had elapsed the Act abolishing the representation of Coloured voters in parliament was passed.

In 1966 Dr. Verwoerd had, thus, been returned to power with an increased majority, both of seats and of voters. On 6 September, just before he was going to make his first important post-election speech in parliament, he was assassinated in the House of Assembly by Demetrio Tsafendas, a parliamentary messenger who was subsequently found by the courts to be insane and unfit to plead, and was committed to an institution.

The Nationalist Party caucus chose Mr. B. J. Vorster as leader and, therefore, prime minister. Dr. Verwoerd was a dominating leader who held rigidly to the apartheid line and did not easily yield to pressure. While he was alive the Nationalist Party had the appearance of an un-broken wall of granite. No one was prepared to challenge his leadership. Under Mr. Vorster, divisions that had been suppressed began to emerge and the vague outlines of two groups within Afrikanderdom appeared: these came to be known as the *verkramptes* and the *verligtes*—roughly, the 'narrow-minded' and the 'enlightened'. These groups first appeared in the cultural field. The previously-noted writers, the *Sestigers*, were *verligtes*, and so were most of the artists. Alarmed by the apparent success of the *verligtes*, the *verkramptes* organized a counter-attack on well-tried lines: defence of the Afrikaans language; preservation of Afrikaner traditions, particularly in the matter of colour; adherence to Christian-National policies; and rejection of anything 'foreign'. This counter-attack brought the quarrel from the cultural into the political field, and by mid-1968 centred round Mr. Vorster's so-called 'outward' policy towards neighbouring African states and in the slight relaxation of the colour bar in sport. While, at that time, there had been no overt challenge to Mr. Vorster's leadership, political differences were sufficiently marked to affect voting at by-elections.[1]

This brief sketch of South African political history from 1910 has been necessary as a background to the understanding of political divisions. Without this, party policies appear confused and unreal. The time has now come to discuss the different party policies, to try to discover what

[1] See Note on p. 189.

the reactions of the parties are to the social and economic problems that beset South Africa, and to see to what extent they differ fundamentally from each other.

The two major political parties in South Africa agree over a wide range of subjects. Where they differ, it is frequently a matter of degree rather than of kind, or of a difference of method in arriving at the same result. Policies in such matters as agriculture, industry, mining, and railway development have, for both parties, the same general objectives—to encourage agricultural production and export, frequently at the expense of the South African consumer; to encourage industrial expansion by means of tariffs; to tax the mines as much as possible without actually discouraging them; and to use the railway rates to further these aims. Native policy[8] is part of all these activities, since African labour is a basic factor in them all.

There are four main issues that separate the two parties. The first is the relations between English-speaking and Afrikaans-speaking South Africans which have been discussed in various parts of this book. It will be seen later how it affects educational policy. The second and third issues are Native policy and foreign affairs; and the last is constitutional.

NATIVE POLICY

One of the ablest and best-informed parliamentarians in South Africa, Mrs. Margaret Ballinger, who was one of the three representatives of Africans in the House of Assembly, once remarked that 'all Union politics are Native Affairs'. It is with an examination of Native policies that we may best begin in order to arrive at an understanding of some of the fundamental differences in party politics.

The necessity for a positive Native policy first began to impress itself on South African statesmen after the 1914–18 War. This is not to say that, long before that, many South Africans, in and out of politics, had not realized the vital nature of the problem nor foreseen the time when policies would have to be framed to meet it; but, before pressure of population and industrialization had brought the question squarely into the centre of political thinking, it had always been possible to regard relations between black and white as susceptible of treatment along the lines of benevolent paternalism—maintaining law and order, Christianizing, kind but firm treatment of the 'child race'. By the 1920's the 'child' was adolescent and showing every sign of growing to lusty manhood, and it was no longer possible to deal with him on an administrative level only, however sound that administration might be. Good government could no longer be regarded as the equivalent of self-government.

---

[8] 'Native policy' means policy in regard to Africans. It would be confusing to call it 'African policy'.

At the highest political level it was Hertzog who first turned his attention to this problem. His thinking, like that of the vast majority of whites in South Africa, was historically and temperamentally grounded on the need to segregate the races. Hitherto a reasonable amount of segregation at the social and economic levels had been the general rule—a rule which broke down in industries, in domestic service, and in other places where it proved inconvenient or uneconomic. Now the question of political segregation became prominent. Africans in the Cape Province had been on a common electoral roll since 1853. The educational and property tests that had then limited the number of African voters had less restrictive value after the First World War; the value of money had fallen and literacy increased. If the number were allowed to grow, and if Africans in the other provinces too began to demand the franchise, African voters would in due course outnumber the white. In 1926 Hertzog put forward a comprehensive programme for dealing with the Native question. Africans were to be removed from the electoral roll in the Cape and all Africans were to participate, directly or indirectly, in the election of a representative council; they would be given representation in the Senate; and more land would be made available for African occupation.[9]

To carry a policy that deprived Africans at the Cape of their common franchise rights would require, by the terms of the South Africa Act, a two-thirds majority of both houses in a joint session. This Hertzog was unable to achieve because the South African Party opposition, being itself divided on the matter, refused to support him. The whole of his policy, since he regarded it as one and indivisible, remained in legislative cold storage. The Nationalist Party, however, did not allow the matter to drop. The 1929 election was fought on the issue and was preceded by a document known as the 'Black Manifesto', which warned the country of the dangers of letting the question slide. When Smuts and Hertzog fused their parties, the latter made it a condition that his policy, possibly amended in details, should receive priority treatment. Accordingly, in 1936 the policy was once more before Parliament. In spite of vigorous agitation by liberals, the necessary two-thirds majority was obtained for the Hertzog Bills; but Hertzog had been compelled to compromise by allowing the Cape African franchise to remain, albeit on a separate roll. African voters in the Cape were permitted to elect three white members, while Africans throughout the Union elected, by means of chiefs, local councils, and local advisory boards—all acting as electoral colleges—four senators. An additional $7\frac{1}{4}$ million morgen of land were to be made available for African occupation, and a South African Natives' Trust Fund was established to finance land purchase and to encourage Native agriculture and education. Finally, a Natives' Representative Council was instituted,

[9] It is important to note, for future reference, that Hertzog regarded the Cape Coloured population as falling on the European side, industrially and politically.

to consist of twelve elected African representatives, four nominated African representatives, and five white officials, with the Secretary for Native Affairs as chairman.

Although most whites hailed these parliamentary Acts as a new and satisfactory solution, and although Smuts called the Natives' Representative Council a second 'parliament', it was evident to J. H. Hofmeyr and the liberals, in and out of parliament, who supported him, that the policy had in fact solved nothing. More land was indeed bought to be added to the Reserves; but adding to badly farmed and inadequately capitalized land more land in the same condition created problems rather than solved them. In any case, the increasing rate of industrialization and the ever-growing demand for African labour made the legislation out of date almost as soon as it was enacted. As for the Natives' Representative Council, it was soon clear that Africans would not long be satisfied with an advisory council whose advice was treated with scant attention. The impotence of the council was demonstrated as soon as it began to advise the removal of the many administrative restrictions that controlled African freedom of movement. The Hertzog policy was an attempt to reach a permanent solution, but the factors in the situation were all moving so fast that, as his brother said of Louis XVI of France, it was like trying to balance a number of billiard balls—a clever, though not a wise, statesman might juggle with them, but he could not balance them.

The 1939–45 War increased the rate of change in the factors that constitute the Native question—urbanization and industrial development, progressive deterioration of the Reserves, and the political awakening of the African. Smuts's government, representing both rural and urban opinion, industrial and farming, liberal and conservative, Afrikaans and English, was pulled in different directions. A small group within the United Party pulled in the direction of more freedom for Africans, for more education, better housing, more social services. Through the Army Education Services during the war many young South Africans had, for the first time in their lives, come to realize some of the disabilities under which Africans lived. Studying these matters in an economically secure position in the Army, they were eager for reforms; and though the eagerness tended to wear off once they returned to the competitive economics of civil life, for a short time they did exercise influence in United Party circles, and found backing from industrialists who welcomed the idea of relaxing colour bars in industry.

Pulling against this force was a stronger force composed of those United Party supporters who, by tradition, by inclination, and by what they considered to be their economic advantage, were fearful of 'going too fast'. They professed to believe in what they called Christian Trusteeship, a vague term that was for ever begging the question of what happened when the wards came of age. Torn between their anxiety to satisfy the rural districts that their supply of labour would be safe and that the government was able to 'look after the Communists', and the needs of the urban areas that were unable to cope with the influx of Africans, the Smuts Government did little besides try vainly to restrict the movement of Africans to the towns. It did, however, set up the Fagan Commission to inquire into the situation. This Commission, one of the most authoritative that have reported on Native affairs, came among many others to the following conclusions: that more than half the African population lived in white areas; that an examination of the carrying capacity of the Reserves showed that it was utterly impossible to put the whole Native population into the Reserves; that the urbanization of the African in white areas had to be accepted, and the process could not be reversed; and finally that it was impossible to 'confine Native labour in South Africa to the migratory type'.[10] The *Fagan Report* bore out what many other commissions and individual authorities had said, most notably the Social and Economic Planning Council under the chairmanship of Dr. ven Eck.[11]

Meanwhile the Native's Representative Council, goaded to despair, refused to co-operate any longer in what had become, to them and to many other people, a political sham, and they took little notice of Smuts's rather vague offer to increase their powers. In one of the three Cape divisions representing Africans, a member of the Communist Party was elected to parliament.

The Nationalist Party inherited the Hertzog policy of segregation, rooted, as it was, in white fear of being 'swamped'; but, just as they shed Hertzogism in English-Afrikaans relations, so they shed some of his Native policy. Sensing the popular alarm at the developing situation, and realizing that the 'black danger' was a winning election card, they appointed a party committee to work out a policy that could be put before the electorate in the first post-war general election. From this committee came the policy known as apartheid, which means 'separation' or 'segregation'. The word was chosen partly because it had the advantage of being new, and partly because the word 'segregation' was associated with earlier political parties and policies such as Botha's. A minor reason for its choice was that the word 'segregation' was disliked by the Africans.

Apartheid, as a policy, may mean a number of things, from social and residential separation to the establishment of separate African and white states. As an election cry it was extremely useful just because of its vagueness. As a Native policy, it had the weaknesses of its electioneering strength. To many people in 1948 it sounded like a policy that might solve the black-white question, a question that the United Party did not appear to be doing anything about. The Nationalist Party, supported by Havenga's

10 See *Native Laws Enquiry Commission*, 1948, popularly known as the *Fagan Report* from the name of its Chairman, Mr. Justice Fagan.
11 See *Social and Economic Planning Council*, *Sixth Report*.

Afrikaner Party, had the advantage of being homogeneous. It was almost entirely Afrikaans-speaking; its real strength lay in the rural areas; it had been welded, during the war, into a closely knit, cohesive party. It had a few of the weaknesses of divided opinion from which the United Party suffered. When, therefore, the Nationalist Party came forward with the policy of apartheid it found considerable response. It pointed to the undoubted danger of allowing things to drifit; it played with skill on the fear which most whites in South Africa have of an ultimate 'black domination'; and it asserted emphatically that its purpose was not to do the African an injustice but, rather, to give him ampler room for developing his own national identity separately from the whites. It rejected the recommendations of the *Fagan Report*. The upshot was that the Nationalist Party won the election.

General election policies are of necessity imprecise; and when Malan's party came to power it found itself embarrassed by the vagueness which had been useful at the election. What, precisely, was apartheid to include? During the early days of the new government, separate railway coaches for whites only were provided on the Cape suburban railway line, and in a great many, though by no means all, post offices separate counters were provided for whites and non-white customers. This move was widely claimed as apartheid. But, rather obviously, it was, if anything, an extremely minor part of a policy. It affected chiefly Coloured people, since, in the other provinces, Africans had long been accustomed to separate, and inferior, facilities in these matters. Moreover, it seemed an acceptance of the fact that Africans, Coloured, and white would long continue to live and work in the same areas.

Nor did the next steps which the government took affect the African population as much as they did the Coloured. The Prohibition of Mixed Marriages Act, 1949, prohibited marriages between white and non-white, since, in 1946, there had been 75 such marriages out of 28,000 white marriages,[12] the Act hardly seemed to have been necessary. Another Act which claimed in part to aim at apartheid was the Population Registration Act which provided for personal identity cards and for a register on which 'race' is shown. In its draft form, African women and African males under 18 years of age were excluded, which seems to indicate that the government was not mainly concerned with the African population. The intention of the Act, in so far as the question of race was concerned, was to fix once and for all the 'race' of everyone carrying a card, and was, in fact, another attempt to prevent Coloured people from 'passing'.

In 1950 the Group Areas Act was passed, empowering the government to declare any area a group area for Coloured, European, African, or Asian.[13] It was a complicated Act, but its intention was that, in due

---

[12] See *Union Year Book No. 24*, 1948.

[13] In certain areas further subdivisions of Malay and Chinese are provided for.

course, the various 'racial' groups would live in distinct areas, and property in such areas might not be acquired by a member of a different group. Here, again, it was hardly the African whom the government had in mind. The principle of separate areas, nationally and locally, had, as we have seen, long been accepted in South Africa. The Group Areas Act, therefore, added little to the restrictions already borne by Africans, but it powerfully affected the rights of Coloured and Asians. Finally, the Act that placed Coloured voters in the Cape on a separate electoral roll and set up a separate Department of Coloured Affairs did not touch the African, but was designed to limit the influence of Coloured voters.

These measures were all part of the policy of apartheid but they hardly touched the vital question of black–white relations. Between 1951 and 1968, however, a whole series of Acts of Parliament and policy statements gave a clearer picture of what apartheid involved in regard to the African population. Starting with the Bantu Authorities Act of 1951 and culminating in the Promotion of Bantu Self-Government Act of 1959, both of which Acts were described in chapter 5, what emerged was a policy to revive and restore tribalism and to make the Reserves into national homes which, according to Dr. Verwoerd, might eventually become independent states. In white areas, Africans were to be regarded as migrants, subject to rigid control in such matters as domicile, employment, and freedom of movement.

Briefly, the case of the academic apologists for the policy of apartheid is this: Africans and Europeans are two different 'races' and can never live in one political state without producing either injustice to the African or the decline of white power. Whites, on the one hand, dare not allow Africans political rights because Western civilization would then be swamped by Bantu civilization. On the other hand, if Africans are working in white-controlled industries it is unjust not to grant them civil rights. Moreover, the African, like the Afrikaner, is entitled to develop his own language and culture; in fact, without that development he will never become a really integrated personality. As long as he remains part of the white state he will become an imitation European instead of a good African. In the white state he cannot be allowed equality, and he cannot be allowed to attain to positions of trust and power and responsibility, as he could if he were in his own country.

Therefore, the argument continues, Africans must have their own homeland, territory that they can call their own and where they can attain to the highest positions of which they are capable. The existing Reserves, augmented by more land to the extent of $7\frac{1}{4}$ million morgen, must constitute this homeland of Africans. When they leave their homeland to work for whites, they do so as temporary migrant labourers and can expect no civil or political rights. They will, in effect, be visiting white South Africa, knowing that they must return to their own country. It is admitted that the Reserves must be rehabilitated; and that South Africa must accept responsibility, financial and otherwise, for helping Africans to industrialize the Reserves so as to increase their carrying capacity. And for some considerable time to come the whites will have to act as trustees over the Reserves since Africans have not yet reached a stage where they can entirely govern themselves.

In somewhat general terms, that is the basic theory of apartheid. There are other important aspects of the policy. Great stress is laid on mother-tongue instruction and on the encouragement and development of Bantu languages and culture; and the restoration of tribal authority and the cultivation of tribal loyalty are essential. It must be remembered that apartheid is an Afrikaner policy—conscious of the importance of their own language and culture in the preservation of the identity of his people, the Afrikaner believes that what is true for Afrikaners is true for Africans. As a good nationalist he cannot deny to any other nation its right to develop its own identity; but, equally, he cannot allow Africans to do this if it is to be at the expense of the Afrikaner people.

To the policy of apartheid as set out here, and as it is applied legislatively and administratively, there are a number of practical and immediate objections. Earlier chapters have shown to what extent white agriculture, industries, and mining depend on African labour, and how much of that labour has already become permanently divorced from its tribal homes in the Reserves. It is accepted as a fact by supporters as well as by opponents of apartheid that to a considerable extent Africans have already become integrated into the economy which whites have erected in South Africa. The supporters ask that the process of integration should be stopped and a reverse process gradually introduced and that as it will take a long time it is imperative to begin at once.

The theoreticians of apartheid do not appear to have given sufficient consideration to the economics of making the Reserves capable of bearing an increased population, or to have faced the consequences, if their policy were logically applied, of black states competing industrially with white. Clothing factories were set up on the borders of the Reserves where, free from wage determinations, they could pay lower wages than obtained in the urban areas. This was in accord with government policy, and the unemployment it caused in the clothing industry in Johannesburg gave grave concern to industrialists.

The Nationalist Government, responsible for carrying out the policy of apartheid, was more acutely aware of the practical difficulties than the academic apologists. When, in 1950, an important national conference of Dutch Reformed Churches wholeheartedly approved the policy of territorial apartheid and urged the government to put it into force, Malan was compelled to issue a public warning that processes that had taken a long time to mature could not be reversed in a few months. The fact is that no government in South Africa would lightly undertake to put into force a policy that must, if it is to do what it says, result in a diminished labour supply for farms and industries. Academicians may speak about the need to make economic sacrifices in the interests of the principles of apartheid; but practical politicians may be forgiven if they are not so sure that the electorate will accept these sacrifices. And the clearer the extent of the sacrifice becomes the less prospect does there appear to be of its being acquiesced in. Afrikaners who participate in the establishment of new industries will not easily dispense with African labour.

The dilemma of the Nationalist Party is made clear by the somewhat contradictory public statements on apartheid. In an address given in September 1950, Dr. Eiselen, who had been appointed Secretary for Native Affairs, against the advice of the Public Service Commission, because of his sympathies with the ideals of apartheid, said that four major administrative steps were required to create a contented and efficient labour force: a realization of diverse aptitudes of Africans, occupational selection, recognition of continuous and efficient service within each labour category, and building schemes by which bona fide urban Africans might invest savings in home ownership.[14] This policy undoubtedly envisaged *local* apartheid, which largely existed already, and made suggestions for the improvement of urban conditions; but it cannot be said to include the conception of African urban labour as migrant and temporary, since it advocated home ownership for Africans in urban areas.

On the other hand the then Minister for Native Affairs, Dr. Verwoerd, announced four months later that the Cabinet had decided that no African would be allowed to own land outside the Reserves.[15] In addressing the Natives' Representative Council in December 1950, Dr. Verwoerd said that whites did not demand overlordship over the whole of South Africa, but only over their own areas. He adumbrated agricultural and industrial development, under white supervision and with white capital, in the Reserves, which would in time become self-supporting and self-governing. How long this would take depended largely on the Africans themselves. Dr. Verwoerd did not speak about the majority of Africans, who live in white areas, and the Council adjourned because the Minister refused to allow it to discuss the political aspects of apartheid, though he invited the members to do so with him unofficially as private persons.[16]

There are aspects of the theory of Bantustans that are not clear. Except for Zululand, the Transkei, and the Ciskei, the Reserves are fragmented and few people believe that even these three can become viable States. Unless South Africa were to surrender to these homelands far more land, including access to ports, the proposed Bantustans could never be any-

[14] See *S.A. Outlook*, October 1950.
[15] See *Die Burger*, 15 January 1951.
[16] See *Die Burger*, 6 December 1950.

thing else than appendages of South Africa. The prospects of persuading any white electorate to agree to the purchase of more land for this purpose are negligible. Moreover, assuming that one or two Bantustans do achieve independence, would that not merely put South Africa back to the border wars of the nineteenth century? It is inconceivable that Africans would for long remain content with a small fraction of what they regard as their own country. Again, the Tomlinson Commission was emphatic that tribalism and a modern economy are incompatible. How then can the industrial development of the Reserves take place if tribalism is to be revived and strengthened? Finally, more than half the African population lives in what is considered the white part of South Africa, and African leaders are clamouring for political rights now. To call them migrants, and at the same time help to provide them with permanent homes in urban areas, would not for long satisfy either the leaders or their followers.

The conditions in the Native Reserves, and their administration, were described in chapters 2 and 5. It is against that background that the policy of self-government for the Transkei, announced by Dr. Verwoerd in January 1962, must be assessed. The Nationalist Party, sensitive to the criticism that its apartheid policy was negative, hailed the announcement as proof to the world that here, at last, was the positive apartheid towards which Afrikaner nationalism had been striving. Dr. Verwoerd had enabled Nationalists to escape from the moral dilemma: on the one hand the determination to maintain their white entity, and on the other the desire not to be unjust towards Africans.

It is clear, however, that in trying to escape from the moral dilemma the government created more problems than it solved. If ultimate independence for the Reserves was seriously meant, the result must be the fragmentation of the Republic, leaving millions of Africans in the 'white' areas. If ultimate independence was not the aim, African nationalism would soon make it so, and talk of self-government, parliaments, and cabinets would strengthen the resolve of African nationalists. In effect, the government attempted to create 'colonies' so as to be able to grant them 'freedom', forgetting that the process of freeing colonies is a long and arduous one. The plain economic facts of the Transkei, as of the other Reserves, are grinding poverty and over-population on a sadly ravished earth. These facts will always drive Africans to seek work in white areas, and as long as that continues, talk of self-government is illusory and serves only to befog the situation. To alter the conditions in the Reserves demands an economic and political price that neither of the two big political parties in South Africa is as yet prepared to pay.

The Nationalist Party has always accused the United Party of having no real Native policy and of having allowed things to drift until they reached the dangerous state from which only the policy of apartheid could rescue them. Another accusation was that the United Party dog was wagged by its small liberal tail and the Party would, if returned to office, abolish all colour bars and promote complete equality. There is some justification for the first accusation; none at all for the second. The United Party, by its very nature, lacked the unanimity of opinion that characterizes the Nationalist Party; and there was a small liberal wing of the party, associated with the name of the late J. H. Hofmeyr, which, while it did not go as far as to advocate complete equality between white and non-white, was determined that the rights of Coloured and Africans should be defended within the existing situation. On the whole, the United Party accepted the fact that Africans had become integrated into white economic affairs, and it would agree with Dr. Eiselen in his diagnosis of what was needed to ensure a contented and efficient labour force. It was prepared to meet social and administrative difficulties as they arose rather than by any clear-cut and comprehensive policy. The basis of this policy was not merely a division of opinion within the United Party; it was also a realization of the fluidity of conditions not susceptible of easy solution by cast-iron policies that neglect important economic considerations.

The United Party consistently opposed that part of apartheid that applies chiefly to the Coloured population, and until 1967 had promised, if returned to power, to restore Coloured voters to the common roll. At its congress in October 1967, however, a new policy was announced: to provide for the representation of Coloured voters, on a separate roll, by six members of parliament and two senators who might be white or Coloured as the voters desired. On the issue of black–white relations there is a considerable area of agreement, or near agreement, with moderate Nationalists. The United Party is in favour of residential and social separation and accepts the principle of the Group Areas Act, but wishes to make it less drastic by curbing the powers of the Minister, by promoting voluntary separation, and by paying full compensation where property rights are interfered with. Probably a large majority of the United Party would agree to some form of industrial colour bar but is opposed to rigid legislation on the matter, and believes that colour bars should be administered by agreement between workers and employers, and the Party is opposed to job reservation by race. It opposed the Extension of University Education Act largely on the ground that it interfered with university autonomy; but a large number of United Party members would probably agree that mixed universities are not desirable.

The greatest disagreement between the two parties was over the representation of Africans in parliament and the establishment of Bantustans. The Nationalist Party believes that Africans should not be represented in parliament while the United Party believes they should, albeit to a very limited extent, on a separate roll, and by whites. In 1957 the United Party put forward a complicated plan for reforming the Senate in such a way as to extend representation to non-whites, to protect minority groups, and to entrench white leadership. Both parties believe that the Reserves must be economically rehabilitated, but they disagree on how this is to be done, and the United Party is opposed to the establishment of Bantustans which might eventually balkanize the country.

By 1961 there were signs that in both the major political parties further consideration was being given to race policies. Within the Nationalist Party there was criticism that the economic restoration of the Reserves was going too slowly and would have to be speeded up if the world was to be convinced that apartheid was being seriously applied. Moreover, a number of Nationalist intellectuals began openly to doubt whether apartheid as applied to the Coloured population was either moral or wise; and, while maintaining the validity of the conception of the Reserves as independent national African homes, they advocated some form of representation for those Africans who had left the Reserves for good. The United Party, on the other hand, supported the restoration of the Reserves but strongly opposed their possible future independence. Instead, Sir de Villiers Graaff, leader of the Party, envisaged increasing self-government in the Reserves leading to a South African federation, to the central parliament of which African areas would elect representatives. The new policy, announced by the United Party congress in October 1967, retained the federal principle and seemed to accept as permanent the existence of the Indian and Coloured councils as well as such legislatures as may be set up in the Reserves.

Neither of the two parties has put forward a policy that, on the long view, takes full cognizance of two fundamental facts in inter-racial affairs. The first is that the economy of South Africa depends on all its 'races' which have been integrated to such an extent that they cannot be separated without damaging the economy beyond repair. In the second place, relations between the different population groups are fluid, not static, and any policy that neglects that fact is unlikely to be workable. The danger in the South African racial situation is that those who wield political power habitually and traditionally start with the fatal handicap of failing to consult the Africans themselves. It is they who constitute the large and variable factor in the equation and must, somehow, be linked to the other factors to make political sense. By short-sighted policies on the part of the whites, Africans have been driven in on themselves to a nationalism that becomes increasingly anti-white. Most whites think either in terms of a 'once-for-all' clear-cut policy or in terms of *laissez faire*. The racial situation has reached such dimensions that neither policy can hope to succeed.

There is in South Africa a body of liberal opinion that expresses itself on race and on other questions through such bodies as the English churches, the South African Institute of Race Relations, and the Civil Rights League at Cape Town. It consists of men and women of all racial groups drawn from the universities, from among teachers, business men and women, and from the churches. It is not a cohesive body and is difficult to weld into a political party because it is scattered and does not command sufficient votes in one constituency to be able to elect a candidate. It exerts what influence it has by conferences, Press statements, protest meetings, and by briefing members of parliament on proposed legislation. After the establishment of the Liberal Party in 1953, this opinion was most nearly represented in the House of Assembly by Mrs. Margaret Ballinger and Mr. Walter Stanford, and in the Senate by Senators Rubin and Ballinger, all of whom were elected by African voters. These parliamentary representatives of Africans were totally opposed to apartheid and were among its ablest and most trenchant critics. Liberal Party policy advocates the extension of the franchise, on a common roll, leading to the eventual enfranchisement of all South Africans regardless of race; it proposes the abolition of all forms of colour bar and is opposed to any legislation that restricts the free movement of Africans or invades the rights of any section of the population on grounds of colour. Under the Promotion of Bantu Self-Government Act, however, parliamentary representation of Africans ceased in 1960, and the Liberal Party was no longer represented in Parliament.

Liberalism in regard to race is, of course, not confined to the Liberal Party. Liberal views usually receive considerable publicity because of the reputation and standing of those who express them. Both major political parties, however, depend so much on the conservative rural vote that neither can afford to pay much attention to such views. Undeterred by this or by the harassing attention of the security police, liberals have continued to express publicly what they believe to be reasonable and just policies. Although the Liberal Party ceased to exist in 1968, liberal views continue to be publicly expressed.

The advent of the Progressive Party, in the latter half of 1959, indicated that liberalism was on the increase. That Party declared itself against the colour bar and in favour of a common (though not a universal) franchise; it took its stand on the fact that there is one nation in South Africa embracing different groups, and that each group is entitled to protection and to a share in the government; it proposed constitutional safeguards, in the form of an entrenched Bill of Rights, to guarantee the fundamental human rights and liberties of the individual and of minorities. Both the Liberal Party and the Progressive Party represented liberalism in its various stages; both parties rejected the Nationalist Party doctrine of apartheid; and neither Party had any faith in the United Party's ability to deal with race problems in their modern form. The difference between the Liberal Party and the Progressive Party was mainly one of emphasis: while both advocated a common franchise, the Liberals would go faster and further than the Progressives; while neither party shirked the essential political and economic facts in South Africa, the Progressive Party was keenly aware of, and laid great stress on, the need to safeguard the rights of minorities in a mixed society.

There is no socialist party in South Africa. The small Labour Party depends for its strength on white trade unions, many of which support a colour bar in industry. The Labour Party had gradually become more liberal after the Nationalists had come to power; but it could never be called socialist. After the 1958 general election the Party was no longer represented in parliament.

The Communist Party was made illegal in 1950 but dissolved itself before the Bill became law. Communists advocated complete and immediate equality for all, but for none of the population groups did their doctrine have any but a limited appeal. Nevertheless most whites fear, or can easily be made to fear communism, and the Suppression of Communism Act and its amendments are a reflection of that fear. With the threat of communism as the ostensible motive, legislation was passed giving wide powers to the Minister of Justice, powers that were not subordinated to the judiciary and for the exercise of which responsibility in parliament could be evaded under the plea of 'the interests of the state'. These powers could be and were used to destroy the personal freedom of outspoken liberals who were themselves fundamentally opposed to communism.

FOREIGN AFFAIRS

Until South Africa became a republic and left the Commonwealth in 1961 it was convenient to divide her foreign affairs as follows: relations with Britain and other Commonwealth countries; with non-Commonwealth countries; and with other states or colonies in southern and central Africa. It might have been supposed that there would be no special reason for maintaining these divisions after 1961, and more particularly for regarding Britain and the Commonwealth as falling into a separate category. The truth is, however, that though political bonds may be broken with relative ease, those of trade and culture are more durable. In 1968 Britain was still South Africa's largest customer, taking 30 per cent of her exports and supplying 33 per cent of her imports. If the Commonwealth were added, more than half South Africa's trade was with her former Commonwealth associates, Moreover, more than R2,000 million of British capital had by 1968 been invested in South Africa, and industrial relations in the form of manufacturing under licence or the establishment of local assembly plants are close. There is, therefore, substantial reason why relations with Britain should still, in 1968, fall into a special category.

In so far as external relations are a matter of trade, there is not a great deal of difference between the policies of the main parties. Both are anxious to extend South Africa's trade relations by exploring new markets and negotiating trade treaties with other countries. Individual firms and local authorities do, it is true, sometimes show a preference for buying 'British', or 'non-British', as the case may be; but, in general, sentiment does not play a large part in trade relations.

Until 1961 it was in political relations, in peace and in war, that differences of outlook occurred. The majority of white South Africans, possibly as many as 60 per cent, realized the need for close alliance with Britain and the Commonwealth. Community of interests, of culture, of language and of traditions were all strongly on the side of a foreign policy whose corner-stone was close relations with Britain. The desire for such relations was shown by the part South Africa played in two world wars, and feelings springing from common experiences in the wars themselves reinforced the policy. There was only a small section of South Africans who had an emotional attachment to England, or who even gave much conscious thought to the matter unless it was challenged. But the majority accepted the fact that cordial relations with Britain and the Commonwealth were both natural and desirable. There existed a vigorous and growing feeling of national independence and pride, but for the majority of South Africans this was not an anti-British sentiment. Among white South Africans this cordiality towards Britain extended to the other dominions that were pre-dominantly white. When the Prime Minister, Mr. B. J. Vorster, spoke about South Africa's racial policies and sport, he said that if South Africa's 'traditional opponents' wished to include non-whites in their teams the government would not refuse them entry. He was referring more specifically to Britain, Australia, and New Zealand and to rugby and cricket. But Mr. Vorster added that South Africa would not seek 'new' opponents—probably a reference to West Indies and cricket.

Within the Nationalist Party, on the other hand, there was a strong section of opinion that hoped to see a republic, cut off from the Common-wealth, established in South Africa. Those who held this opinion maintained that they were not anti-British; that they wanted a republic because it suited the South African temperament; that association with Britain dragged South Africa into war; and that, as long as South Africa was 'tied to Britain', English-speaking South Africans would always regard Britain as their motherland and South Africa only as their second home. Once the republic was established, they said, English-speaking citizens would co-operate more readily with Afrikaners because they could no longer regard England as having first claim on their loyalty.[17]

There was little substance in these arguments. In spite of a nostalgic and sentimental attachment to the idea of a republic, there is no proof that

[17] Malan (then Prime Minister) was reported in *Die Burger* of 23 May 1951 as follows: 'We shall be free from a divided loyalty only when we have a republic.' This view was re-iterated by Dr. Verwoerd in January 1959 when, speaking in the House of Assembly on the republican issue, he said: 'I go further and say that the republic will bring peace in South Africa, not only peace between us but also peace as regards the suspicion being spread abroad.' *Hansard* (1959) Col. 57.

the republican form of government is more suited to the South African temperament than is a constitutional monarchy. As for her attitude in time of war, South Africa's position astride the Cape route has made neutrality impossible ever since the Napoleonic Wars. But this is only in time of war. Harbour facilities at Cape Town are of great international importance, enhanced when the Suez Canal is closed; and South Africa will, in peace time, sell those facilities to any ships, no matter under which country's flag they may sail. When a world war breaks out South Africa alone cannot for long defend the Cape route against a world power and she would perforce have to choose sides. Until 1967 the ally she chose would certainly been Britain, and the agreement by which the Naval Base at Simonstown was handed over to South Africa in 1955 was based on this assumption. At the end of 1967, however, Great Britain began withdrawing from defence commitments in the East, and Simonstown became less important to her. It is possible that modern armaments have reduced the strategic value of Simonstown, but whatever importance it still has will ensure that South Africa will not be able to maintain a neutral position in a world war. The fact that she has become a republic will not prevent her from being 'dragged' into war; and at whatever inconvenience she may be compelled to look around for alternative allies.

There is, historically at any rate, much substance in the argument that political and cultural bonds exist between English-speaking South Africans and England. South Africa's first cultural and political ties were with Holland, but the political ties were cut in 1806, and the cultural ties, though maintained for many generations, languished and were gradually supplanted by those of British origin. For more than a hundred years the majority of Europeans living in what has become the Republic of South Africa were closely linked, economically, socially, and politically, with Great Britain. Those Afrikaners who, by temperament and political history, were antagonistic to Britain were unable to look to an overseas country for moral or cultural support. In this way Afrikaans nationalism was born and grew up in a context where to be an Afrikaner meant to be opposed to Britain. Twelve years after the Boer War Britain was at war with Germany, and Afrikaner nationalism, being anti-British, tended to be pro-German, English-speaking South Africans and those Afrikaners who followed Botha and Smuts, quite naturally looked to Britain for physical support and spiritual comfort.

These habits of thought persisted. During the Second World War those members of the Nationalist Party who did not positively hope that Germany would win did, at any rate, regard the anticipated break-up of the British Empire with equanimity; at all events, they prepared for the coming republic. Followers of Smuts, English- and Afrikaans-speaking South Africans, looked all the more eagerly to Britain to stand between them and conquest by Nazi Germany. Thus the gulf between those who

'looked to England' and those who did not, widened. The more the Afrikaner in the Nationalist Party spoke about a republic, the more strongly
did non-Nationalists feel the need of close ties with Britain. This was the
more so since, during the war years, various Nationalist Party groups and
individuals defined the republican constitution as one that was authoritarian in character, and had, moreover, no room for 'unAfrikaans' elements.
Such a republic held no attractions for non-Nationalists. Moreover, many
non-Nationalists who might, in 1948, have been indifferent on the question
of a republic became increasingly antagonistic to a republic established and
dominated by an Afrikaner nationalism that showed few signs of having
purged itself of authoritarian leanings.

There is, therefore, some justification for Nationalists who said that
English-speaking South Africans looked to England for their salvation.
It is, however, a saying that can easily be misinterpreted. The generation
that used to refer to England as 'home' had, for practical purposes, passed
away well before 1968. Britain did not interfere in South African affairs,
nor was there any justification for suggesting that, consciously or unconsciously, English-speaking South Africans relied on Britain to 'take their
part' in South Africa. But the fact remains that many South Africans had
close cultural and linguistic associations with Britain, that they admired,
and copied, many British institutions, and that Britain stood, in general,
for an interpretation of Western civilization that fitted most closely with
their own ideas. Furthermore, the two countries were bound by economic
interests. The establishment of a republic in South Africa did not and would
not break these affiliations so long as Britain stood for those ideas that were
acceptable to most South Africans.

The Nationalist Party was not unanimous in 1960 on the republican
issue. Possibly half the party favoured a republic provided that a large
majority of the voters supported it and, probably, provided it remained
within the Commonwealth. The remaining half consisted of the two
extremes—those who were not republican, and those who wanted a republic
soon and outside the Commonwealth. The constitution of the Nationalist
Party of 1951 (when the Nationalist and Afrikaner parties united) contained
a clause maintaining that a republican form of government, outside the
Commonwealth, was best suited to South Africa. In 1957 this clause was
changed to make the republic and association with the Commonwealth
separate issues—a change which may indicate that there were a number of
Nationalists who might vote for the republic provided they were assured
that it would be within the Commonwealth. That assurance was freely
given at the time of the referendum by Nationalists of all ranks, and Dr.
Verwoerd himself, while saying that no guarantee could be absolute, was
insistent that he was asking for a republic inside the Commonwealth.
Indeed, had the assurances not been given it is highly probable that there
would have been no majority for the republic. As it is, there were many

warnings from non-Nationalist opponents of the republic against relying on such assurances.

Cultural ties with Britain are not confined to South Africans of British descent and a minority of Afrikaans-speaking whites. The most die-hard Afrikaner nationalist is continuously exposed to cultural influences that are expressed through the English language; and even when he consciously isolates himself from such influences he has not yet broken his ties with Britain. That a kind of love-hate relationship still exists between nationalist Afrikaners and Britain (though the ordinary Briton is blissfully unaware of this) may be seen by the reactions at the end of 1967 when Britain decided to cut her overseas commitments though that meant 'abdicating as a great military power'. Had any other country been involved the Afrikaans Press would have treated the news objectively and realistically. As it was Britain, there was ill-concealed glee that she could no longer be called 'Great Britain', and this was combined with the bitter accusation that she was, unworthily, opting out of her obligations and thus increasing the burden on her allies—of whom South Africa was one.

Though it is impossible to speak with any degree of accuracy about the views of the non-white population regarding a republic, it is tolerably certain that the vast mass of it was opposed to the idea. The Coloured people of the Cape associated their political rights with Britain, for it was under British rule that they attained the franchise on equal terms with whites. That equality was removed in 1956 by a parliament in which the Afrikaans-speaking Nationalist Party was in power. Africans in the Cape Province, too, associated their political rights with Great Britain, and the loss of those rights with Hertzog and, subsequently, with the Nationalist Party. In the other provinces most Africans, whether justifiably or not, have always tended to think of the Afrikaner as a worse 'oppressor' than the British. British colonial policy in the 1960's appeared to thinking Africans as more hopeful for the future than the policies of South African governments. There seems little doubt, therefore, that Coloured and African opinion, had it been sought, would have been overwhelmingly opposed to a South African republic, particularly one outside the British Commonwealth. In any case, the severest criticism of the republic is that it was brought into being without consulting the non-white citizens of South Africa.

So far we have discussed South Africa's relations with Great Britain. With regard to the rest of the Commonwealth, the Nationalist Party's attitude was, broadly, either sceptical or hostile. It did not feel that there were any special advantages in belonging to a Commonwealth of such diverse peoples—advantages, that is, that could not be as well obtained by direct dealings between South Africa and Australia or Canada. Although the word 'British' had been dropped, it was still felt that the Commonwealth was British, and that South Africa, as a member of it, might become involved in undesirable international policies through that connexion. When certain Commonwealth nations sided against South Africa at U.N. over the Asian question, Nationalist newspapers asked whether there really was a Commonwealth. Further, when the Secretary of State for Colonies, early in 1951, expressed the hope that the Gold Coast would in time become a member of the Commonwealth, the Nationalists were up in arms. If the Commonwealth really existed they asked, who gave Great Britain the right to invite additional members? Nevertheless, when Ghana became independent in 1957 the South African Government was represented by a high official at the inaugural ceremonies, as she was subsequently when the independence of other African states was inaugurated.

The United Party, on the other hand, regarded the Commonwealth as a positive achievement, as something which gave South Africa greater security. True, the United Party found that relations with India and Pakistan were not easy; but it was prepared to put up with such difficulties for the sake of the advantages to South Africa and because it liked the idea of a Commonwealth association.

In actual practice, there was no difference in peacetime between the policies of the two parties in regard to their day-to-day relations with other Commonwealth countries. The differences that have been discussed were those of general attitude; and it was only in time of war that practical action flowed from these attitudes. The Nationalists were opposed to South Africa's participation in the two world wars. If Britain and the Commonwealth were to become involved in a third world war against Communist countries, however, there is little doubt that, for the first time in her history, the white population of South Africa would be united over foreign policy. Whatever government was in power, South Africa would go to war against Communism. It is probable that the enthusiasm of the whites for a war against Communism would not be shared by the non-whites. This does not mean that Communism has any particular hold on the non-white population, but rather that they might not regard as an unmitigated evil conquest by a country that acknowledges no colour bar.

South Africa has trade and diplomatic relations with a number of non-Commonwealth countries, either at the consular or at the ambassadorial level. Two countries are mentioned here only for the sake of rounding off the picture and not because they reveal any marked differences between the two parties. In the post-war atmosphere of the 1950's it was to be expected that South Africa, with a large non-white population, would be sensitive about Communism. When it came to power in 1948 the Nationalist Party set about taking vigorous measures to combat the danger that, it was convinced, threatened South Africa from this source. The Suppression of Communism Act of 1950 made the propagation of Communism illegal and gave the Minister of Justice powers to 'deem' any person a Communist and subsequently to 'name' him and prohibit him from attending meetings or belonging to specified organizations; against these powers there was no effective legal redress. Under pressure from the Afrikaans churches and other bodies this Act was in due course followed by the closing down of the U.S.S.R. Consulate. It may be added that this has not stopped trade between South Africa and the U.S.S.R.

In the post-war world the United States of America became as interested as the U.S.S.R. in Africa, and it was natural that a great deal of this interest should have been centred on South Africa where the advent and actions of the Nationalist Government were attracting world-wide attention. Encouraged and largely financed by the State Department in Washington, the Carnegie Corporation of New York,[18] and the Ford Foundation, a steady two-way traffic began to develop in journalists, editors, professors, professional and business men, and government officials. The Americans came to study the situation on the spot, and South Africans went to find out what lessons might be learnt from American practice. The South African Government was somewhat embarrassed by this intense interest in its apartheid policies, particularly when an American television company sent a camera team to make what turned out to be an unflattering film of apartheid in practice. On two occasions ministers rather petulantly referred to 'dollar imperialism in Africa' and to the support given by an American foundation to so suspect a body as the South African Institute of Race Relations. On the whole, however, the government was not anxious to alienate the sympathies of so economically and politically powerful a State, and the exchange of personnel continued even after American interest had to some extent shifted its emphasis to Central and West Africa.

Until the end of the Second World War South Africa's relations with other territories in southern and central Africa were economic rather than political. Johannesburg, the centre of an economic empire, draws most of its labour for the mines, and a good proportion of its labour for industries, from outside its borders. Moreover, South Africa has valuable trading relations with other African territories and is intent on developing these markets. With the exception of German East Africa and South-West Africa in the First World War, relations between South Africa and other African territories have always been peaceful. Belgium was, in two world wars, an ally; and Portugal was an ally in the first, and neutral in the second; the remaining territories were British or French.

Cecil Rhodes dreamt of a united South Africa that would include

---

[18] It was announced in 1968 that, as from the end of 1969, Carnegie travel grants would no longer be available to Australia, New Zealand, and South Africa. Thus came to an end a magnificent programme which, over forty years, had enabled hundreds of South Africans to visit the United States.

Southern Rhodesia; and when union was being debated, at the National Convention of 1908, Southern Rhodesia was represented by observers. The most serious attempt to unite her with South Africa took place in 1922 when Smuts toured the country and tried to persuade Rhodesians to throw in their lot with South Africa. They were, however, afraid of an Afrikaner majority, and refused. In the last years of the Second World War Smuts talked a good deal about pan-Africanism; but it is doubtful whether he had any specific policy in mind beyond the need for closer co-operation in the exploitation of natural resources, the development of transport, and in fighting pests such as locusts. Smuts, like others, was impressed by the smallness of the white population in southern Africa.

After 1945 other factors began to influence South Africa's political relations with territories to the north of her borders. In the first place, there was an increasing immigration of South Africans into the two Rhodesias. These two territories were expanding rapidly and there was a demand for technicians, railwaymen, and civil servants. Land was cheaper there than in the Union, and young South Africans found the conditions for settlement attractive. Many of these South African immigrants were Afrikaners, and a language problem soon made its appearance. In 1950 Afrikaners in Southern Rhodesia were sufficiently numerous to have their own newspaper, and they petitioned the Rhodesian Government for Afrikaans-medium primary schools. The government refused, and the Nationalist Press in South Africa took strong exception to the refusal. Even in Kenya the language question arose. In 1951 a party of Afrikaans children from Kenya toured the Union to raise money for the establishment of a private school, and they were received cordially in official and unofficial circles. The reaction of the Nationalist Party Press to this question of Afrikaners who have trekked to other African territories seems to indicate that, in due course, the government of the Republic might be under pressure to interfere on behalf of the emigrants.

The second political factor that began to assume increasing importance was the question of the part that Africa might have to play in another war. From the point of view of strategic position, of European manpower, and of ability to manufacture war materials, South Africa must be regarded as the dominant single state south of the Sahara; and it is obvious that she will play an important part in the co-ordination of military plans. There are, however, difficulties in the way of effective co-operation. South Africans in general, and the Nationalist Party more particularly, are opposed to the use of armed non-white troops. During the First World War Coloured troops were armed, and fought well, while Africans were used as a labour force only. In the last war, Coloured troops were used chiefly as transport drivers, but they were usually armed when on active service. Africans were not used as fighting troops and this caused great dissatisfaction among them and hindered recruiting. It may well be that, in another war, Africans will be reluctant to volunteer in sufficient numbers unless they are armed, and this may have repercussions on the African populations of other countries.

The third and most important factor that affected South Africa's external relations was the astonishing speed with which political events in the rest of Africa marched after 1950. Within two decades, territory after territory in Africa achieved independence. Immediately after the Second World War, most people with a knowledge of Africa knew that fresh and more progressive colonial policies would be adopted in Africa and that such policies would, in the fullness of time, lead to responsible government. Few would have believed that, within ten years' time, more than half the population of Africa would be politically independent, and that the white governments of the territories occupied by the rest would be faced with urgent and immediate problems of extending political power to their African subjects. Changes in the political climate of Europe and the world, the wooing of Africa by the two greatest Powers, and the simultaneous bursting into flower of African nationalism are among the main general causes of the revolution that took place. But whatever the causes, the result is indisputable: by the early 1950's it was no longer a question of *whether* political rights and power would be extended to Africans; it was only a question of *when* and *how* this would happen.

The full import of these startling events was not at first realized by the white population of South Africa. The first reaction of the Nationalist Party Press to the independence of Ghana was to accuse Britain of a policy of scuttle and of leaving the white man in Africa to his fate. This was followed by a strongly expressed belief that the experiment in self-government could not possibly succeed because Africans were not ready for it; but when it became clear that this belief was not necessarily well founded, and that other territories were soon to follow Ghana's example, the uneasy realization began to dawn that the Union would have to come to terms with events. The Nationalist Press and ministers then began to take the realistic line of recognizing and welcoming any new States and of offering, in advance, to co-operate with them in solving common African problems; at the same time, great stress was laid on the need to respect South Africa's right to deal with her interracial problems in her own way—that of apartheid. There were debates and discussions on whether to exchange diplomatic representation with the new States and on the social difficulties of having black diplomats in South Africa; there was even talk of erecting a multi-racial hotel to house distinguished non-white representatives; and in 1967 it was announced that the government proposed creating a diplomatic suburb where embassies might build their own residences immune from normal racial restrictions. Both the Nationalist Party and the United Party were, however, extremely cautious about these matters and left it to individuals to make the bolder suggestions that could, if necessary, be disowned officially.

There are aspects of South Africa's relations with the emerging States of Africa that require further discussion. In the first place, there is a community of outlook among the majority of Europeans who have made their home in Africa and who have entrenched themselves economically and politically in Rhodesia and the Republic, and to a lesser extent in other territories, namely a powerful incentive to protect their vested interests by retaining and increasing their political hold on the countries they inhabit; they regard themselves, as indeed they are, as small communities surrounded by an alien civilization; and they are convinced that no mother-country government can really understand the problem of dealing with Africans. There are minorities in all these territories who do not share these views and who look forward to a common citizenship regardless of race; but the majority will not lightly surrender their privileged position. The largest body of whites live in South Africa, and many of those beyond her borders look to her hopefully as a possible protector. Indeed, many of them have immigrated to the Republic with whose race policies they find themselves in sympathy if not in entire agreement. Those who have remained behind have strong doubts about the wisdom and feasibility of apartheid. Moreover, they suspect that Afrikaner nationalism is anti-British. Nevertheless the urge to stand together in face of a threat to vested interests will become stronger as African freedom and authority grow. White settlers in the rest of Africa may not believe complete apartheid to be practicable; but they find it difficult to face African rule with equanimity. If the Republic were to modify her race policies and shew that Afrikaner nationalism is neither anti-British nor anti-African, white settlers would readily accept her leadership.

The second attitude is the converse of the first: Africans in the Republic look with growing pride and admiration at the new independent African states, and contact between African leaders in those states and in South Africa has become closer as young African intellectuals escape from the Republic under whose laws their freedom of movement and action is threatened. Leaders in the newly independent African states talk about liberating their brothers in the south, and have instituted boycotts of South African products; and Mr. Julius Nyerere's statement on the eve of the Prime Ministers' Conference in March 1961, that Tanganyika would not wish to remain a member of the Commonwealth if South Africa did, was probably decisive. South African governments may, for a time, be able to regard such threats lightly or use them as a reason for banning African leaders and organizations; but their significance cannot be overlooked by anyone, white or black, who thinks of Africa as home and for whom a ganging up of black against white spells disaster. The test of statesmanship in Africa, and of South African foreign policy, must lie in warding off that disaster.

For the Republic of South Africa to pass that test depends, in the first place, on considerable modifications of her internal race policies and on her contact with the rest of Africa. In 1961 the Republic was represented in the Central African Federation and in Portuguese East Africa. With the rest of the new and turbulent Africa she had no direct contact, but her membership of the Commonwealth gave her inestimable advantages of first-hand information and indirect representation through British sources. Dr. Verwoerd's decision to withdraw from the Commonwealth would, in due course, compel the Republic either to seek direct contacts or to depend for vital information on casual reports. By 1968 the Republic had exchanged diplomats with Malawi and with the Smith government in Rhodesia and had developed close contacts with her three immediate neighbours, Botswana, Lesotho, and Swaziland. Her relations with these three states will be discussed in chapter 10.

CONSTITUTIONAL QUESTIONS

The fourth question that divides the two major parties is constitutional. It is not merely a question of whether South Africa should be a republic, in or out of the Commonwealth, but whether she should be governed on the lines of a parliamentary democracy in which respect for constitutional conventions plays a considerable part.

By the time the Union was constituted South Africa had had experience of two kinds of popular government. In the Cape there was parliamentary government which was based on the British model and had inherited and developed the traditions of British parliamentary democracy. The Transvaal, on the other hand, had a republican constitution that was unstable and subject to such continual stresses that constitutional traditions had no chance to mature. Constitutionalism in the Cape connoted adherence to the spirit of parliamentary democracy as well as to the letter of the written constitution; in the Transvaal the practice of constitutionalism was empirical. Natal had followed the British model, and the Free State was closer in spirit to the Cape than it was to the Transvaal.

Broadly speaking, the United Party adhered to the British conception of constitutional government, and the Nationalist Party showed a tendency to hark back to the republican constitution of the Transvaal. Many Nationalists expressed strong opinions against what Malan called 'British parliamentary democracy', and maintained that it was not suited to the Afrikaner temperament or to South African conditions. The first of these contentions has no substance. The histories of the Cape Parliament, and of the Union Parliament after 1910, show that Afrikaans-speaking South Africans were foremost among parliamentarians and the staunchest upholders of constitutional conventions. The second contention, that British parliamentary democracy was unsuited to South African conditions, is based on doubtful premises. Soon after Germany and Italy popularized the idea of the one-party state, it became customary in Nationalist Party circles to maintain that the Boer Republics were one-party states and that that system was more suited to the Afrikaner temperament. The cry, therefore, became: Back to the Boer Republics. As the Council of the Dutch Reformed Churches pointed out, however, the theory that the Boer Republics were one-party states is an illusion.[19] In the *Volksraad* there were, as yet, no clearly defined parties, but that was because there was general agreement on the simple fundamental issues that faced its members. Towards the end of the nineteenth century there were clear signs that parties were beginning to emerge, and presidential elections had become contests between two groups.

Another argument against British parliamentary democracy was that it does not work where there is a non-homogeneous population. The system might work, say the critics, where there are a common language and a common cultural background. But, in South Africa, there is no such bond between whites and non-whites, and even between the two main white groups there is a lack of common background. This argument, too, is of doubtful validity. Cape statesmen of pre-Union days were practically unanimous in maintaining that a common voters' roll of citizens of all colours, and based on civilization tests, was practicable, and they fought hard to have that well-tried system adopted in the South Africa Act. The history of South Africa from 1948 to 1968 shows that the mere existence of a parliament is in itself no guarantee of individual liberty; but that was not because the population is non-homogeneous but because parliament was elected by one-fifth of the population. There is indeed a danger in a non-homogeneous society that a majority, or even a well-organized minority, may use the control of the parliamentary machine for its own purposes and, in the process, deprive other groups of rights and liberties. The remedy for that lies in a more rigid constitution in which individual and group rights and liberties are entrenched, and this is the remedy that the Progressive Party strongly advocates.

Where the Nationalist Party differs from other parties is that many of its members are less firmly attached to the constitutional principles and conventions of parliamentary democracy. Like those who worked the nineteenth-century Transvaal constitution, they tend to be empirical and to justify constitutional changes whose main object is the advancement of the interests of a racial group or of a political party. This tendency was evinced in the passage of the Separate Representation of Voters Act which has already been described. In the debate on that Bill the United Party declared its intention, if the Bill was passed, of testing its validity in the courts, and Malan replied that if the courts found against the government he would have to consider action similar to that taken by President Kruger

[19] See *Fundamental Principles of Calvinist Political Science*, quoted in chapter 9.

when he dismissed his Chief Justice for pronouncing against the validity of a resolution of the *Volksraad*.[20] The subsequent history of the Separate Representation of Voters Act, as well as other legislation introduced by the Nationalist Government, shows a curious mixture of respect for the letter of constitutional forms and a disregard for their spirit. Moreover, the tendency to give far-reaching and arbitrary powers to ministers, though not unique to South Africa or to the Nationalist Government, has been pushed to lengths which argue, at the least, an impatience with the legal and legislative safeguards that a parliamentary system is presumed to provide.[21]

Parliamentary democracy assumes an independent judiciary whose status all parties are concerned to uphold; only thus can individual freedom be safeguarded against arbitrary government. In 1952, when the Appellate Division of the Supreme Court declared the Separate Representation of Voters Act invalid, ministers permitted themselves and their followers to refer in public to the judges as 'paid officials' who should be brought under control; and in 1959 the Minister of Justice introduced a Supreme Court Bill which contained a provision empowering the Governor-General to suspend a judge for 'misconduct', subject to the subsequent approval of parliament. Under the South Africa Act, a judge might not be removed except by the Governor-General on an address from both Houses of Parliament, and the proposed Bill would, virtually, have made judicial tenure subject to the executive. There was so much criticism of this proposal that it was dropped; but the fact that the proposal could have been brought forward at all augurs a lack of steadfastness of belief in the importance of an independent judiciary.

The value of an independent judiciary as a bulwark against arbitrary government may be reduced by means other than direct interference with judicial officers. Acts of parliament that deliberately exclude the jurisdiction of the courts effectively undermine the rule of law. Thus, the Suppression of Communism Act empowers the Minister of Justice to deprive citizens of their liberty without telling them precisely of what they are accused or giving them an opportunity to have the matter tested in open court. The Criminal Procedure Amendment Act of 1965 empowers an attorney-general (officials appointed and controlled by the Minister of Justice) to arrest and hold a state witness for 180 days at a time. The Act expressly excludes the jurisdiction of the courts and denies the individual the right to consult legal opinion. The Johannesburg Bar described this law as 'a grave and totally unwarranted interference with the liberty of the subject, the rule of law, and the administration of justice.' There are other laws of this nature and Nationalists defend them on the grounds that

[20] See Walker, *A History of South Africa*, pp. 464–6, 472.
[21] For a carefully documented account of the extent to which the rule of law has been eroded see Brookes and Macaulay, *Civil Liberty in South Africa*.

they are necessary for the protection of the State against communism. More-over, they deny that in passing such laws parliament itself has undermined the rule of law.

It is important to determine whether this attitude towards constitutional conventions and the rule of law was inherent in Nationalist Party policy or whether it grew up in justification of acts which its opponents stigmatized as unconstitutional. Nationalists are divided on this as they are on republi-canism or the Commonwealth. Many have a deep respect for constitutional forms and were concerned when their own government appeared to be disregarding them; some resigned from the Party because of this dis-regard. Nevertheless, it is possible to discern a link between what might be called Krugerism and the dominant group in modern Afrikaner national-ism: in both are to be found an impatience with opposition and criticism, a conviction that Afrikaners are the real 'people' (*die volk*) of South Africa, and a determination to retain political control in Afrikaner hands even if that involves flouting constitutional procedures.[22] Whatever the truth, the issue is one of paramount importance to South Africa, for on its resolution will depend whether the Republic will continue to be governed according to the forms of parliamentary democracy and the rule of law which came from Britain and were nourished and developed in the Cape Parliament. A distinction must, of course, be drawn between the forms and the principles of democracy, for a country in which four-fifths of the popu-lation is unenfranchised can hardly be said to be democratic in principle. Nevertheless the forms are important, even if they are regarded only as the tribute that authoritarianism pays to liberty.

A discussion of political parties and policies would be incomplete unless it mentioned political pressure groups, those extra-parliamentary forces that attempt to influence legislation and administration. There are many such, and counterparts to most of them are to be found in all countries. Agricultural unions, chambers of commerce and of industries—both English and Afrikaans—the Chamber of Mines, and the trade unions, all use their organizations to obtain favourable legislation and administration and, thus, to further their economic interests. In the same general cate-gory are English and Afrikaans teachers' associations, the Public Service Association, and the various professional associations. There are also a number of disinterested organizations that use their influence for the advancement of specific or general social aims. Such are the various child

---

[22] On 21 January 1968 Mr. Dirk Richards, editor of the influential Nationalist Party paper, *Dagbreek*, maintained in an outspoken article that rhe Afrikaans Press had in the past been a willing slave of the party. He quoted as a 'classic instance' the notorious High Court of Parliament Act of 1952 which had been designed to circumvent the constitution. The Nationalist Press of the day, said Mr. Richards, had reviled anyone, including Nationalists, who dared suggest that the Act made inroads into the whole judicial system with its high ethical standards. This seems to suggest that the Nationalist Party is indeed prepared to sacrifice constitutional principles for party advantage.

welfare organizations, the English and Afrikaans women's councils, the churches, and the South African Institute of Race Relations, which has acquired a considerable reputation as a body that makes an objective study of interracial affairs and is concerned to influence public opinion and parliament by the presentation of facts. On the borderline between political and cultural organisations are a large number of Afrikaans societies which exist to promote Afrikaans culture. Owing to the close connexion between the Afrikaans language and nationalism, these societies have exercised a direct influence on political thought, and the *Federasie van Afrikaanse Kultuurverenigings* may not unfairly be regarded as a powerful unofficial ally of the Nationalist Party.

There are a few organizations that require further description because of the influence they have had on party politics. The War Veterans' Torch Commando came into being in May 1951 as a spontaneous movement of ex-servicemen and women who opposed what they regarded as unconstitutional actions by the Nationalist Party Government, such as the alteration of the South Africa Act without observing the constitutional terms laid down in the Act, and the removal of free access to the courts under the anti-Communist legislation. Led by 'Sailor' Malan, the Torch Commando's declared object was to evict the Nationalist Government, by constitutional means, because it considered that it was tampering with the freedom for which the ex-servicemen had fought. The movement spread rapidly and attracted to its ranks a large number of men and women who were not normally active in politics. It was not confined to ex-servicemen, though only they might hold executive positions and so control policy.

The Nationalist Party and its Press took the Torch Commando seriously as a new political force. From Dr. Malan downwards, the Commando was accused, alternatively, of being an adjunct of the United Party and of usurping the functions of that Party; of being Communist-inspired and of being financed by the United South Africa Trust Fund, a capitalist foundation; of being a new political party and of being subversive of parliamentary institutions. In actual fact, the Torch Commando was none of these things. It was a manifestation of the frustration of men and women who suddenly realized that they were being governed by a political party that had sympathized with the enemy during the war. Few of the members of the Torch Commando had political ambitions and they regarded their activities as called for by exceptional circumstances; they had no common policy except to evict the government at a general election. In the 1953 election they threw all their energies and enthusiasm on to the side of the opponents of the Nationalist Party, which was, nevertheless, returned with an increased majority; and its initial momentum spent, the Torch Commando dissolved, some of its more active members joining the United Party or the newly formed Liberal or Federal parties.

The Black Sash, originally called the Women's Defence of the Constitution League, was founded in 1955 to rouse public opinion over the government's proposal to enlarge the Senate and, thus, to secure the necessary two-thirds majority for taking Coloured voters off the common roll. The women who founded the movement, and those who joined it in large numbers, regarded the Senate Bill as an attempt to circumvent the constitution as embodied in the South Africa Act—hence its original name. The movement chose as its emblem a black rose, and in public demonstrations members wore black sashes. It rose with startling rapidity, like the Torch Commando; but unlike the Torch Commando it developed objectives that were not those of protest only and it was able to maintain an effective organization after the initial momentum had died down.

At first it was by means of 'vigils' and 'haunts' that the Black Sash registered its protest against the Senate Act and subsequent discriminatory legislation introduced in parliament. A 'vigil' was a stand of women in black sashes with bowed heads outside the Houses of Parliament or some public building, and a 'haunt' consisted of a double row of women, in black sashes but with heads up, to meet any minister who, in his official capacity, arrived or departed at airports, railway stations, or public buildings. Ministers were so embarrassed by the gaze of these women that they resorted to secrecy about their movements to avoid them.

The undoubted impact that the movement made on the public was owing partly to the dignity and impressiveness of its vigils, which also won it much respect and sympathy even from Nationalists, and partly to the novelty and surprise of seeing women using such methods to attract attention to public affairs. As the novelty wore off vigils became less frequent, and after a couple of years 'haunting' ceased altogether. At the same time the organization widened the scope of its activities, and while it continued to protest against the passing of discriminatory legislation, it embarked on a programme of political education, both of its own members and of the public, by means of public lectures, brains trusts, articles and letters in the Press, and a magazine. Since then it has assisted African women and men with their difficulties under the pass laws; in the Transvaal it exposed conditions of virtual slave labour on a number of farms, and during and after the emergency of 1960 it assisted the families of those who were killed, wounded, or imprisoned. It has further initiated various activities that have hived off into independent movements, either alone or in collaboration with other societies.[23]

The South African Bureau of Racial Affairs, usually called Sabra, was founded some years ago by Afrikaners who supported the policy of apartheid, and it had considerable influence on Nationalist Party thinking. It drew its support largely from the Afrikaans-speaking universities and the Afrikaans churches, and its annual conferences attracted much attention

[23] For the early history of the movement see *The Black Sash*, by Mirabel Rogers. Its activities are mirrored in a monthly periodical called *The Black Sash*.

because Sabra provided intellectual support for government policies in race matters. Unlike the older South African Institute of Race Relations, Sabra was open to white membership only; but, though its policy was basically one of apartheid, it by no means rejected contact between white and non-white. On the contrary, Sabra emphasized the cultural and social contact, at a responsible level, is essential if non-whites are ever to be persuaded that territorial separation is a sound policy, and that, unless they are persuaded, apartheid will never be possible. Though Sabra had close contact with the Nationalist Party government, that contact became less cordial for two reasons: the government paid scant attention to the recommendations of the Tomlinson Commission Report which Sabra believed provided the only economically sound basis for apartheid; and Dr. Verwoerd, soon after he became prime minister, openly expressed his disagreement with Sabra's insistence on discussions with African and Coloured leaders. In 1959 several prominent members of Sabra resigned from the Nationalist Party because they felt that it was not carrying out either the letter or the spirit of apartheid as Sabra understood and expounded that policy. By 1961 there was open division in Sabra between those who supported and those who opposed Dr. Verwoerd's determination to reject any compromise on the policy of strict apartheid, and in 1962 Dr. Verwoerd's supporters captured the most important positions on the executive committee. However, five years later there was once more a serious divergence of view between Sabra and the government: the leaders of Sabra were urging that much more money should be spent on the Reserves and ministers were unwilling to commit themselves to increased expenditure. Sabra supports Nationalist Party policies in general and could, therefore, have considerable influence on these policies. That influence will vary with the degree to which it is content to be an adjunct of government instead of a friendly but forthright critic.

The *Afrikaner Broederbond* is a secret society, although the names of a few of its more prominent members, including cabinet ministers, are publicly known. Because of continued accusations that the Broederbond was a secret power behind the throne, the Dutch Reformed Church Council decided, in 1949, to investigate the matter. The committee of investigation reported in 1951 and its conclusions were published in that year.[24] This report says that the Broederbond came into being in 1918, at a time when there was great confusion in Afrikaner ranks, as an attempt on the part of a few people to end the division among Afrikaners. The objects as set forth in the constitution, are to establish unity among all who desire to promote the welfare of the Afrikaners; to arouse a national self-consciousness among Afrikaners; and to promote the interests of the Afrikaner nation. Membership is open to Afrikaans-speaking Protestants

[24] See *Agenda vir die Twee-en-Twintigste Vergadering van die Raad van die Kerke*, 1951, pp. 49–52.

of good character who regard South Africa as their only fatherland. It is a cardinal principle of the Bond, says the report, that the names of its members and all its proceedings are strictly confidential, though any member has the right to make his own membership public. It was explained to the committee of inquiry that this secrecy was a matter of efficiency, just as cabinet discussions are secret until they come before the public.

The committee of inquiry of the Dutch Reformed churches said that it was assured that politics were not allowed in the Broedervond and that matters affecting the moral, intellectual, social, and political progress of the nation were discussed on a non-party-political basis. Among the many subjects to which the Broederbond devoted attention were the Native question, immigration, usury, mother-tongue instruction, and libraries. The committee of inquiry came to the conclusion that the Broederbond was sound and salutary, that it did not wish to harm anyone, but merely aimed at serving the best interests of the *Afrikanernasie* (the Afrikaner nation).

That this report of the Dutch Reformed churches did not satisfy those who regarded the secret activities of the Afrikaner Broederbond as dangerous was due partly to the belief that some ministers of the Afrikaans churches are members of the Bond and that the committee of inquiry could, therefore, not be regarded as impartial. Moreover, the committee had to depend on information supplied by the Broederbond itself and, since it is a secret society, it is to be presumed that the Bond did not necessarily reveal all its secrets. Critics of the Broederbond recall that, in 1935, Gerenal Hertzog, then Prime Minister, publicly castigated the Bond in these words:

They are sworn not to entertain any co-operation with the English-speaking population and thereby they stand in direct racial conflict with our fellow English Afrikaners, and are striving by way of domination on the part of the Afrikaans-speaking section to put their foot on the neck of English-speaking South Africa.... The Broederbond has become a grave menace to the rest and peace of our social community, even where it operates in the economic-cultural sphere.[25]

Towards the end of the 1939–45 War General Smuts yielded to pressure in his own party and banned membership of the Broederbond to public servants. Those public servants who were known to be members were given the option of resigning either from the Bond or from the public service, and in justifying this measure Smuts referred to the Broederbond as 'a dangerous, cunning, political, Fascist organization'. Before 1948, while Afrikaner nationalism was struggling for power, the Broederbond was a secretly-operated pressure group infiltrating the top ranks of the public service, the Afrikaans churches, the Afrikaans-medium universities

[25] Quoted in *The Friend*, 21 May 1951.

and schools, and the professions. After 1948, however, its role changed to that of policy making and more direct control of Nationalist Party strategy and tactics. During the latter half of 1963 the *Sunday Times* of Johannesburg published facsimiles of secret documents that gave strong evidence of this new role. The authenticity of these documents was never denied and they had, in fact, been supplied to the Press by two leading Afrikaner churchmen, Dr. Geyser and Dr. Beyers Naude; the latter had been a member of the Broederbond for 22 years but had come to regard its activities as inimical to the spiritual health of the church.

This exposure revived the controversy as to whether the Broederbond did in fact constitute a serious threat to parliamentary democracy. To such assertions the usual Nationalist reply was that it was no different from the Sons of England and the Freemasons, which were also secret societies. In 1964 Dr. Verwoerd, by way of a challenge in parliament, offered to appoint a judge to investigate the Broederbond if the Leader of the Opposition, Sir de Villiers Graaff, would agree to include the Sons of England and the Freemasons. Sir de Villiers at once agreed and in due course Mr. Justice Botha reported that none of the bodies was guilty of subversion, graft or nepotism, or of undermining the rights and liberties of any section of the population. Nevertheless, the belief that is still widely held had not been proved false: that the Broederbond is a secret society of some 5,000 members; that it does in fact exert pressure and wield considerable influence on government; that, unlike the Sons of England and the Freemasons which exert their influence on behalf of *individual members,* the Broederbond exists to promote the interests of the *Afrikanernasie* which it wrongfully equates with the *South African nation.* The Broederbond, in fact, is not interested in the welfare of its individual members except in so far as they are able to advance the interests of true Afrikanderdom as the Broederbond understands that term.

The vast majority of non-whites in South Africa have no vote. Nevertheless, non-white political organizations have assumed increasing importance as extra-parliamentary bodies of great potential strength. There are a number of these organizations, but there is no one national body representative of non-white opinion, for they are divided on how to achieve what all non-white leaders want: to share political power with the whites. At one extreme are those who argue that their aim will never be achieved by co-operation with whites and that their only hope is to strengthen their own organizations to the point where their demands will be irresistible. At the other extreme are those who believe that such action will breed a non-white nationalism and that a more hopeful approach is to seek co-operation with white liberal organizations. The strongest bodies were the African National Congress and the South African Indian Congress, and in practice both followed a policy between the two extremes: while strengthening their own organizations and using their own methods to exert political pressure, they co-operated on an *ad hoc* basis with such groups as the Liberal Party and the Civil Rights League, and were prepared to take part in discussions with Sabra. In 1960, the Pan African Congress, a breakaway from the African National Congress, came to the fore with a policy that aimed at the control of South Africa by Africans; its leaders, however, were insistent that they were not anti-white. The A.N.C. and the P.A.C. were both banned as unlawful organizations in 1960. So acute an observer as Prof. Gwendolen Carter has noted that non-white leaders in South Africa are not revolutionary and that, in contrast with other parts of Africa, they 'seek changes within the existing system, not its overthrow'. 'They want', she says, 'a share in political power, not to oust the Europeans. They want a fuller return for their contribution to the economy, not to change its character. They want to become more Western, not less.'[26]

[26] Gwendolen M. Carter, *The Politics of Inequality.*

Note: It is important to note that the terms *verligte* and *verkrampte* are essentially derogatory epithets. Towards the end of 1968 the quarrel intensified and Mr. Vorster, *pour encourager les autres*, dismissed Dr. Albert Hertzog, the leader of the *verkramptes*, from the cabinet. At the same time he found it expedient to impress on rank-and-file Nationalists that the *verkramptes* were maligning him by calling him a *verligte:* he and his followers were perfectly capable of maintaining the true principles of Afrikanderdom. In order to re-assure his followers he went out of his way to attack the English-language Press, the English-medium universities, and the English-language churches.

January 1969

8

EDUCATION

ORGANIZED education in South Africa, as in the rest of southern Africa, is a product of Europe. What African or Coloured educationist there are, are themselves the product of an educational system that has its roots in Western culture, planned, instituted, and largely paid for by Europeans. The early settlers found southern Africa inhabited by heathen tribes, whose lives were dominated by witchcraft and superstition. They brought with them from Europe the spiritual and intellectual equipment of Western civilization, and both unconsciously and of set purpose they imparted this to the heathen with whom they came into contact, and, in doing so, they began to free the spirit and mind of Africa. In the course of bringing Western civilization to Africa the Europeans made many mistakes— mistakes that sprang from an impatient desire to speed up the process of civilization as well as from greed and selfishness, mistakes due to over-zealousness as well as to indifference. But for better or worse, European education has left the indelible impress of the West on South Africa.

Until the last quarter of the nineteenth century it was common in the Cape Colony for white and Coloured children to attend the same school for the first few years of their education. More than half the schools in 1860 were state-aided mission schools, and in 1883 almost 6,000 of the 38,000 children in mission schools were white. It gradually became the practice, however, to have separate schools in the Cape and in Natal. In the Transvaal and Free State Republics there was strict separation between black and white, though Coloured children not too pronouncedly dark were to be found in white schools.

Until industrialization began to draw them to the towns, the vast majority of Africans lived in their own tribal areas, which had been conquered by the whites. The different governments regarded mission education as a valuable instrument in pacifying these conquered territories and gave grants to missions for this purpose; and by the time that the four colonies united, it was well-established practice that white and non-white education were administered separately, and that the former should be completely financed by the state while the latter was conducted through state-aided mission societies. It is convenient, therefore, to discuss the white and non-white educational systems separately.

EDUCATION OF WHITES

Primary and secondary education and teacher training other than that given in universities are controlled by the provincial councils. In each province there is an education department in charge of a Director or Superintendent-General. Although the directors and the school inspectors are regarded as servants of the central government they are controlled by the provincial authorities. The education departments are responsible for the establishment and maintenance of schools, and they conduct their own school examinations and prescribe their own syllabuses; the school-leaving or matriculation examination is subject to the supervisory control of a Joint Matriculation Board on which the universities are represented. Education is financed to the extent of about 50 per cent by the central government, the balance coming from provincial taxes, and with minor exceptions it is compulsory and free for all whites. In 1964[1] there were, in round numbers, 698,000 scholars. 29,000 teachers, and 2,500 schools. In addition to these state schools there are about 217 private schools, most of them run by the Roman Catholic, Anglican, or Methodist churches, with about 50,000 pupils. Some of these private schools are state-aided and all must be registered and open to inspection by the education departments. The largest are independent of government aid and are among the oldest and best-known schools in South Africa, enjoying a reputation akin to the public schools of Britain on which, with local adaptations, they are modelled.

The primary school ranges from standard I to standard V. Below the primary school are sub-standards A and B; above it are the secondary standards VI to X, which is the school-leaving or matriculation standard. Each sub-standard and standard implies a year's schooling, and ages range from 8 years in standard I to 17 plus in standard X. About 31 per cent of all children are in secondary schools.

In all the large towns, and in small towns that have acquired a reputation as education centres, there are separate schools for boys and girls, but in all the smaller centres and in the large number of farm schools co-education is the rule. Separate education is, in fact, the accepted principle except where sparsity of population makes it too expensive. Many secondary schools, and a few primary schools, have boarding departments, usually known as hostels.

An important feature of primary and secondary education, except in Natal, is that each school has a school committee elected by the parents.[2] The committee selects and appoints teachers, subject to the approval of the education department, and has limited powers of control over the

---

[1] The figures here given are from *Statistical Year Book* 1966.
[2] There are also, except in Natal, elected school boards for districts. These have administrative rather than educational functions.

school. The practice of having school committees is an old one in South Africa and, given a principal and a committee who are in sympathy, the system has many advantages. The committee strengthens the hands of the principal and staff; it helps to create local interest in the school; and it serves as a useful link between the school and the impersonal education department. But the system is not without its faults and its dangers. Party politics loom large in South Africa, and many committees are elected on a party-political basis. When that happens either there is friction between staff and committee, or, what is worse, the staff accepts decisions that are based on considerations other than educational. In neither case are the best interests of the school served.

There is another danger inherent in the system. In a great many of the country districts one of the three Dutch Reformed churches is the strongest religious body. The minister of that Church is an important man in local affairs and is frequently chairman of the school committee. His influence in the matter of appointments is considerable, and the result is that staff appointments are frequently and increasingly made on religious and denominational as well as on party-political grounds. In the larger urban centres, where the authority of the Church is less than that of the business and professional world, political rather than religious considerations may be a determining factor. Moreover, applicants for teaching posts are required to submit testimonials from a minister, often the chairman of their previous school committee, and many less liberal ministers demand strict religious conformity before giving these.

The result of all this is that a great many teachers must, for bread-and-butter reasons, be careful of the opinions they express, whatever they may think. A teacher who openly expressed so-called 'liberal' views on race relations would find a large number of country schools closed to him. On the other hand, it is improbable that one who held pronounced Nationalist Party views would be appointed in an English-speaking urban centre, however good his qualifications, except, possibly, to teach Afrikaans. There is, therefore, a strong temptation to conform for the sake of a job.

Lack of intellectual and religious freedom on the part of teachers must affect adversely the standard of professional work, and when considerations other than those of character, professional qualification, and intellectual integrity obtrude themselves in the appointment of teachers, the schools are bound to suffer. An editorial in the official organ of the Afrikaans-speaking teachers in the Transvaal drew attention to the 'unpleasant wire-pulling which occurs in various places among churchmen when a teacher is to be selected for a post by a parent body such as a school board or school committee'. It pointed out that all three Afrikaans churches were Calvinist and that they should co-operate to ensure that education was Christian and National. 'No school in the Transvaal', it continued, 'serves the members of one Church only; therefore no Church has the right to demand the services of one of its members as a teacher.'[3] Coming from Afrikaans teachers, this is indicative of the extent to which denominational considerations may count in the selection of teachers, and at the same time it suggests that teachers who do not belong to one of the three Afrikaans churches are unlikely to be appointed in strongly Afrikaans centres.

One of the thorniest problems in South African education is that of language, a problem that has become virtually identified with party politics. Just after the Boer War, in the early years of the century, teachers were largely English-speaking men and women who had been imported from Britain. Many of them were fine teachers to whom South African education owes a great debt. Not many of them, however, learnt to speak Dutch or Afrikaans, with the result that Afrikaans-speaking children were taught through the medium of a language which was not their mother tongue, though many of them did have some knowledge of English. We have seen how the rise of nationalism coincided with the rapid growth of the Afrikaans language, and it was to be expected that Afrikaaners should insist upon mother-tongue instruction. It was a reasonable demand, but there were three difficulties that had to be faced. The first was the lack of trained Afrikaans-speaking teachers, an obstacle that was soon overcome. The second was, and is, one of finance. During the first two decades of the twentieth century, urban areas were predominantly English-speaking, and it was beyond the resources of the State to pay for two sets of teachers. Even when they were efficiently bilingual, it would still have required increased staff to provide complete mother-tongue instruction.

The third difficulty, which still exists, was that many Afrikaans-speaking parents preferred to send their children to English-speaking schools so that they should become proficient in a language which had so much social and economic prestige. The Nationalist Party, aware that this was a threat to nationalism, began to agitate for unilingual schools and for compulsory mother-tongue instruction, at least in the primary schools. In the Free State and the Transvaal it became compulsory for a child to receive primary school education through his mother tongue, no matter what the wishes of the parents were. For the time being, the choice of medium in secondary classes was left to parents or to the dictates of circumstances.

By 1940 there were two main types of secondary school. The majority were either parallel medium or dual medium schools. In the first, parallel classes were provided in English and Afrikaans; in the second, some subjects were taught in English and some through Afrikaans. The second type of school was the single medium school, where the second language

[3] *Die Onderwysblad*, November,1951. The available evidence is that, since 1951, the influence of 'Christian' and 'National' considerations in the appointment of teachers has not diminished.

was taught as a subject, but where all other subjects were taught through the mother tongue. This type was economically possible only in those centres where the school population was large enough to warrant two separate schools; but it remained the object of Afrikaner nationalism to make single medium schools the general rule.

As a reaction against the insistence on single medium schools there arose a strong movement for the use of dual medium or parallel medium. The arguments for and against the single medium school are partly educational and partly political. The chief argument for parallel medium schools is that boys and girls from each language group get to know those from the other, and their language and traditions, in a natural and friendly way. It is socially and politically necessary for South Africans to be completely bilingual; and the only way of achieving that is to have bilingual instruction at school. The principle of mother-tongue instruction in primary schools is admitted as sound; but if the children are taught in separate schools, the gap between Afrikaner and English will never be bridged. Single medium schools make for cultural isolation, and in them the standard of bilingualism deteriorates,[4] and English-Afrikaans differences are perpetuated, while parallel medium schools make for tolerance in racial matters. As neither English nor Afrikaans is a completely *foreign* language to any white South African, the principle of mother-tongue instruction need not be violated by parallel medium schools. There is also the academic argument put forward in favour of bilingual education, that it opens the door to two sources of culture—two literatures and two ways of thought. Unfortunately this is very often lost sight of amid political pressures.

Those who favour single medium schools maintain that children not educated entirely through their Afrikaans mother tongue do not become genuine Afrikaners. The Afrikaner has a right and a duty to preserve his language and traditions, and the atmosphere of parallel medium schools is not favourable to these; if he relinquishes his language he will soon become anglicized. Bilingualism, they maintain, with some justice, is usually interpreted to mean that the Afrikaner must speak English, not that the English must speak Afrikaans. Why therefore, should the Afrikaner be penalized for not being proficient in English?

How thoroughly this question has become a party-political one is illustrated by the dominant part it continues to play in provincial elections.

[4] Whatever the reason, the standard of bilingualism continued to fall. The Public Service Commission, concerned to recruit bilingual candidates, said in its report of 1950 that of the total number of candidates appointed in 1949 only 21·8 per cent could be regarded as 'reasonably bilingual'. Those who entered the service in 1949 were, by 1968, reaching for the higher posts in the service. In its report for 1966, published in 1968, the Commission noted a sharp decline in the number of serving officials required to take language tests. This is ascribed to a new approach to bilingualism in which officials are tested for their proficiency in 'functional language' rather than academic knowledge. This may be realistic but it seems to bear out the contention that the standard of bilingualism is falling.

In 1943, for example, the United Party won the election and began to introduce dual medium instruction in the Transvaal. Staffing difficulties hindered progress and when the Nationalist Party won the election in 1948, it reversed the policy. In that province mother-tongue instruction became compulsory in all State and private schools.[5] The lengths to which the Transvaal administration is prepared to go in insisting on single medium schools is shown by the case of the Hendrik van der Bijl school at Vanderbijlpark. This was a parallel medium school about which the parents were happy and where, according to all accounts, the pupils of both language groups got on well together. In 1956 the Administrator disestablished the school with the intention of making it an Afrikaans-medium school and providing elsewhere for the English-speaking children. A unanimous petition by the parents to keep the school bilingual was rejected, whereupon the parents applied to the Supreme Court to restrain the Administrat r and Executive Council on the ground that the wishes of the parents had been ignored. The parents won their case, but in 1957 the Education Ordinance was amended to give the Administrator power to decide the language medium of any school.

In Natal, in May 1951, a Nationalist Party member petitioned the Provincial Council to take away the right of parents to decide through which medium they wanted their children educated. The petition was decisively rejected, but the agitation has continued. Mother tongue as a medium became compulsory up to and including matriculation in the Transvaal and Orange Free State, and in the Cape Province to standard VIII; and it is the department's inspectors, not the parents, who decide what the mother tongue is. The right of the parents to send their children to private schools, and thus to decide the medium through which they want them educated, has not been taken away in the two latter provinces as it has in the Transvaal.

Related to the question of language is what is called Christian National Education, usually referred to as C.N.E. Immediately after the Boer War the Dutch Reformed churches saw the need for rehabilitating the shattered Boer morale. Ministers of the Afrikaans churches took the lead in demanding from the British administration the right to establish church schools subsidized by the state, as had been the case in republican days—schools in which Afrikaner children would receive religious instruction according to the tenets of the Calvinist churches. The agitation for C.N.E. schools was not successful but, as the Dutch churches played a prominent part on school committees, and were thus able to influence policy, the need for separate church schools became less pronounced, and undenominational

[5] The right of parents to send their children to a private denominational school where the medium was not the mother tongue of the children was tested in the courts. The Supreme Court of the Transvaal decided, by a two to one majority, that the parents did have this right: but the decision was reversed, by a three to two majority, in the Appeal Court (June 1951).

schools financed by the state became the accepted rule. But the agitation never quite died down, and was stimulated by the fact that the Roman Catholic and Anglican churches had their own private denominational schools to which many Afrikaans children were attracted.

In the 1940's when the struggle over the language medium became acute, the agitation for C.N.E. was revived. It was led by the most conservative of the Dutch Reformed churches, the *Gereformeerde Kerk,* whose headquarters and whose inspiration was the University of Potchefstroom in the Transvaal. A group of university professors and Nationalist Party politicians (including two who subsequently became cabinet ministers) prepared a programme for Christian National Education in which they went very much further in their demands than the supporters of C.N.E. after the Boer War had done. Under the influence of ultra-Calvinist churchmen, extreme fundamentalist doctrines were put forward as principles on which to base education. The theory of evolution was condemned as opposed to predestination; history and geography were to be taught as divinely inspired in the narrowest sense of the word—God had given to each people a country and a task, and it was the Afrikaner task to rule South Africa, and no one had the right to question what was divinely ordained. Teachers who were not prepared to subscribe to these doctrines would not be appointed.

The publication of this programme in 1948 aroused a storm of protest from teachers, from University staffs, and from the general public. An Education League was formed to combat C.N.E. and to defend liberty of conscience in the teaching profession. While English-speaking teachers' associations condemned the proposals, Afrikaans-speaking associations declared themselves in favour of C.N.E. A number of prominent Afrikaners publicly opposed the programme; but many, while privately disapproving, were not prepared to go against the stream of Afrikaner nationalist opinion. So strong is the influence of the Dutch Reformed churches that, in the country districts, few teachers would brave church disapproval by opposing C.N.E.

In 1948 the Nationalist Party, having newly come to power, was not sufficiently sure of itself immediately to pursue the policy of Christian National Education vigorously. But the men who had prepared the programme were for the most part men of considerable standing in the community: two became cabinet ministers in 1948; one subsequently became Superintendent-General of Education in the Cape Province; two were university professors; and three were ministers of religion, and the history of South Africa between 1948 and 1961 is evidence that, as the Nationalist Party proceeded from strength to strength, C.N.E. as an official policy gained ground. In the Transvaal and Orange Free State it had become the official policy; in the Cape Province it was all but officially laid down; only in Natal did the provincial council refuse to accept it.

There are other parts of the C.N.E. programme, as published in 1948, that have been put into practice. The use of the mother tongue as a medium of instruction in the primary school, in the early years of a child's life, is a reasonable educational principle though there is plenty of evidence that, in a bilingual country, its educational importance has been exaggerated. What is less reasonable in a bilingual country is the application of that principle in the secondary school, in the teeth of parental opposition. Yet that is what has happened in three provinces since 1948, and it follows closely the C.N.E. programme which states, 'We will have nothing to do with a mixture of languages, of culture, of religion, of race'. This conception runs through much of the legislation concerning university education and African and Coloured education, as will be seen presently.

In this programme the word 'Christian' is explicitly equated with the Calvinist creed, and the word 'National' is implicitly equated with Afrikaner nationalism. So close has the association of C.N.E. been with Afrikaner nationalism that, in its South African context, C.N.E. means Calvinist Nationalist Education, and the church, the language, and the political party are three mutually supporting pillars of Afrikaans culture.

Two questions remain to be discussed: officially sponsored though the C.N.E. programme is, to what extent is it in fact carried out in schools, and what are the effects? Do teachers in fact teach the kind of fundamentalist history and geography advocated by the programme? The idea that divine providence has allocated to each 'nation' its geographical place on earth, and has given it a divine mission, is not one that ordinarily commends itself to educated men and women, particularly in a country where the known facts of history and geography seem so singularly unable to endorse those theories. Nevertheless, the history of the world, more especially perhaps since the 1930's, is a warning not to underestimate the capacity of men and women to reconcile the irreconcilable. In 1959 the Transvaal Education Department placed on its list of approved books a series of history text-books based on the theory that the world was created some eight thousand years ago. In that province, too, a conference of teachers held in 1959 to discuss methods of guiding and advising pupils was told by an inspector of schools not to worry too much about psychological theories but to base their advice on sound Christian National principles. Under this kind of pressure there is, of course, an incentive to conform for fear of losing one's job or of missing promotion. And it must be borne in mind that many of the normal and training colleges, and the education courses at universities for training primary and secondary school teachers, have been greatly influenced by C.N.E.

It is impossible to be specific either about the extent to which C.N.E. is being applied or about its effects. It seems clear that one of two things is happening, and is bound to happen if the upholders of C.N.E. push their programme hard: either the teachers are teaching according to C.N.E.

principles from conviction, or they are finding it expedient to combine outward conformity with inward scepticism. Neither of these results can be anything but unhappy. More than 80 per cent of the towns of South Africa have populations too small to support two separate schools, and in three of the four provinces the small town school is predominantly Afrikaans-speaking. In these three provinces the provincial authorities accept the principles of C.N.E., and it is already evident that the pupils in those schools are being more and more isolated from the main currents of European thought. Unless the progress is halted the chief sufferers from C.N.E. will be the Afrikaners themselves.

During the campaign for the provincial election of 1959 the leader of the Nationalist Party Congress in Natal protested that the 1948 C.N.E. document was not Nationalist Party policy. It is very probable, however, that this was an endeavour to pacify Natal voters whose provincial executive was at that time engaged in a struggle with the Union Government over the appointment of an Afrikaner of known C.N.E. sympathies to high office in the education department. Moreover, the Nationalist Party had several times mooted the desirability of making school education a national rather than a provincial matter; and there had been, on the eve of the election, an immediate and strong reaction to yet another such pronouncement by the Prime Minister, a great many voters believing that this would mean the enforcement of C.N.E. throughout South Africa.

A bill to establish a Union Advisory Council was, in fact, introduced by the Minister for Education in 1960. While many parents and educationists had for some time felt the need for a body that would co-ordinate a number of matters connected with syllabuses, standards, and salaries, a large body of opinion, including many Afrikaans teachers, opposed this Bill strongly on several grounds. The most important were that the members of the Council would all be appointed by the minister, no provision being made for appointing or consulting educationists, other than one in each province; and that it was given wide powers to 'investigate' any school. These powers would, in fact, enable it to enter private church schools whose independence had long been frowned on by extreme Nationalists. There seemed little doubt that the purpose of the Bill was not purely educational, but that it aimed at greater political control of schools.

The Bill was withdrawn under heavy opposition but reappeared in 1961 and, after reference to a select committee, was passed as the National Education Advisory Council Act of 1962. Minor changes had been made, but most of the features of the original Bill to which there had been such strong objection, appeared in the Act, notably the wide powers vested in the Minister, even over provincial authorities whose function it is to control primary and secondary education. In October 1962 the Minister appointed 29 members of the Council and at the end of 1963 announced that, after consultation with the Council, he would introduce legislation to counteract the effects of divided control of education of whites and to develop an acceptable national education pattern.

The National Education Policy Act of 1967 empowered the Minister of Education, after consultation with the Council and the provincial authorities, to determine the general policy for education of white pupils. It was to be christian, though not sectarian, and national; instruction had to be through medium of the mother tongue, English or Afrikaans; and education was to be free. Syllabuses are to be nationally co-ordinated and service conditions and salary scales for teachers to become uniform. No legislation, except for the appropriation of funds, relating to school education for whites may be introduced in parliament or any provincial council without prior consultation with the minister; and if a provincial authority fails to give effect to the Minister's policy he may make regulations to enforce compliance. Finally, the Minister has wide powers to inspect any school to find out whether the national education policy is being carried out.

There was widespread and strong opposition to the Act. The United Party opposed it at every stage, including the formal first reading; the Natal Provincial Executive asked the State President to refuse consent; the English-speaking teachers' associations objected to the Bill with well-informed professional criticism; and public protest meetings were held. All this had no effect and, by 1968, the education of white pupils in South Africa was, in theory at any rate, conducted according to the principles of Christian National Education.

The social status of teachers has, during half a century, suffered a change. In the early years of the twentieth century the schoolmaster, particularly in the rural areas, had a social position comparable to that of the Scots dominie. Together with the minister, he represented learning and culture, and despite his small income he was looked up to by all. He was referred to, affectionately and with respect as *'meester'* (master), and his advice was sought by the community in which he served. With the spread of education and the growth of a more sophisticated urban civilization, the rest of the community caught up with the minister and the schoolmaster, and their status and influence have, relatively, declined. Teachers still enjoy much of the prestige that attaches to their office, but it has become the exceptional headmaster who commands widespread respect and affection.

Teachers are not allowed to take an active part in party politics, and a teacher who wishes to stand for parliament or for a provincial council must resign his post and lose pension and other benefits. In the Transvaal he may be given six months' leave without pay and without loss of privileges to fight an election, and in exceptional circumstances, he may be allowed to take part in local government and to become a town councillor, but such permission is rarely granted.

White teachers in all the provinces have professional associations. Except in the Orange Free State, these are divided into English- and Afrikaans-speaking associations, which have their annual conferences separately. The executive councils of the two teachers' associations in the Cape meet each other from time to time, and the two bodies co-operate in matters such as pressing for better service conditions. But on academic matters they deliberate separately, and on the question of Christian National Education they hold entirely opposed views. African, Indian and Coloured teachers have their own organizations, separate from each other and from the white associations. There is, thus, no one body in South Africa that represents all those who are engaged in teaching.

AFRICAN EDUCATION

The problems connected with African education have exercised many minds, and in South Africa they are complicated by the need to consider them in the social environment of a multi-racial society. It is not merely a question of what and how to teach, but of what the evolving African society asks, and of what the European society will be prepared to pay. The early missionaries believed that the quickest way of christianizing and civilizing Africans was to open schools where European education in a European language was made available. Later generations doubted the wisdom of a policy that ran counter to much psychological theory of education. The belief grew that greater emphasis should be laid on the mother tongue; that school education for Africans had become too bookish and not sufficiently 'practical'; and that greater attention should be paid to the cultural background of Africans. The early missionaries took it for granted that the cure for barbarism was European civilization. Later, people began to ask whether, by foisting their civilization on to Africans, they might not turn them into a bad imitation of Europeans instead of making them good Africans.

In the Cape Colony and in Natal the policy of state aid for mission schools was begun in the middle of the nineteenth century, but it was only after the Boer War that the system was introduced in the Transvaal and Free State Republics. By the time of Union, in 1910, it was general. African education was financed and controlled by the provinces, but, as in the case of education for whites, they soon found that the costs were beyond their resources. In 1922 the central government took over financial responsibility for aiding African education, leaving the control of it to the provincial authorities. That year it contributed a block grant of R680,000 to African education, and this sum was to be a fixed annual grant. It was inadequate for existing needs, let alone expansion, and in 1925 a proportion of the Native poll-tax was added to it. Ever-increasing demands led successive governments to increase the proportion of the Native poll-tax to be allocated until, in 1943, four-fifths of the tax (about R1,800,000) went to African education. Then in 1945, government acceded to the wishes of those who had for years been asking that African education should not be made dependent on the amount of direct taxation Africans could pay, and from then until 1953, funds for aiding African education were drawn entirely from general revenue.

The story of the financing of African education is relevant because it illustrates the changes that took place in white public opinion. There was a time when educating Natives was strongly disapproved of—it gave the Africans 'ideas beyond their station' and unfitted them to do manual labour. Money derived from taxation of whites should certainly not be spent on such an object; if the African wanted education he should pay for it himself. Very gradually, public opinion changed. In the beginning, small annual grants were made to mission societies for schools. As the demands grew, the grants expanded; but the principle that Africans should pay for their own education was adhered to, and the Native poll-tax was used to finance it. Then, as late as 1945, the principle that African education should depend on what the Africans could pay was abandoned, and the state accepted financial responsibility. As we shall see presently, the Bantu Education Act of 1953 brought about radical changes in organization and financing and in the relationship between the state and the mission societies that had until then had a major control.

While Africans asked for European education, white public opinion was divided on what education for Africans should be. The Dutch Reformed Church missions and Afrikaner educationists were, on the whole, in favour of a specifically 'African' type of education, and other missions tended to regard differences between European and African education as temporary and negligible. There are historical reasons for this. Dating from the early nineteenth century, the missionaries, who were then for the most part English-speaking,[6] were cordially disliked by Afrikaans farmers. They said that the missionaries treated the blacks as equals and 'spoilt' them—a view by no means confined to Afrikaans-speaking settlers, as missionaries elsewhere in Africa could testify. They said, moreover, that the missionaries 'blackened' the name of the Afrikaner. When the Dutch Reformed churches entered the mission field they did so with a different outlook from that of the English-speaking societies. The Dutch Reformed Church has a fine record for mission work in Africa, as far north as Nigeria; but while it by no means neglected education, it was not enthusiastic for academic education on European lines.

This differences between the Afrikaner churches and the English-speaking churches was accentuated by the growth of Afrikaans nationalism and its insistence of the doctrine of apartheid. Although there is still a

---

[6] German, Swiss, French, American, and Swedish missions also worked in southern Africa; but English was the dominant language.

great deal of opposition among Afrikaners to any but an elementary and severely practical education for Africans, the Afrikaans churches realized that formal education could not be withheld from them. Since, however, the doctrine of apartheid postulates the perpetual overlordship of the whites, educational theory based on that doctrine must differentiate sharply between European and African education. This leads Nationalist theorists to stress mother-tongue instruction and to insist that tribal traditions must be the foundation on which African education is built.

It is improbable that tribal traditions can survive the impact of Western economy and culture, and it is, therefore, difficult to see how an educational system can be constructed on what is, at best, a shifting foundation. More and more Africans are adapting themselves to European standards and will increasingly demand European education.

As far as the use of the various Bantu languages is concerned, it is not easy to forecast what will happen. They are living languages, and since missionaries and scholars reduced them to writing they have developed a growing literature. But, unless Africans develop a new civilization based on Europe and yet African, it is fairly evident that they will become absorbed into the stronger Western civilization to which they will undoubtedly bring their special contribution to its enriching. It is probable, therefore, that English and Afrikaans will remain the chief means of communication of a society embracing Western culture, and that all Africans will, in due course, acquire one or both of these languages. The various Bantu languages will in all likelihood long remain in everyday usage; but the two European languages have a survival value far greater than that of any Bantu language in South Africa.

The Bantu Education Act of 1953 transferred the control of African education from the provincial education departments to the Department of Native Affairs of the Union Government; and in 1958 a new department of state, the Bantu Education Department, with its own Minister, took charge of all African education. Until 1954 about 90 per cent of all schools were state-aided mission schools under the control of more than forty mission bodies, and in that year these bodies were given the option of handing their schools over to the government or of retaining control under a diminishing state subsidy; all teacher-training institutions were either to be handed over or closed down; and all schools for Africans, whether privately run or state-aided, had to be registered. This placed the missions in a difficult position. Most of them believed that the time was not ripe to relinquish control of African education, thus removing from it the religious influences that had played such an important part in moulding it. Moreover, many of the institutions founded by the early missionaries had by 1954 gained well-merited reputations beyond the borders of South Africa and had developed traditions of which they and their past students were justifiably proud. Two such only need be mentioned:

Lovedale in the eastern province of the Cape, and Adams in Natal; but there were many more. On the other hand, apart from the buildings and equipment, for which the government offered compensation, practically all the money to run these institutions was by then coming from the state, and mission institutions could not shoulder the financial burden if state subsidies were diminished and finally ended. It was a cruel dilemma. The Roman Catholic Church and the Seventh Day Adventists refused to relinquish control of their schools, and the former set about establishing a two-million rand fund against the day when subsidies would end. With the exception of the Anglican diocese of Johannesburg, where the well-known St. Peter's school[7] was situated, all other mission bodies handed over control to the state, though at least two teacher-training institutions closed down rather than surrender control.

The Department of Bantu Education next set about organizing the many schools it had taken over and reconstituting the form and content of African education. That this was a task of some magnitude can be seen from the figures. In 1954 there were, in round numbers, 5,700 schools at which 940,000 African children were taught by 21,500 teachers. By 1967 the numbers had risen to 9,000 schools, over 2 million pupils, and 35,000 teachers. In 1954 only 5 per cent of schools were government schools, and by 1967 this had risen to over 70 per cent. From 1945–1953 expenditure on African education had been a charge on general revenue and the annual expenditure was about R17 million. The Bantu Education Act reverted to the old system of a fixed annual block grant from general revenue plus a proportion of the poll-tax, a tax paid by African only. By 1959 the total expenditure on African education was about R19 million of which R13 million came from general revenue.[8]

The department introduced other new features into the organization of African education. By far the most important of these was the attempt to secure the active participation of Africans themselves in the management of schools by setting up school committees and school boards, as in the education of whites but with one vital difference: white school boards and committees are elected, while their African equivalents are nominated by chiefs and headmen and their continuation in office subject to the approval of the minister or his deputy. It was a criticism of mission-controlled education that it did not give Africans sufficient training in managing their affairs, and in setting out to correct this the department laid great stress on the restoration of tribal authority;[9] but the tribal authorities set up by

[7] This was a school of the Community of the Resurrection and Father (later Bishop) Huddleston was in charge. It was closed down by the Community rather than accept the Act.

[8] After 1962 the figures for the Transkei were separated from those for the rest of South Africa and it is impossible to give accurate figures comparable to those before 1962. It is probable that the total expenditure on African education, including the Transkei, had by 1958 reached R35 million.

[9] See Report of the Department of Native Affairs, 1954–1957, p. 17.

the Bantu Authorities Act were themselves rigidly controlled by the Department of Bantu Administration and Development, and with this double control on their activities the school boards and committees were more apt to become instruments for carrying out departmental policy rather than organs of local self-government. By 1968 it was estimated that some 80,000 African parents were members of school boards, school committees and other local school governing bodies.[10]

The form and content of African education was considerably altered by the great stress laid on Bantu languages, by the introduction into the syllabus of a second official language, and by the separation of the junior certificate examinations from those written by whites. It had formerly been the rule that, in the lower primary school, the African child learnt his own language and one of the two official languages of the Republic; both languages were now made compulsory. During the first four years the vernacular was used as the medium of instruction and, thereafter, one of the two official languages; now the vernacular was made compulsory as the medium of instruction throughout the primary school and subsequently in the secondary school as well. This policy involved creating technical terms for which the Bantu languages had no words and of producing the necessary text-books, a task which the various language boards of the Department of Bantu Education performed with energy and skill.

Much criticism was levelled at the Bantu Education Act, some, though not all of it, ill-informed. Sooner or later African education would have had to be taken over by the State, and whenever that happened there would almost certainly be opposition from the bodies that had previously controlled it. The government underestimated the strength of the opposition, and in its hurry to complete the operation was impatient of criticism. In extenuation it must be said that the operation was gigantic. The small staff of officials who had previously been responsible for supervising African education was called upon at short notice to create the machinery for a job a hundred times larger and more complex; and this had to be done in an atmosphere of suspicion and in the face of opposition from white and black alike. That errors of judgement and delays should have occurred was inevitable.

Criticism by African teachers was stifled by the Department of Bantu Education but it is well known that many of them agreed with white educationists who directed sustained and informed criticism at the Bantu Education Act. The main ground of criticism was the excessive emphasis laid on tribalism and on the vernacular. Granted that the use of his mother tongue during the first few years of a child's schooling was necessary, it was believed that from that stage onwards a European language should gradually be introduced as medium. To adapt themselves to a modern Western way of life and economy Africans would have to equip themselves

[10] See *Bantu*, February 1968, p.8.

in a language in which the West expressed itself. Though it is no doubt possible, if cumbersome, to express even simple mathematical and scientific concepts in Xhosa or Tswana, an African who is unable to do so in a European language would be unable to use this knowledge outside his tribe. Even for the elementary purpose of finding employment in the Republic, some knowledge of English or Afrikaans is a great advantage. African parents were well aware of these facts and regarded the new policy with grave suspicion. It is an interesting commentary that when education in the Transkei became the responsibility of the Transkei government in 1963, the old policy was scrapped and the English language was re-instated as the principle medium of instruction.

A second ground for criticism was that, in making the education of African children different from that of whites, an inferior brand of education was being foisted on Africans. African education has always been greatly inferior to that of whites, but it is doubtful if the authors of the Bantu Education Act deliberately set out to maintain or to institute an inferior system of education. More probably those charged with implementing the Act were devoted officials whose aim was to establish a sound system of education; but they were bound by the inhibiting ideology of apartheid and the crippling lack of funds that resulted from it. Parliament, elected by a white electorate, agrees to the expenditure of R252 million on 750,000 white pupils but with difficulty approves of spending R29 million on 2,000,000 African pupils. The difference between R325 and R14 per white and African pupil respectively is some measure of the superiority of white education over African.

Nevertheless, the Department of Bantu Education has a few achievements to its credit. By 1968 more schools had been built and many more children were at school than formerly; more educated Africans were able to find employment as clerks and secretaries of school boards, and the policy was introduced of making higher posts, such as that of sub-inspector, open to Africans; finally, whatever criticism there may be about school boards and committees, it is obviously sound policy to associate the African community as closely as possible with the education of its children. To list these achievements is not to share in the belief that a modern education system can be built on tribalism or to deny that grievous mistakes have been made. Rather, it is to welcome what advances have been achieved in the belief that when tribalism has disappeared a more durable system of education can be built.

COLOURED AND ASIAN EDUCATION

In Natal, where the large majority of the Asian population lives, there are separate schools for Indians; in the Transvaal there are a few separate Indian schools and, for the rest, Indian and Coloured attend the same schools, as in the Cape Province. In the Orange Free State there is no Indian population, and Coloured pupils attend separate schools. In 1968 there were, in round numbers, 390,000 Coloured children at school, 86 per cent in the Cape Province, and 133,000 Asian children, 84 per cent in Natal. Until 1963 Coloured schools in the Transvaal were financed by the province; in the Orange Free State more than half the schools were financed in this way and the rest were aided; and in Natal and Cape Province the great majority of Coloured or Asian schools were aided and the rest fully financed by the province. The total expenditure on Coloured and Asian education in 1968 was in the neighbourhood of R45 million.

With slight differences, Coloured children follow the same primary and secondary school syllabuses as white children do. The language, culture, and general outlook of the Coloured population are European, so that the problems of Coloured education are not those of African education. In such matters as equipment, salaries and state expenditure per child, Coloured education stands about half-way between white and African education. Coloured teachers are, as a class, conscious of the social distinction between white and Coloured. Many of them are well educated, with the same academic and professional qualifications as white teachers, but they receive smaller salaries and have to teach under far more difficult conditions. They are, not unnaturally, embittered and resentful of a social system that closes so many doors to them and to their children.

Although the Cape Province did not spend as much money on Coloured as on white education, it had always regarded Coloured schools as an integral part of the Cape education system. The theory of apartheid, however, demanded a complete separation between white and Coloured education, and in 1957 a Nationalist Party majority in the Cape Provincial Council voted in favour of Coloured education being taken over by the Union Government. This was done by the Coloured Persons Education Act of 1963 which placed the control of Coloured education throughout the country in the hands of the Department of Coloured Affairs. Most Coloured people were strongly opposed to the Act on the grounds that they were part and parcel of Western civilization and that however plausible an excuse there might be for separating African education from white, there was none for isolating Coloured education. It was an argument with which many whites, including Nationalists, agreed. A serious defect of the Act is that, as with the Bantu Education Act, it includes service conditions that effectively tie teachers down and forbid any public criticism of government policy or of any department of state. In 1968 an Act was passed setting up a Coloured Representative Council to which parliament would delegate powers. It is probable that the responsibility for Coloured education and its financing will then be placed on the new Council.

In 1965 the Indians Education Act provided for the gradual transfer of Asian education to the Department of Indian Affairs, and the government has stated that a policy similar to that for Coloured is to be adopted for Asians.

UNIVERSITY EDUCATION

Until the early 1920's the majority of the teaching staff of South African universities came from overseas, chiefly from Britain, and, to a lesser extent, from Holland and Germany. Till then, too, it was the ambition of South African students to complete their university education at an overseas university. Those who wished to become medical doctors were compelled to go overseas, and the rugby football teams of Guy's Hospital, Edinburgh, Trinity College, Dublin, and other universities drew great strength from their South African students. It was not, however, only British rugby that benefited by this happy arrangement. South Africa was, and is, a thinly populated country; it was, and is, of the utmost importance that she should keep intellectual contact with her cultural motherlands in Europe. The constant stream of students travelling to Europe to study medicine, law, engineering, the humanities, and the arts, and the returning stream of qualified men and women, immensely enriched the intellectual life of South Africa.

It was, no doubt, necessary for South Africa to develop her own university institutions so that her students should no longer have to travel 6,000 miles to qualify in foreign countries; and it was inevitable and desirable that those universities should, gradually, be staffed by South Africans. But the country had lost something in the process. One of the most necessary and difficult things in South Africa's multi-racial society is for the representatives of Western civilization to maintain high intellectual standards and codes of behaviour, and in seeking to do this they were greatly strengthened by the influx of men and women trained in European universities with their traditions in both. The best of the 'imported' professors and lecturers became South Africans without losing contact with Europe. They brought to their task a breadth of learning and a standard of intellectual integrity that left a deep mark on South African life. The stream of importations has, fortunately, not quite dried up; the tradition of studying in Europe still lives, and many university professors and lecturers have had a period of oversea study. But by 1961 there was ominous signs that the Republic of South Africa was entering on a period of semi-isolation in intellectual matters. Universities were finding it increasingly difficult to attract first-rate teaching staff to a country where academic freedom and human rights seemed to be held in low regard. Moreover, and for the same reasons, some of South Africa's best university men and women were leaving the country and by 1968 it was officially stated that some 70 per cent of white South Africans doing post-graduate work abroad had no intention of returning to the country.

The University of the Cape of Good Hope was the first statutory university authority in South Africa. Established in 1873, it was nothing more than an examining body; the actual university training was at that time carried on at the Victoria College at Stellenbosch and at the South African College in Cape Town. It was at those institutions that men like Smuts, Hertzog, Rose Innes, and Schreiner took degrees before going to England or Holland to complete their training. The two Boer Republics had no university institutions, and their young men went to Cape Town and Stellenbosch. By 1918, university colleges had been established at other centres, and in that year Stellenbosch and the University of Cape Town became full universities, while the University of South Africa, successor to the old University of the Cape of Good Hope, consisted of constituent colleges at Grahamstown, Bloemfontein, Pietermaritzburg, Pretoria, Johannesburg, Wellington, and Potchefstroom. One by one the university colleges achieved full university status, except Wellington which went out of existence; and the University of South Africa remained as an examining body and to cater for the large number of external students who were unable to attend a university. In 1964 a dual medium university was established at Port Elizabeth and opened in 1965; and in 1968 the Rand Afrikaans University was opened in Johannesburg. The Minister of National Education has since then said that he was contemplating the setting up of three more universities.

Not all the universities are able to offer full courses. Only at Cape Town, Witwatersrand, Pretoria, Natal, and Stellenbosch, for instance are there medical schools. Theology may be studied at Stellenbosch, Pretoria, Grahamstown, and Potchefstroom. At all the universities the normal arts and science courses may be taken for a degree. The universities do not conduct their own entrance examinations but accept the provincial examinations and those of the Joint Matriculation Board for this purpose and are content to exercise a control over the syllabuses prescribed for these. For many years there has been considerable complaint that the standard required for provincial examinations is too low and that students enter the universities at an immature stage, with the result that a good deal of the work at the universities is merely a continuation of school teaching. There has been talk of instituting a preliminary year of training at the universities, but the difficulties of expense have, so far, defeated this project.

University education is financed from two main sources: State grants and fees. The grant is based on a subsidy formula that is revised every five years and takes into account factors such as numbers of student in each faculty and capital requirements. In 1968 total university revenue was approximately R23 million of which over 64 per cent came from government subsidies, 29 per cent from student fees, and the balance from endowments and donations. The report of the University Advisory Committee has recommended a considerable increase in government subsidies. The universities are, thus, dependent on government support and on numbers of students. Moreover, government support depends partly on the number of full-time students at each university and partly on the extent of private donations. There can be little doubt that this dependence has had a deleterious effect on the freedom of the universities. In the first place, universities are forced to compete for students. It is not unknown for universities to advertise extensively and to appoint special canvassers to travel the country to recruit students. In order to make the universities more attractive, courses are included that are more suitable for technical institutions—such as courses in domestic science and in physical culture— and academic standards tend to be lowered so as to avoid too many failures.

There is another way in which dependence on numbers undermines university freedom. The Dutch Reformed churches have a powerful influence on schools and on parents in the *platteland* or rural areas; and the close connexion between the churches and the Nationalist Party places a further restriction on university freedom. University appointments, expressions of opinion by university professors and lecturers, and even student social activities, are all matters in which those universities that depend on the support of the Dutch Reformed churches have to be 'careful'. Until the 1960's this would have applied principally to Afrikaans-medium universities, though English-medium universities were subject to com- mercial industrial, and mining pressures that are, possibly, less insidious and more easily disregarded. But of recent years the co-called 'liberalist' tendencies in English-medium universities have attracted adverse criticism from those sources within the Afrikaans churches and the Nationalist party that regard anyone who does not wholly accept Afrikaner nationalism as a danger to the *volk*. The English-medium universities are, therefore, under increasing pressure to conform to the outlook of rural conservatism.

Until 1950 every Act of Parliament for the establishment of university colleges and universities contained a so-called 'conscience clause' which provides that no religious test may be applied to students or staff in making appointments. This clause has always been jealously guarded by university staffs and by those who are concerned to maintain independence of thought in the universities. In 1950, when the old Potchefstroom University College for Christian Higher Education achieved university status, the Act omitted the usual conscience clause in so far as it affected the staff and substituted a clause forbidding the application of dogmatic tests in the admission of students.

Taken by itself, there could be little objection to the application of a religious test at an institution that, professedly, exists to promote Christian higher education. The main objection is that public funds should finance such an institution. However, the omission of the 'conscience clause' in this one instance cannot be taken by itself. There exists an organized move to abolish the clause altogether, a move supported by Afrikaans teachers' associations, by the Dutch Reformed churches, by some, though by no means all, of the staffs of Afrikaans universities, and by the promoters of Christian National Education. Unofficially, religious tests are already frequently applied in the appointment of teachers; and even in the Afrikaans universities membership of one of the Dutch Reformed churches and strong Nationalist sympathies are sometimes powerful recommendations. It is improbable that the deletion of the 'conscience clause' will be made compulsory; it is more likely to be done at the request of the university concerned, as happened in 1961, when the University of the Orange Free State promoted a Private Bill to delete, the 'conscience clause' from its charter.[11] The University of Port Elizabeth Act of 1964 contained the conscience clause, but the Rand Afrikaans University Act of 1965 omitted it.

Until 1962 it was possible to say that, though harm had been done to academic freedom and university autonomy by direct legislative interference, there was no evidence that government subsidies to universities had been used to curtail their freedom. The Minister of National Education has charge of university education and no new post may be established without approval from him and from the Treasury. Universities have always been severely hampered for lack of funds and the grants from government are inadequate for their growing needs; but the grants were given impartially. It will be seen presently, however, that by 1968 it was no longer possible to take this state of affairs for granted.

In 1916 there was established at Fort Hare, in the eastern province of the Cape, the South African Native College. It was founded and supported partly by missionary and private funds and partly by government aid which, increasing year by year, assumed an ever larger proportion of the College's total revenue. Of the revenue in 1957 of R220,000, about four-fifths was from government funds. Although the college was intended to provide university education for Africans, Asians and Coloured were admitted, and of the total enrolment of 438 in 1958, just under 100 were Asians or Coloured, in about equal numbers. The staff was originally entirely white, but by 1958, 12 of the 46 members of the academic staff were Africans; the principal has always been white, but the vice-principal, who frequently acted for the principal, was for many years the late Z. K. Matthews, one of the most intellectually distinguished Africans in South Africa. Another African of great distinction who served the college for many years was Professor Jabavu who died in 1959.

[11] The Bill was postponed until 1962 when it was re-introduced, this time without the section to delete the conscience clause. The promoters of the Bill, meeting with unexpected opposition in their own ranks and anxious to have the remaining sections of the Bill passed as non-contentious, dropped the conscience clause section.

Under the Education Act of 1923 the college was incorporated as an institution for higher education and students were prepared for degrees of the University of South Africa, and in 1951 it became affiliated to Rhodes University and changed its name to Fort Hare University College. The college has thus always prepared its students for university degrees common to the rest of South Africa and has wisely eschewed the idea of separate examinations that could be stigmatized as inferior. Until 1950, when government prohibited the admission of students from outside the Union, African students at Fort Hare came from many parts of Africa, and Fort Hare graduates are still to be found occupying responsible positions in South Africa, southern and central African territories, Kenya, Tanzania, and Uganda.

Until 1959 there was no legal colour bar in the various Acts establishing universities. Nevertheless, there were only two universities at which non-whites were admitted to the same lectures as whites: there were the so-called 'open' universities of Cape Town and Witwatersrand; at a third, the University of Natal, there were three constituent colleges—one at Pietermaritzburg for whites, one for whites at Durban, and one (which included a medical school) for non-whites at Durban. In none of these did non-white students live in the same residences as white students, and they were excluded, by general practice and tacit agreement, from many student social (as distinct from academic) activities. No non-white student would, for example, be chosen to represent the university in any of the athletic sports. In Cape Town and Witwatersrand non-white students could be, and normally were, elected to the Students' Representative Council. No distinction of colour was made at graduation ceremonies at Witwatersrand and Cape Town; in Natal, such distinction was made until the combined pressure of staff, students, and convocation, together with a boycott of the ceremony by non-white students, brought about a change of policy. Outside of actual university functions there had been increasing social contact between white and non-white at the open universities.

There are great differences of opinion on the question of university education for non-whites. Most thoughtful South Africans, of all shades of opinion, agree that it should be provided and the only question is what form it should take. The majority of Afrikaners—though by no means all—say that the two groups must have entirely separate facilities. To do anything else is to go contrary to all the traditions and beliefs of South Africa and is in the interest neither of the whites nor of the non-whites. The majority of English-speaking South Africans—but, again, by no means all—would agree to mixed universities as at Cape Town and Witwatersrand. It may be doubted, however, whether they would continue to agree if the number of non-whites increased considerably.

Those who favour the compromise of Natal argue that a small group of non-whites among white students means that the former are always in an abnormal situation. Either they are merely tolerated, when they are not ostracized, or else they are treated on a somewhat emotional basis. In neither case are they really treated on their merits, simply as human beings. In such circumstances they miss the opportunity of developing powers of leadership which a university should provide. If they are in a separate institution, as in Natal, they form a coherent 'natural' group, and are not subjected to the emotional stresses of life in a mixed university where they are excluded from many social activities.

Finally, an increasing minority of white South Africans from both language groups not only agree to mixed universities, as at Cape Town, but actively favour them. Where, they ask, can educated people from all racial groups meet if not at a university? It is, they maintain, essential that future leaders of the different population groups should mix on equal terms, and the universities should provide facilities for this. Non-whites in segregated universities may not suffer social strains, but they suffer the worse strain of frustration, and they prefer to go to a mixed university whatever the social disabilities may be.

Soon after the Nationalist Party came to power in 1948 it became apparent that pressure would be brought to bear on the open universities to compel them to conform to the pattern of apartheid. For a time, the Minister of Education resisted the pressure from party congresses to take active steps; at two such congresses he maintained that, while he personally was opposed to mixed universities, he was loath to do anything that might infringe the autonomy of universities. By 1955 the pressure had become too strong and in the following year it was announced that a Separate Universities Education Bill would be introduced in parliament in 1957. Before the Bill was published the open universities began actively organizing opposition. The Universities of Cape Town and Witwatersrand set up a joint Academic Freedom Committee which was responsible for drawing up a full statement that would inform the public on the issues involved.[12] After the Bill was published, in March 1957, these activities were intensified and were backed by strong public reaction against a measure that proposed to prohibit the open universities from admitting non-white students, to place the University College of Fort Hare under the Department of Native Affairs, and to separate the non-white medical school from the University of Natal and place it under the Department of Education, Arts and Science. Protest meetings were held, petitions were drawn up and presented, deputations visited the minister; solemn processions of students and academic staffs, in academic dress and led by their respective chancellors, marched through the streets of Cape Town, Johannesburg, Durban, Pietermaritzburg, Grahamstown, and the little

[12] This was published as a book, *The Open Universities in South Africa*, and widely distributed both in South Africa and to universities overseas.

town of Alice near which Fort Hare is situated. Statements were issued by convocations, by groups of prominent citizens, and by a number of national organizations; mass meetings of students at the English-language universities issued protests against the Bill, and at the Afrikaans-speaking universities resolutions strongly favouring the Bill were passed by students. At Cape Town the students lined the main roads carrying placards proclaiming their ideals of open minds in open universities, and women of the Black Sash held vigils in the main centres. Private and public appeals were made to the academic staffs of the Afrikaans universities, as colleagues, in the belief that they would realize that a threat to the academic freedom of some universities was a threat to all. There is evidence that members of the staffs of Afrikaans universities used their influence as individuals to dissuade the government, but with a few exceptions they would not associate themselves publicly or concertedly in opposition to government proposals, and their influence was insufficient to restrain the government from passing the Bill and thus depriving the open universities—and consequently all South African universities—of their freedom to decide who should be admitted to their fellowship.

The Separate Universities Education Bill was sent to a Select Committee which became, when the session ended, a Commission of Enquiry. In giving evidence before the Commission, individual members of Afrikaans universities did indeed oppose the proposed interference with the open universities and attacked the proposed new university institutions for non-whites on the ground that the regulations controlling these, as published in the Bill, would deprive those institutions of all real autonomy or academic freedom. As the Bill finally emerged and was passed in 1959, it was renamed the Extension of University Education Bill and, under that title, became law.

Fort Hare was dealt with in a separate Act which, briefly, brought to an end the existence of that college as an independent university institution and placed it under the control of the Minister of Bantu Education. The Extension of University Education Act provided for the establishment of three more university colleges, one in Natal for the Zulu, one in the Transvaal for the Sotho, and one in the Cape for the Coloured. In 1961 a university college for Indians was established in Durban. Students at these tribal university institutions are prepared for examinations conducted by the University of South Africa, but it is government policy that they will, as soon as possible, conduct their own examinations. The regulations laid down for the management and control are calculated to restrict, rather than promote, intellectual independence. All appointments of staff, senate, and council are under ministerial control; since there are not enough non-whites to fill the academic posts, whites are appointed, but white and non-white are segregated and do not share a common room or sit on the same senate or council, as was customary at Fort Hare; there are two separate

senates and councils for each institution, and it is envisaged that the black
senate and council will eventually take charge. Stringent regulations are
laid down for the conduct of staff and students by which they are, among
other things, forbidden to take any part whatsoever in politics or to criticize
government policy or the conduct of any government department; and the
Minister has far-reaching powers of dismissal. Within three months of the
passing of the Act the Minister of Bantu Education dismissed eight white
members of the staff at Fort Hare. In doing so he stated that he would not
hesitate to dismiss any member of staff who 'sabotaged' apartheid, but he
did not specify in what manner the eight members had been guilty of this.
At the same time, the Department of Bantu Education made it clear to
African members of staff that political activities, such as membership of the
African National Congress, at that time a legal organization, were contrary
to regulations. Rather than accept such limitations on their academic
freedom, several African professors resigned, thus forfeiting all pension
rights. One of these was Professor Z. K. Matthews, the first graduate of
Fort Hare, who had taught at the College for twenty-four years and was
within two years of the retiring age.[13]

The final passage of the Bill was accompanied by renewed protests and
demonstrations. The parliamentary opposition parties combined to fight
the Bill at every stage, including the first reading, and it was only by all-
night sittings and the application of the guillotine that the government was
able to secure the passage of the Bill before the end of the session. On the
night when the Bill was finally passed, members of the Black Sash stood in
silent all-night vigil at the entrances to Parliament. After it had become
law, the universities of Cape Town and Witwatersrand held solemn
official ceremonies to mark the passing of their autonomy and to dedicate
themselves to the task of recovering it; and they decided to have annual
ceremonies in order to keep alive the idea of university autonomy and to
restate their belief in academic freedom. At the University of Cape Town
a bronze plaque was unveiled by the Chancellor in July 1960 recording the
removal of academic freedom in 1960 and leaving a blank space for the
date when that freedom would be restored.

After the passage of the Act, non-white students already at the open
universities were allowed to complete their courses; but no new admissions
were allowed unless the applicant wished to study a subject not yet catered
for at the new university colleges. Permission for this was readily granted
but could be withdrawn at the discretion of the Minister. The following
enrolment figures are for 1958, the year prior to the Act, and 1967, the
latest available. These figures exclude the Rand Afrikaans University which
opened in 1968.

[13] Prof. Matthews subsequently took an appointment with the world Council of Churches
in Geneva, and in 1967 later became Botswana's permanent representative at U.N. He
died in 1968.

All university institutions, excluding correspondence course at University of South Africa.

	white	Asian	African	Coloured	Total
1958	26,293	717	618	500	28,128
1967	45,131	2,160	1,449	865	49,605

University of South Africa Correspondence Courses

1958	6,144	601	1,179	204	8,128
1967	22,163	134	431	66	22,794

Combination of above

1958	32,437	1,318	1,797	704	36,256
1967	67,294	2,294	1,880	931	72,399

While these figures are possibly more a reflection of growth of population and rapid economic expansion than a result of the Act, they reveal interesting features. Total enrolment of non-whites students declined relatively to white enrolment which was 89 per cent of the total in 1958 and 93 per cent in 1967. On the other hand, the number of non-whites taking courses at institutions other than the correspondence courses of the University of South Africa increased from 7 to 10 per cent of the total.

Enrolment at the three open universities

	white	Asian	African	Coloured	Total
1958	11,694	658	298	441	13,091
1967	18,964	700	137	293	20,094

The number of non-white students at open universities declined from 1,397 to 1,120, but the proportion of non-white to white declined from 12 to 5·5 per cent. The total number of non-white students taking university courses is 5,105, which, in a non-white population of over 15,000,000, represents 0·03 per cent of the population. It used to be said that South Africa had more non-white university students and graduates than the rest of Africa put together. Though that boast is still endlessly repeated it is no longer true.

Until 1959 South Africa was, perhaps unconsciously, experimenting with different solutions to the problem of university education in a mixed society. These experiments were of immense social importance to Africa, for on their results would depend in no small measure the extent to which European and non-European in Africa would be able to co-operate. That they will have to co-operate is certain, but whether the co-operation will be fruitful or not will depend on the extent to which white South Africa can provide effective and constructive university education for non-whites. It was all to the good, therefore, that different experiments were being carried on, and to put a stop to them was a short-sighted policy which could not but cause serious worsening of relations.

The attitudes of students to national questions are important. Since language, politics, and religion are all connected in South Africa it is generally speaking true to say that the Afrikaans-medium universities are nationalist and enjoy the support of the Dutch Reformed churches, while the English-medium universities are more cosmopolitan and, the conservative Afrikaner would say, more irreligeous and 'liberal'. The Afrikaans universities are Stellenbosch, Pretoria, Bloemfontein, Potchefstroom, and Rand; and the English-medium universities are Cape Town, Rhodes, and Natal. Port Elizabeth is dual medium. It must not, however, be thought that there are no English-speaking students at the one nor Afrikaans-speaking students at the other. At the English-speaking universities in particular there is a healthy mixture of students from both language groups. Nevertheless, there remains a close association between the Afrikaans universities and the Nationalist Party and the Afrikaans churches that constitutes a threat to the intellectual independence of those universities.

These facts are reflected in the two main national unions that exist. In 1924 a National Union of South African Students (commonly known as Nusas) was established and all university centres were members. By 1932, however, it had split and the main body of Afrikaans students hived off to form the *Afrikaans-Nasionale Studentebond*, usually known as A.N.S. The split was political and cultural, as Nusas was felt to be too liberal and unnationalist. When it had shed the more conservative Afrikaner element, Nusas became increasingly liberal in its political attitude. As we saw in chapter 7, the period 1932–48 was one during which the Nationalist Party was divided. These divisions were reflected in the Afrikaans universities, and A.N.S. went through a lean period. In 1948 a new body was formed, the *Afrikaanse Studentebond*, known as A.S.B.

Nusas and A.S.B. have made various attempts to find a common basis for student co-operation in inter-university matters. Both bodies organize student tours to Europe, and inter-university student activities in South Africa. But all attempts at co-operation have failed, largely because of fundamental difference on the question of non-white students. Nusas does not distinguish between students on grounds of race or colour; A.S.B. does. A.S.B. declares that it is prepared to confer with non-white students provided they come from a separate university institution and are neither represented by nor represent white students. Students at non-white university colleges are forbidden by their governing bodies to affiliate with Nusas and it is improbable that they would wish to join A.S.B. Individual non-white students at the tribal colleges who have contact with Nusas immediately become a matter of interest to the security branch of the police.

There are, of course, other points of difference. Nusas decisively rejects the ideas of Christian National Education, while A.S.B., officially at any rate, supports these principles. Then, too, A.S.B. speaks in terms of Afrikaans culture, which it defines in a manner that excludes English-speaking South Africans, while Nusas claims that it speaks in terms of a broader South African culture. All in all, therefore, the division between the English and the Afrikaans university students is deep. As with single medium schools, single medium universities have tended to perpetuate divisions between the two white groups in South Africa.

Many students at the universities of Cape Town and Witwatersrand, and to only a slightly lesser degree at Rhodes and Natal, have for long been determined and vocal opponents of Nationalist Party race policies. Nusas represents the students at these universities and claims to speak on their behalf; and Nusas itself is outspoken in its condemnation of apartheid and the legislation that inevitably flows from the attempt to implement it. Individual members of staff, too, are informed critics of apartheid. All this has not endeared the English-speaking universities to a government that has striven to convince its followers and the world that apartheid is a sound and just policy. Those universities have long been an object of suspicion, fear, and hatred to extreme Afrikaner nationalists who regarded them as hotbeds of communism in the guise of liberalism, of atheism, of un-South African attitudes. Individual ministers and members of parliament have not hesitated to condemn them and to warn parents not to send their children to such morally dangerous places.

This antagonism between the Nationalist Party and English-medium universities naturally increased when the government took away the universities' right to decide, irrespective of race, who should be admitted. It increased still further after 1960 when a whole series of laws was passed restricting freedom of association and personal relations and empowering government, under the pretext of suppressing communism, to deprive individuals of their liberty without allowing them to defend themselves in open court. These laws are described elsewhere in this book; so too is the wave of sabotage between 1962 and 1964 in which a small number of young men and women who had previously been prominent in university life and in Nusas, and a few who were still connected with a university, had been involved and were, on conviction, sentenced to imprisonment for varying periods. The point to be made in this chapter, however, is that during the sixties the government consistently used arbitrary powers conferred on it by parliament to attack and to harass the English-language universities and Nusas.

These attacks take various forms and it is their secret rather than their open nature that constitutes a serious assault upon academic freedom. A watch is kept on students and members of staff who show liberal tendencies, and it is generally accepted that the security branch employs informers planted on the campuses. Raids have been carried out on Nusas offices and on the homes of members of university staff a number of whom have been arrested under the so-called 90-days Act and subsequently been released without being charged. Furthermore, the government resorted to banning under the Suppression of Communism Act to silence outspoken critics. Thus, in 1964 the Minister of Justice placed a President of Nusas under arrest for 28 days and then released him without charge; and in 1965 it banned another President. When the Minister of Justice, then Mr. B. J. Vorster, was challenged in parliament about this he gave a few reasons but made various errors of fact that were immediately disproved. Nevertheless, the ban remained. At the end of 1966 the then President was refused a passport to go overseas on a scholarship. He was entitled to take an exit permit which would prevent him from returning to South Africa without permission, but this he refused.

There were a number of bannings and of imprisonment without trial of members of staff at English-medium universities. In Cape Town, Professor Jack Simons, an expert in African law, was banned in 1962; and in 1967 Dr. R. Hoffenberg, an endocrinologist of international repute on the staff of the Medical School at Groote Schuur Hospital, was banned from continuing his work as a medical teacher and as a research scientist. Both immediately obtained university positions in Britain. The Minister of Justice imposes bans on secret information supplied by the security branch, so that he now has a deciding voice on who may teach at universities.

Another matter on which the government, through the Minister of National Education, has been at odds with the English-medium universities is that of so-called closed and open societies. This applies more particularly to the University of Cape Town where the Students' Representative Council had a rule that official recognition on the campus would not be accorded to any society that had a colour bar in its constitution. In 1966 this rule was challenged by a group of students. The University Council upheld the S.R.C. but, under threat by the Minister of legislation, revised the S.R.C. constitution and removed its power of refusing recognition to a colour bar society. Eventually a compromise acceptable to the majority of students was reached.[14]

[14] During the last few months of 1968, relations between the government and the English-medium universities worsened. The Council of the University of Cape Town, on the recommendation of Senate, appointed an African, Mr. Mafeje, to a lectureship. Under direct threat from the Minister of Education the Council rescinded its decision, an act for which it was severely blamed by the students and by many others who believed that the Council should have forced the government to take upon itself the odium of applying a colour bar to an academic appointment. The students of the University of Cape Town staged a sit-in which attracted world-wide attention but failed to achieve its object. The Prime Minister and three other ministers publicly berated the students and threatened police action to prevent a recurrence; and the Minister of Education promised legislation in 1969 to control student activities. The President of the S.R.C. at Cape Town, who was subsequently elected as President of Nusas, was refused a passport to enable him to use a much sought-after travel scholarship.

January 1969

Students at the English-medium universities, and as organized in Nusas, have sustained a vigorous fight for academic and personal freedom. During the past two decades there have been many assaults on liberty, and in every one of them students from the English-language universities have been in the forefront of opposition and protest.

There is one further aspect of universities in South Africa that must be mentioned, and that is research. Facilities for research are very limited. In most of the universities, but particularly in the smaller ones, the professors and lecturers are so busy teaching that there is no time for independent research. Some of the universities have extra-mural or part-time students, who earn a living and can attend classes after working hours only, and the extra teaching load on the staff that this involves further reduces any free time that might be devoted to research. Instead of making more money, and thus time, available to the universities, governments have concentrated on establishing research laboratories which have, for the most part, no direct connexion with any university. The South African Council for Scientific and Industrial Research and the National Council for Social Research are government bodies. The universities are, indeed, well represented on these councils, which make grants for individual pieces of research. But research tends to become divorced from the universities and controlled by government departments; and in a country where control by a government department too frequently involves conformity to government policy, the quality of research is bound to deteriorate. Industry, too, donates money to universities for research, but experience in the United States and elsewhere is that when universities too readily accept large and tempting research grants from government departments or industry they are in danger of losing their independence. Research on specific assignments from government or industry may involve secrecy, for security reasons or because of commercial rivalry. Moreover, specific asignments not of the scientist's own choice divert his energies and the quality of the research tends to decline. If this tendency is not checked it will deprive the universities of the services of those who must have un-fettered research facilities and who will seek them elsewhere if South Africa cannot provide them.

9

RELIGION

ALMOST half the African population of South Africa is classed as 'heathen'. The word connotes barbarism, lack of contact with the ways of civilization, and the practice of witchcraft. In previous census returns 'heathen' were classified as 'others and indefinite', a loose description which probably covers all the grades between complete heathenism and mere religious indifference. But it is significant that, out of a total population of over 18¾ million people, about 3½ million are, officially at any rate, classed as having no affiliation with any Christian community. It illustrates, once more, the lack of homogeneity in the South African population, and what a long road civilization still has to travel.

Since Christian missions have played such a large part in the history of non-white education it is instructive to compare the relative strengths of the major Christian communities. The figures reveal that there are almost twice as many whites in the Afrikaans churches as in the other Protestant churches put together. On the other hand, there are nine times as many Africans, and almost twice as many Coloured, in the other Protestant churches as there are in the Afrikaans churches. These facts are significant as showing the great influence of the Afrikaans churches on the social and political life of the whites, and the predominant influence on non-white education of the English-speaking churches, which, together have played a far greater part in missionary work than the Afrikaans churches.

It must not be assumed that the Afrikaners have been lacking in missionary enthusiasm. The comparatively small part they played in mission work was due partly to the fact that the missions were in close proximity to the white congregations, among whom there was considerable prejudice against educating these 'children of Ham'. In nineteenth-century Britain, on the other hand, there was great enthusiasm for foreign missions, and the English churches in South Africa, which had originated in Britain, were able to draw on a fund both of good will and of money. The Afrikaans churches had no such outside means, and were entirely dependent on their own resources. Financially these were meagre, for although the Afrikaners possessed land they had little cash, and it was only after the 1920's that there were those who could make reasonably large donations to church funds. Even among the well-disposed, contributions towards missions came from people who had little money themselves, and many a Dutch Reformed Church parson and his wife have collected pennies from people who, in Britain, would be considered extremely poor, pennies that went to support a missionary or an evangelist in Nigeria, in Nyasaland, in China, or in the local African location. The Afrikaans churches have certainly played their part in establishing Christianity in Africa, and they are taking an increasing share of the common burden.

There are over 2,400 African separatist churches, and their number as well as the numbers of adherents fluctuates considerably, since most of the churches have little stability. Some are established for reasons such as personal jealousies and ambitions, the temptation to make what seems to be a comparatively easy living, and dissatisfaction with the too irksome discipline of the white-controlled parent church. Others are founded from a desire to adapt the Christian religion to primitive beliefs or an awakening nationalism that demands a separate and independent organization. The former are often the result of dissatisfaction with church discipline and are unlikely to live long; the second are, in prevailing social and political circumstances, likely to attract increasing numbers of Africans who suffer from a sense of frustration. It has been estimated that between 1946 and 1961 the number of adherents to separatist churches increased from 701,000 to 2,188,000.[1]

The Roman Catholic Church in South Africa is organized under the Apostolic Delegation of Southern Africa. The English-speaking Protestant churches, deriving from Britain, are today all separate from any control by the parent churches overseas and are governed by their own synods or conferences or assemblies. After considerable controversy during the 1850's and 1860's a constitution was drawn up for the Church of the Province of South Africa, which is governed by a provincial synod under the presidency of the Archbishop of Cape Town, and is the legally recognized representative of the Anglican Communion in South Africa.

There are three Dutch Reformed churches of which the smallest is the *Gereformeerde Kerk van Suid-Afrika*, with about 144,000 adherents. It was established in 1859 as a breakaway from the main Dutch Reformed Church in the Cape Colony and is more rigidly Calvinist. Its headquarters are at Potchefstroom, where it controls the university and trains its own ministers. It has no moderator or permanent executive, and the control of the church rests mainly with the individual congregations. Although the *Gereformeerde Kerk* has a small membership, it has exercised a considerable influence on theological thought and on education, partly because of the rigour of its doctrine and largely because it has produced at Potchefstroom a succession of able and vigorous ministers.

The *Nederduits Hervormde Kerk* was the first state church of the Transvaal Republic in 1858. The parent church at the Cape had been slow in

---

[1] Figures in this Chapter are from *A Survey of Race Relations in South Africa* for 1959–60, and 1966 and 1967, compiled by Muriell Horrell and published by the South African Institute of Race Relations. Figures are here given in round numbers.

following up the Trekkers who had left the Cape and established the two northern republics. The Transvaal, being farthest away from the Cape, established its own church and looked to Holland rather than to the Cape for its ministers and for its spiritual guidance. When, in 1866, the church from the Cape did establish itself in the Transvaal, a number of members of the *Hervormde Kerk* joined the new church. The *Hervormde Kerk* remained a separate institution, though not differing greatly from the parent church, and it has about 214,000 adherents, most of whom are in the Transvaal.

By far the largest church is the *Nederduits Gereformeerde Kerk* (usually abbreviated to N.G.K.), which has 1,696,000 white adherents, or almost half the total white population. When people refer to the Dutch Reformed church in South Africa it is chiefly the N.G.K. that they have in mind.

The N.G.K. is organized on a federal basis, each of the four provinces and South-West Africa having its own synod which meets annually and is presided over by its own moderator. Until 1962 a federal council advised on and co-ordinated the work of the church but it had no constitutional authority over the provincial synods. In that year the five synods united and constituted a general synod to meet every four years. Though the general synod has more than advisory and consultative powers the structure of the church remains federal. The unit of organization is the congregation, in which church matters are regulated by a representative church council of elders and deacons presided over by the minister. Ministers are 'called' by the church council and, in accordance with an old custom, if the voting for two candidates is equal, lots are cast. Several congregations form a presbytery, which functions as a link between the church councils and the synod. Both in its separate congregations and as an organized church the N.G.K. does a great deal of social welfare and mission work, which is co-ordinated by such bodies as the Federal Mission Council and the Federal Poor Relief Council.

In religious dogma the N.G.K. is Calvinist and stems direct from the seventeenth-century parent church in Holland. The doctrine of predestination is a cardinal belief, and many of the church's social attitudes on such matters as dancing, card-playing, and the sabbath are strictly Calvinist. Members of the Orange Free State Synod have at various times deplored the fact that at the University of the Orange Free State students were allowed to have dances; and the church at Kimberley protested strongly because a local rugby football team, touring in Rhodesia, was to play one match on a Sunday. South African rugby teams playing in France insist, to the bewilderment of the French, on Sunday observance. The church is strong enough to be able to secure a certain outward conformity in these matters, but a large number of its members, particularly in the big urban centres, no longer conform even outwardly. To many of them Sunday is their only day for recreation.

Candidates for the ministry in the N.G.K. are trained at the Theological Seminary at Stellenbosch or at the University of Pretoria. Coloured ministers are trained at a separate institution at Wellington, and Africans were trained at the Stofberg-Gedenkskool in the Orange Free State until it was declared a 'white' area, in terms of the Group Areas Act, and the institution was split into four and removed to Reserves in the four provinces. On the completion of the course a few white ministers go overseas, either to Europe or to the United States, for further study; more frequently, however, they go straight to work, usually as temporary assistant to an experienced minister, from where they are called to a congregation of their own.

Traditionally and by the very nature of the positions they occupied, ministers of the N.G.K. played a prominent part in the history and development of the Afrikaner people. During the nineteenth century it was the ministers of the Afrikaans churches who organized congregations and built churches and schools. When the Boer War broke out ministers in the Republics went on commando, usually as ministers, but, in one case at least, in a prominent combatant role.[2] And the sympathies of ministers in the Cape and Natal were almost all with the Boer forces. Lord Milner regarded what he called the 'Predikants' (Ministers of the N.G.K.) with equal detestation and suspicion as dangerous opponents of his policy.

After the Boer War the ministers took the lead in restoring the shattered morale of the Afrikaner. Most of them loyally accepted the terms of peace and worked hard to promote understanding between Boer and Briton. Some of them voluntarily reduced their salaries because their congregations were too poor to pay them. With self-sacrificing devotion, they rebuilt churches and established schools, and turned the thoughts of their people from the bitter defeat of the past to a more hopeful future. In doing so they helped to awaken the spirit of Afrikaner nationalism, which, when political conditions became favourable, turned aside from its original course and developed into a strong political movement which they were powerless to control. The First World War, and the rebellion in South Africa, split the church, and a new generation of ministers, strongly imbued with nationalism, partly followed and partly led the new political movement.[3]

We saw in chapter 7 how rapidly Afrikaner nationalism developed during the period between the two world wars and how close its association with the growth of the Afrikaans language was. The Afrikaans churches were deeply involved in these twin developments. There are numbers of ministers and church adherents who have never been politically associated with the Nationalist Party, but they are in a minority. Whether passively or actively, the majority of those who control the Afrikaans

[2] The late General Roux, who, after the Boer War, returned to his congregation.
[3] Dr. D. F. Malan, for example, was a N.G.K. minister until 1915, when he entered politics as a Nationalist. He became Prime Minister in 1948.

churches are supporters of the Nationalist Party, to whose policies the churches lend all the considerable weight of their moral influence. During the 1939–45 War, for example, it was extremely difficult to find Afrikaans chaplains for the Forces, despite the fact that an estimated 60 per cent of the troops were Afrikaans-speaking, because the Nationalist Party was opposed to South Africa's participation in the war.

Relations between the Afrikaans churches and other Christian communities suffered because of the cleavage between Afrikaners and English-speaking South Africans. There was a time, in the 'twenties of this century, when co-operation between all the Protestant churches was cordial. In many centres a Ministers' Fraternal met regularly, inter-church meetings discussed common problems and took combined action, and the inter-denominational Christian Council was well supported by Afrikaans ministers. The language used at such meetings was always English because most of the ministers from English-speaking church could not understand Afrikaans. This fact, combined with the increasing emphasis on nationalism, gradually destroyed the spirit of co-operation, and the Afrikaans churches began to isolate themselves from the English-speaking Christian communities.

A few Afrikaans ministers continued to co-operate actively with those of other denominations, and they worked together amicably enough on official educational and welfare boards; but inter-church co-operation between the actual churches ceased for the time being. Many ministers on both sides felt this state of affairs to be unfortunate; but the political forces were strong, and the Afrikaans churches found it extremely difficult to go against the current of nationalism of which they had for so long been an integral part.

In 1953 the Federal Missionary Council of the Dutch Reformed churches convened a three-day conference of European Protestant church leaders of all denominations to discuss common missionary problems. It was a notable achievement to bring together men of such widely differing ideas, but the conference revealed just how wide the differences were on the question of relations with non-whites.

Private meetings and unofficial discussions between leaders of the different churches continued, but political events after 1953 increased, rather then reduced, the differences. As we shall see presently, however, successful efforts to re-establish contact between the Protestant churches were made in the late 1950's.

Relations between the Protestant churches and the Roman Catholic Church have never been cordial, since the latter does not usually co-operate with non-Catholic churches. On the part of the Afrikaans churches there has always been a marked hostility towards the Roman Catholics. There are various reasons for this. Being staunch Calvinists, the Afrikaner churchmen have an ingrained fear and distrust of Roman Catholicism, and, as nationalists, they fear any organization that has a foreign governing body. The Roman Catholic Church appears to have plenty of money and has set up many excellent schools, which have, rightly or wrongly, acquired a reputation as good 'finishing' schools, and of being able to 'get pupils through their examinations'. Some Afrikaners send their children to these schools, despite the warnings of the Afrikaans churches who fear that the children will become Romanized and denationalized. Under an ordinance in the Transvaal[4] it became illegal in that province for parents who were Afrikaans-speaking to send their children to church schools where the medium of instruction was English, but the Roman Catholic Church overcame this obstacle by establishing an Afrikaans medium school.

Antagonism on the part of the Afrikaans churches to Roman Catholicism is openly expressed in many ways.[5] There is an annual 'Reformation Sunday' on which the breakaway from the Roman Catholic Church is remembered and the virtues of Protestanism as well as the 'dangers of Rome' are stressed. When Mr. te Water, then South Africa's Ambassador Extraordinary, paid an official visit to the Pope in 1949, there were strong protests from synods and from Nationalist Party congresses. Finally, at a provincial congress of the Nationalist Party in 1949 it was proposed to exclude Roman Catholics from holding office in the Nationalist Party; but the proposal was withdrawn under pressure from the party executive.

It is in theory and, to a lesser extent, in practice that race relations constitute the greatest difference between the Afrikaans churches and other Protestant communities. Previous chapters have attempted to explain the origins and development of race attitudes and policies in South Africa. The Afrikaans churches are part of the Afrikaner people, and their attitudes and policies both form and are formed by those of the majority of the Afrikaner people. Though there are, no doubt, individual exceptions, the Afrikaans churches believe in separate congregations for different racial groups. They maintain that while it is the function of the church of the white-man, by missionary effort, to help Africans to establish their own separate church, non-whites must not have membership or control in the affairs of the parent church. In this way only will each develop a mature Christian community. This argument, sincerely advanced by men who have devoted their lives to the spiritual welfare of the non-whites, is not to be lightly set aside. It affirms the essential equality in the eyes of God of all men, but maintains that for practical reasons people of different races should worship God, each in their own church.

The English-speaking churches believe that while it may be practically

---

[4] See p. 195.

[5] An editorial in *Die Kerkbode*, official organ of the N.G.K., of 29 September 1951 said: 'It [the Roman Church] wants to catch the Afrikaner in its meshwork of propaganda and to lead him to new points of view. . . . Rome is seeking more and more authority in every sphere of life.'

expedient for white and black to worship in separate churches, they are all members of the same community and should share in the government of the church. In practice there are a small number of Anglican churches where whites and non-whites worship together, but the great majority of congregations have separate churches. When it comes to synodical meetings, white and non-white ministers and elders deliberate together. In the Afrikaans churches such meetings are always separate, one for the European church and one for the mission church, in the latter of which, however, white missionaries and non-white ministers sit together. The English-speaking communities regard the non-white churches as an extension of the white; the Afrikaans churches regard them rather as separate mission churches that will one day be independent. Though the approach differs, all churches are concerned to bring Christianity to non-whites.

It is in political, non-church matters that there is even greater difference of opinion between the two groups. The Afrikaans churches have all expressed themselves strongly in favour of the Nationalist Party's policy of apartheid, while the English-speaking churches have, equally strongly, opposed that policy. At a meeting of the Federal Mission Council of the N.G.K. the policy of territorial and political separation was supported and the government was urged to put it into practice as soon as possible.[6] So strongly worded was the resolution that the then Prime Minister, Malan felt impelled to issue a warning that apartheid could not be implemented in a hurry.

At its 22nd Annual Meeting, the Federal Council of the N.G.K. considered the whole question of the relations between church and state. After affirming the right of the church, warranted in history and in the Scriptures, to express its opinion on political matters, the statement issued by the Council goes on to analyse and describe the origin and functions of the state.[7] Fundamental to all its Calvinist thought is the doctrine of Divine creation, the fall and redemption. Further, the state has been created by God, and exists independently of its citizens; its authority over the individual is ordained by God, and what distinguishes it from other divine creations is that it possesses a monopoly of might, of 'the power of the sword'. It is the duty of the state to organize this power internally and externally, by means of a police force and an army.

In every state God is the fountain of authority and power, irrespective of whether rulers and subjects acknowledge it. The Christian state acknowledges God's sovereignty while the non-Christian acknowledges merely the sovereignty of the people or of those in authority. Strongly opposed to this Calvinist conception are the humanistic theories of individualism and

---

[6] *Die Naturellevraagstuk*, April 1950.
[7] This document was published as Annexure C of the Council's Agenda and was approved by the Council, May 1951.

universalism which regard the state as something created by man for his own use. These ideas are decisively rejected by the Council. God instituted the state to counteract the worst effects of the fall of man, and no Christian may regard the state merely as a necessary evil, as Liberalism does. It is the duty of the state, thus instituted, to hold the balance between its subjects. But it has no right to interfere in non-state matters, and cannot dictate in religious matters.

Although the state is created by God, the form which it may take is the work of man. This accounts for its great diversity of forms. Historically, the establishment of most states was natural and unconscious just because it was divinely ordained. The small number of states that were consciously 'established' owe their origin to men who were, formerly, subjects of natural states.

As regards the relations between subject and ruler, the authority of man over man is not a human invention, but a gracious gift of God to a fallen generation. The authority of the state over the individual is derived from God; it must be exercised according to God's will; it is not unlimited; it cannot be replaced by another authority; and it is indivisible. Consequently, the humanistic conceptions of titular, legal, political, or popular sovereignty have no validity; further, there can be no division of power between legislature, executive and judiciary. The state has the authority and the duty to integrate harmoniously the various interests of its subjects. This doctrine is opposed both to liberal democracy and to totalitarianism. Under the former, for example, workers are compelled to form trade unions to defend their rights, often to the detriment of society as a whole; had government done its duty properly, there would have been no need for trade unions. Totalitarian states, on the other hand, go too far and seek to legislate on matters such as science and religion as well as on those in their own legitimate sphere.

The divinely ordained authority of the state has definite territorial limits. These are part of God's plan, and attempts to wipe them out are of the devil. The humanistic ideal of a world-state must be rejected as contrary to Scripture and an attempt to achieve world peace outside the Kingdom of Heaven.

The state must ensure civic freedom by not interfering in private matters, except that it must protect the individual against exploitation and wrong-doers even if, in so doing, it has to interfere temporarily with individual liberty. Political freedom consists in the right to a voice in political matters, without which no one is politically free; but it does not entitle citizens to a voice in matters relating to the church or the school or the factory. In primitive communities and in dictatorships the only freedom granted to citizens is the right of access to authority to acquaint it with their wants; the only way they can get rid of a government is by assassination or a *coup d'état*. A Christian people may not be satisfied with anything less than the right to replace a government that is not acting in accordance with God's will.

Applying this theory to South African conditions, the statement of the N.G.K. Federal Council continues: the greatest problem lies in the ideas of the revolutionary democratic school of Rousseau. According to those ideas all men are equal and, therefore, every individual is a sovereign and a lawgiver; all, white and black, must participate in the making of laws. The mass of individuals then become the source of state authority; the government becomes the servant of the people instead of the authority over them, it receives its mandate from the people, and is unseated as soon as it no longer serves the wishes and the needs of the people. This is nothing more nor less that the myth of sovereignty opposed to God. To the Christian, on the other hand, the franchise is a means of grace that must be used with the greatest care and responsibility to God. The Christian does not regard the franchise as qualifying him to make laws, which is a function of the state;[8] the vote, for the Christian, is always a symbol of God's sovereignty and every vote cast must reflect the will of God. Thus being enfranchised gives the voter the right to apply a religious test to authority.

In the light of this belief, says the statement, various points in relation to the African become clear. Those who do not have the franchise are by no means slaves or suppressed people. They still have civic rights and are protected by government. The franchise is a treasure which should belong to those who are of age politically and are able to use it responsibly before God. The African does not fulfil these requirements, and, therefore, will not be able to use the vote correctly. Since the franchise implies having a say in the establishment of government, and since government is clothed with such sacred responsibility, it is obvious that not everyone should automatically have the vote. Not only undeveloped groups, but all those who are openly in rebellion against God, such as the Communists, should not be given it. In a Christian state, therefore, the necessary qualification is not only that a man should be of age, but that he should be a Christian.

Political parties are necessary in a state, and no Christian people will tolerate the dictatorship of a clique or of one party, as happened in Germany and Russia. But this is not the only reason why the Christian cannot do without political parties. Where political life is threatened by doctrines born of unbelief—'powerful in Liberalism, much stronger in Democracy, and most dangerous in Communism'—it is without doubt the duty of Christians to try to become the strongest political factor in the country and to establish a Christian government.

The question is raised whether the holders of all forms of political thought should have the right to organize in political parties. In the existing democracies, says the statement, not only has everyone who is of

[8] This seems to contradict an earlier statement that 'the Christian citizen knows just as well as the government what is politically right and wrong'.

age the vote, but the holders of all forms of political thought have the right to organize and, if they are strong enough, achieve power.[9] This is the cancer at the root of modern democracy, because right and truth are made dependent on a mere majority of votes. The Christian citizen may not rest content with this. Only the Christian political faith is valid, and no anti-Christian philosophy should be given the right to form political parties. This applies particularly to Communism; but a Christian people ought to go even further and ought not to allow the right of organization to any group who aim at a dictatorship.

Finally, the actual form of the state is a matter of secondary importance, because a Christian people will organize a Christian state in God's good time; and for each people there will be a particular form of state. It is obvious, then, that there is such a state for the Afrikaner people. While leaving the details of this to Christian citizens, the church declares that any form of government born of unbelief must be rejected as displeasing to God. This applies not only to Communism and National Socialism, but also to 'revolutionary democracy' with its belief in the sovereignty of the people.

This statement by the N.G.K. Federal Council has been set out in some detail because it is an important document. The statement is entitled *Fundamental Principles of Calvinist Christian Political Science*. It was approved as its official policy by the highest council in the N.G.K. and was sent to all members of parliament and cabinet ministers. The N.G.K. plays a major role in the life of South Africa because of its influence over Afrikaans-speaking South Africans, at least two-thirds of whom support the Nationalist Party now in power. We must therefore, analyse further these principles of Calvinist political science and estimate their effect on South Africa.

Speaking of sixteenth-century Calvinism at Geneva, Professor R. H. Tawney says: 'It was a creed which sought, not merely to purify the individual, but to reconstruct Church and State, to renew society by penetrating every department of life, public as well as private, with the influence of religion.'[10] And again: 'He . . . taught them to feel that they were a Chosen People, made them conscious of their great destiny in the Providential plan and resolute to realize it.'[11] There is much in the history of the Afrikaans Calvinist churches to which these two quotations are applicable. Calvinism is a determinist creed which consorts naturally with conceptions of racial superiority and of national separateness. The religious beliefs of the Afrikaners thus powerfully reinforce the tendencies to isolation which arise from the history of the Afrikaner people and from the

---

[9] This statement of the churches was drawn up before the Communist Party was made illegal by Act of Parliament.
[10] R. H. Tawney, *Religion and the Rise of Capitalism*, p. 102.
[11] Tawney, op. cit., p. 112.

fact of their having a distinctive language. Luther's religious beliefs took shape in a peasant society; Calvin's beliefs were formulated in a middle-class commercial society. It is, perhaps, not fanciful to suggest that the statement of the N.G.K. could not have been made while the Afrikaner was still an agriculturist with strong individualist tendencies; the statement became possible only after he had entered the world of business in a modern urban society. If there is truth in this, then Calvinist political doctrines are likely to become increasingly influential.

Historically, Calvinism is revolutionary or authoritarian, depending on whether it represents a minority or a majority in the state. It was revolutionary in England, and authoritarian in Geneva and in Scotland. Now, in South Africa, Calvinism represents both a minority and a majority. In relation to the whole population, adherents of Calvinist churches form a minority; but in relation to the total white population they are in a small majority and will remain so as long as the white population is politically and economically dominant. Within the white group, therefore, there is a tendency for Calvinist political beliefs to become authoritarian. In the statement of those political beliefs which we described above there is constant opposition to the idea of the sovereign will of the people. This is repudiated as liberal and democratic error, born of humanism and utterly opposed to true Calvinist doctrine. It is true that the statement repudiates totalitarianism of the German or Russian model. But it explicitly enunciates the doctrine of the authoritarian state. R. H. Tawney says: 'In the struggle between liberty and authority, Calvinism sacrificed liberty, not with reluctance, but with enthusiasm.'[12] The statement of the Federal Council of the N.G.K. is entirely Calvinist in this respect.

Whether the Afrikaans churches succeed or fail in establishing a theocracy in South Africa will depend on many things. This statement of political beliefs must be taken as representing the official views of the N.G.K., but it may be doubted whether all the adherents of the church accept all the doctrines there enunciated. Even so staunch a Calvinist as the late D. F. Malan stated publicly that the sovereign power in South Africa is the will of the people, and there are many other Afrikaners who would not agree with a political theory that contradicted that democratic principle. Nevertheless, the Afrikaans churches are politically powerful, and authoritarianism is an insidious doctrine, particularly in a multi-racial society where it promises an easy solution to so many problems.

Afrikaner nationalism achieved political power in 1948 and for many years had the support of the Afrikaans churches through thick and thin. Apartheid, vague though it was in the beginning, seemed to be a Christian way of preserving the Afrikaner 'nation' without doing any harm to other 'nations'. But as the legislative fruits of Afrikaner nationalism and of apartheid began to be plucked, a few Afrikaner churchmen wondered

12 See Tawney, op. cit., p. 131.

whether something had not gone wrong somewhere. When the English-language churches were moved to protest against the toll of human suffering involved in such measures as the Group Areas Act, Nationalist politicians could pass those protests off as the manifestations of an anti-Afrikaans complex; Father Michael Scott and Father Trevor Huddleston could be written off as the modern equivalents of the nineteenth-century missionaries who 'blackened the name' of the Afrikaner. Officially, the Afrikaans churches remained silent rather than hamper an Afrikaner government; in many cases they gave active support. Nevertheless, two prominent church leaders spoke out clearly against what they believed to be bad theology and worse Christianity. Professor B. B. Keet of the Theological Seminary at Stellenbosch and Dr. Ben Marais of the Theological Seminary in Pretoria did not join in public protest; but they did what was at that time more important: they wrote to the official Afrikaans church organs and spoke at church conferences; to the members of their own churches they exposed the hollowness of the argument that apartheid is supported by the Bible.[13]

Criticism did not come only from inside South Africa, where it could be discounted as born of anti-Afrikaans sentiment. Race questions are not confined to South Africa, but they are sharply defined in that country, and this sharp definition attracted world-wide attention. Ministers of Afrikaans churches who attended international gatherings, such as the World Council of Churches, found themselves constantly on the defensive, put there by Christian colleagues who could not be accused of lack of sympathy. Moreover, churchmen from other countries visited South Africa and were greatly perturbed by what they found. Dr. Visser 't Hooft, then General Secretary of the World Council of Churches, visited South Africa in 1952. As a Hollander he had every tie of sympathy with the Afrikaans churches—language, religion, history—and in writing about his visit he expressed all this sympathy and begged churchmen not to judge the Afrikaans churches harshly. Yet even he was constrained to say that the danger in South Africa was not that the churches interfered in politics but that 'owing to the historical co-operation between church and nation, the church is far too much inclined to support uncritically the decisions and policies of the Afrikaner political bodies'.[14] Dr. 't Hooft was followed by others, notably by J. J. Buskes jr., a minister from Amsterdam, who visited South Africa in 1955 on behalf of the International Fellowship of Reconciliation. His report, while once more expressing sympathy for the Afrikaner churches in their predicament, is a scathing attack on the government's policy of apartheid.[15]

[13] See *Whither South Africa?*, by B. B. Keet, and *The Colour Crisis and the West*, by B. J. Marais. Both books were first published in Afrikaans and written for Afrikaners.

[14] Quoted from Gwendolen M. Carter, *The Politics of Inequality.*

[15] J. J. Buskes jr., *Zuid-Afrika's Apartheidsbeleid: Onaanvaarbaar.* (In translation: South Africa's Policy of Apartheid: Impracticable.)

Criticism of apartheid, and by implication of Afrikaans churches, came from within the fold. The churches had extended and intensified missionary work among non-whites and their missionaries were finding their efforts frustrated by much of government legislation. Sabra, too, an Afrikaans body that had at first enjoyed wholehearted support from the Afrikaans churches began to find itself openly at odds with the government. Moreover, it was not only criticism that was coming from abroad. From America and Europe were coming accounts of a more positive approach to church unity, particularly in questions of race, and a few South African churchmen began to wonder whether, after all, separation of races was the Christian solution.

By 1960 the stirrings within the two major Afrikaans churches had reached proportions that made it clear that, in matters of race relations, a Nationalist Party government could no longer rely on unqualified or unanimous support from the churches. In December 1959 an Ecumenical Conference in Johannesburg, attended by representatives of all Protestant churches, took resolutions that implicitly condemned much of apartheid legislation, and provided for further consultation between the churches. The shocking events of March 1960, culminating in Sharpeville, led to an invitation to the World Council of Churches for a consultative conference with South African churches to be held at Cottesloe in Johannesburg. At this conference leading churchmen of the World Council of Churches met the representatives of eight Protestant churches including three of the seven Dutch Reformed churches,[16] to discuss the Christian basis of race policy. After a week's consultation in closed session, this body of eighty Protestant churchmen and laymen, including twenty-four non-white members, issued findings that demolished the moral foundations of apartheid as practised in South Africa. One of the three Afrikaans churches disagreed wholly and publicly with the findings, and the other two added a rider that, while still believing that territorial separation of white and black was the only practical solution, a policy that denied to non-white people the right of collaboration in the government of the country of which they were citizens could not be justified.

Shortly before the conference eleven leading Afrikaans churchmen published a book[17] in which they denounced racial discrimination as unchristian. Taken in conjunction, the book and the findings of the conference constituted a serious threat to Nationalist solidarity which was immediately recognized as such by Dr. Verwoerd. In a New Year's message he warned the Nationalist Party that it was being divided by its enemies and added that statements by churchmen did not necessarily represent the opinion

---

[16] The N.G.K. has five autonomous branches, one in each province and one in South-West Africa. Together with the two other churches there are, thus, seven Dutch Reformed churches.

[17] *Vertraagde Aksie*, published in English as *Delayed Action*.

of the churches. This was true, for the statements were subsequently repudiated by the synods, and the churches withdrew from the World Council, while vigorous attacks were made on the authors of the book and the ministers who had taken part in the conference.

Nevertheless, the year 1960 may well be regarded as marking the close of a period of unquestioning co-operation between the Afrikaans churches and the Nationalist Party as then constituted. A small but influential number of churchmen found themselves no longer able to support race policies whose justice they could not reconcile with the teachings of Christ, and they realized that if they remained silent their consent would be taken for granted. In 1962 two professors of theology, members of the N.H.K. which subsidized their chairs at the University of Pretoria, attempted to persuade their synod to test the colour bar in the church's constitution in the light of scripture. The synod, by a large majority, voted against this proposal and resolved that members of the church would in future not be allowed to criticize the church (as the two professors had done) except in church meetings. Professor Geyser refused to obey this instruction and was later found guilty of heresy and deposed as a minister. This jeopardized his chair at the university but he was immediately appointed to a newly-crated Chair of Divinity to the Witwatersrand University. His colleague, Professor van Selms,[18] resigned his divinity chair but remained head of the department of semitic languages. Professor Geyser appealed to the civil courts against his deposition and the matter was settled out of court in his favour. The synod subsequently resolved that no member against whom diciplinary action had been taken might appeal to the civil courts.

In 1962 the Rev. C. F. Beyers Naude, former moderator of the N.G.K. in the Transvaal, and a group of kindred spirits founded a small monthly publication called *Pro Veritate*. It is bilingual and has an interdenominational and interracial board of directors, and it expresses the views of churchmen who, broadly speaking, agreed with the Cottesloe resolutions and with *Delayed Action*. In the following year these men established the Christian Institute with *Pro Veritate* as its mouthpiece.

The Afrikaner churchmen who had taken a lead in establishing the Christian Institute were concerned about the growing isolation of their own churches and their refusal to belong to the World Council or to co-operate with other churches in South Africa. They were greatly concerned, too, by the close relationship between the Afrikaans churches and Afrikaner nationalism, a relationship so close that the churches were ever ready to defend Nationalist Party policies against the world. To the majority of ministers of the three Afrikaans churches such concern, publicly expressed, was akin to treason against the Afrikaner *volk*, and it was but a short step to equate treason with heresy and both with communism and liberalism. Members of the Christian Institute, and particularly the leaders, were

[18] Professors Geyser and van Selms were two of the eleven authors of *Delayed Action*.

subjected to persecution. Rev. Beyers Naude was evicted from his pastor-
ate for editing *Pro Veritate* and—an alarming co-operation between church
and state—his office was raided by the security branch of the police.

In 1961 Professor Geyser and Dr. Naude had attended a World Council
of Churches Consultation at Mindola, in Zambia, and a N.H.K. organ, the
Hervormer, carried a series of articles by Professor Pont in which they were
accused of approving of violence to achieve political rights for Africans.
Against such accusations they vindicated themselves in an action for libel
against Professor Pont. The heresy hunt continued. In 1966 the General
Synod of the N.G.K., at its quadrenial meeting, decided by some 400 votes
to 1 that members of the Church should not belong to the Christian Council
thus forcing a crisis of conscience on all those who had joined or wished to
join that body.

In 1965 and 1966 anti-communism, that ever handy weapon against
unorthodox opinions, was vigorously used against dissidents in the Afrikaner churches. One of the leaders of a movement reminiscent of McCar-
thyism in the United States, was Rev. J. D. Vorster, brother of the then
Minister of Justice who later became Prime Minister. Rev. Vorster occupied
one of the highest positions in the General Synod of the N.G.K. and used
his considerable influence to organize symposiums and conferences on the
dangers of liberalism and communism. At one such symposium, held in
Pretoria in September 1966, one of the speakers was the then head of the
security branch of the police, Major General H. J. van den Bergh; another
was a Major Bundy, of the Anti-Communist Church League of America,
with close connections with the John Birch Society, who stigmatized the
World Council of Churches as a 'communist front'. At this meeting, and at
public meetings elsewhere, the tactics of smearing and guilt by association
were freely used and everything that might remotely be branded as un-
Afrikaner was attacked as endangering the state. The American Field
Service, Leadership Exchange with the United States, the World Council
of Churches, the Student Christian Association, and the Christian Institute
all, in the eyes of Antikom,[19] promoted the aims of communism. From
1967 more moderate councils prevailed, partly for reasons of policy and
partly because common sense began to assert itself over hysteria; but those
who mounted the attack against unorthodox views are still in their positions of power.

One last point must be mentioned in connexion with the relations
between the Afrikaans- and the English-language churches. Afrikaner
politicians have been accustomed to castigate the English-language churches
for preaching against apartheid while practising it in their own churches.
This has compelled the churches to take stock of their position, only to
find that this accusation is very largely true. The South African pattern
that has developed for all churches has been one of social separation. In

[19] The name of the organization founded to combat communism and liberalism.

so far as the African members of the different churches are concerned, this is often a matter of practical expediency dictated by language differences and geographical separation, but that is not an argument that applies to the Coloured population, particularly in the Cape Province where the question of separation in churches is most acute. Yet, in the Cape, many English-language churches practise separation in church attendance, though not in synodical meetings. The attacks on the English-language churches and the visible results of apartheid have induced them to take an increasingly strong stand against it. Dr. Joost de Blank, soon after he became Arch-bishop of Cape Town in 1957, made it abundantly clear that he would not allow separation in any churches under his control. In 1956 already, when a clause in the Native Laws Amendment Bill threatened freedom of worship by making it unlawful for Africans to attend white churches, Dr. de Blank's predecessor, Archbishop Clayton, a few hours before his death, signed a letter to the prime minister on behalf of the Anglican bishops saying that while they recognized the gravity of disobeying the law of the land, they felt bound to state that 'if the Bill were to become law in its present form we should ourselves be unable to obey it or to counsel our clergy and people to do so'. All the English-language churches took similar action, and the Afrikaans churches, though not associating themselves with the protests, sent a deputation to the government.

There is, therefore, increasing pressure on the Afrikaans churches from three sources: from within its own ranks, from the ranks of the Christian Church in South Africa, and from world Christendom. It is difficult to believe that the Afrikaans churches will forever cut themselves off from Christian fellowship in their own country and in the world; but only when they cease to be the handmaidens of Afrikaner nationalism, in or out of power, will they once more be able to enjoy that fellowship.

No description of the part played by religion in the history and politics of South Africa can omit the Jews. There are about 120,000 Jews in the Republic, and the Jewish contribution to the economic and cultural life of South Africa has been considerable. From the early days of settlement, when Jewish pedlars wandered about the country with pack-horse or donkey cart, Jewish traders have been foremost in commerce. When diamonds and gold were discovered, individual Jews helped to develop these industries, and subsequently to start secondary industries and to expand trade and commerce. But the contribution of Jews to South African life is not confined to economics. In the encouragement of the arts, in helping to establish universities, and in the spread of enlightenment, Jews have always been prominent. While clinging tenaciously to their religion and in that respect isolating themselves from the rest of the community, they have, nevertheless, thoroughly identified themselves with South African life. A great many are Zionists, but they manage to combine Zionism with a genuine patriotism for their own country and thus to demonstrate that the oft-maligned 'divided loyalty' may be no bad thing.

South Africa did not escape the evils of Hitlerian anti-Semitism. But until Hitler began to poison the mind of Western Europe, anti-Semitism was never either sustained or virulent. The writer recalls growing up in a typical Orange Free State village where the mysteries of the synagogue and the queer and apparently arbitrary Jewish holidays were a source of wonder to Gentile children; but they were no cause for enmity or for social distinctions. In later years, however, social discrimination against Jews became more common. Headmasters of popular schools are prone, while careful to deny any anti-Semitic feelings, to limit the number of Jewish entrants; and appointments to public posts are frequently decided by whether the applicant is a Jew or not. Discrimination against Jews is so common in many clubs that most Jews would not apply for membership and thus place themselves in the embarrassing position of being black-balled.

Social discrimination against Jews is far more common, and more humiliating, among English-speaking than among Afrikaans-speaking South Africans. The Afrikaner has never been a thorough-going anti-Semite. There have been periods when 'the Jew' has been used as a bogy in Nationalist political propaganda; but the Afrikaner has always respected the Jews and their religion and has, indeed, had a kind of fellow-feeling for them. Until comparatively recent years the Afrikaners were not prominent in commerce, while the Jews were. So were the English-speaking South Africans, and the result was that commercial rivalry with the Jews induced anti-Semitism among the former.

During the second and third decades of the twentieth century, when nationalism was developing fast, so-called 'Jewish' capital was a convenient scapegoat and bogy on to which to fasten responsibility for economic ills and with which to frighten the electorate. The Nationalist Party Press made great play with 'Hoggenheimer', the symbol of Jewish capitalism, who was depicted in political cartoons as an obese Semite smoking a cigar and wearing diamond rings and a top-hat. This mythical creature was presumed to be the financial power behind the Botha–Smuts Party; he represented the mine magnates who pulled the strings to which the political puppets danced. The propaganda paid good dividends and, when no longer required, was put into cold storage. It was revived in order to discredit the United South Africa Trust Fund which was started by Mr. Harry Oppenheimer, then an M.P., and a number of business men, with the expressed aim of furthering good relations between the two main European groups in South Africa. The trustees of the Fund were all supporters of the United Party, and the Nationalist Party Press revived 'Hoggenheimer' in cartoons to show that the United Party was still controlled by big business dominated by Jews.

It would be surprising if Jews were not opposed to the Nationalist Party. Just before, and during, the 1939–45 War that party gave many signs of underwriting Hitler's race theories: The Transvaal Nationalist Party excluded Jews from membership, a prohibition that was removed only in 1951 when the Afrikaner and Nationalist parties united. Moreover, many of the younger professional Jewish men and women were stirred to action by legislation passed after the Nationalist Party came to power in 1948— legislation that seemed to them to bear a strong resemblance to the racial laws in Hitler's Germany. The Jewish Board of Deputies, which regulates Jewish affairs in South Africa, issues statements from time to time to the effect that, as a Board, it is neutral in politics. Indeed, as a Board, it has not joined the controlling bodies of other religions in protesting against such laws as the Group Areas Act. The Nationalist Party Press has, however, always been lukewarm about accepting these statements of neutrality, because most Jews are in fact, openly or less publicly, supporters of parties opposed to the Nationalist Party. Moreover, it is normal for nationalism to regard those who are not for it as being against it.

Relations between Jews in South Africa and Nationalists have for some time been disturbed by the policies that Israel adopts towards Asian and African states, particularly at U.N. where she normally votes with those states in condemnation of South Africa's race laws. Letters and leading articles in the Afrikaans Press from time to time ask why South African Jews fail to bring pressure to bear on Israel in this matter, and it is suggested that this failure must be taken as lack of patriotism for their own country, South Africa. During the Israeli–Arab war in June 1967 Afrikaner sympathy was largely with Israel, partly because she was so brilliantly succesful and partly because Afrikaners have no very high regard for the Arabs.

10

THE REPUBLIC'S NEIGHBOURS

A GLANCE at the map will show four territories, along or near the borders of the Republic of South Africa and either partially or completely surrounded by it, whose history and future are intimately connected with its own. These territories are South-West Africa, Lesotho, Botswana, and Swaziland, and their combined area is one-and-a-quarter times that of the Republic and their total population is about one-ninth that of South Africa.

SOUTH-WEST AFRICA

Settlement in South-West Africa was begun in 1883 by Germans under a charter from the German Imperial Government. By treaties with African and Hottentot chiefs, the country became a German Protectorate, which at that time meant that other nations recognized Germany's right to exploit the country when she was in a position to do so. In 1892 the German Government took over the country and colonization began in earnest. Germans were settled on the land, harbours were built at Lüderitz and Swakopmund (near Walvis Bay), and railways and roads were constructed.

German history in South-West Africa followed a pattern that was common in nineteenth-century colonization of Africa: treaties with chiefs who did not understand what they were agreeing to, followed by rebellion and 'pacification'. German administration, neither worse nor better than that of other colonizing powers in this respect, caused constant discontent. In 1904 a major rebellion of African and Hottentot tribes broke out which took three years to crush and ended only with the near extermination of the Herero. In 1915 South-West Africa was conquered by South African forces in a brief campaign, and the Peace Conference of Versailles decided that the territory should be a C Mandate administered by the Union Government as an integral portion of its own territory. In 1925 a Legislative Assembly of twelve elected and six nominated members was set up. The franchise and membership of the Assembly were open to whites only, and the Assembly was given powers to make ordinances subject to the approval of the Union Government. A long list of subjects such as Native affairs, mines, justice, post and telegraphs, railways and harbours, defence, customs, currency,[1] and banking, was reserved to the Union Parliament.

[1] South West Africa has its own stamps; and commercial banks were formerly permitted to issue their own notes in South African currency. On 30 December 1961 this right was withdrawn in favour of the South African Reserve Bank.

With Hitler's rise to power, agitation for the return of former German colonies became vigorous both in Germany and in South-West Africa. So flagrant was pro-Nazi propaganda among the Germans living there that the Union Government appointed a commission of inquiry in 1936. The report of this commission revealed the existence of Nazi cells, Labour Front Groups, Hitler Youth Cadres, and Winter Help Centres, not only in South-West Africa, but in the Union, and the government, acting on the report, declared Nazi organizations illegal. When war broke out in 1939, many of the German inhabitants of South-West Africa were interned.

Between the two world wars South Africa was responsible to the League of Nations for her administration of South-West Africa, and she had to report annually to the Permanent Mandates Commission of the League. The Mandates Commission was severely critical of the way in which the government had exercised its mandate, and its reports contain constant references to 'complete stagnation' of social work, to the inadequacy of provision for health and education, to the general policy of discrimination on the grounds of colour, and to the 'apparent assumption by the white population that "Natives exist chiefly for the purpose of labour for the whites" '. From the annual reports of the Mandatory and from those of the proceedings of the Permanent Mandates Commission itself it is evident that the Union Government was far more concerned with the interests of the 30,000 white inhabitants than with those of the 300,000 non-white. The government maintained law and order, but despite continuous encouragement by the Mandates Commission it was reluctant to initiate any positive welfare or educational projects or to spend money on the development of the tribal Reserves. As late as 1938 the Chairman of the Mandates Commission said bluntly that in South-West Africa it appeared that taxpayers benefited from public expenditure in proportion to their contribution to revenue, contrary to the practice in most civilized communities. Previous chapters of this book will have made it clear that the South African Government was, in fact, applying to South-West Africa principles that obtained in the Union. Article 2 of the Mandate declared that the Mandatory 'shall promote to the utmost the material and moral well-being and social progress of the inhabitants of the territory subject to the mandate', and, judging by the reports of the Commission, the Union Government had failed to comply with this article.

By 1945 a large majority of whites in the Union and in South-West Africa was in favour of full incorporation of the territory. When, therefore, the question of Mandates was debated at the San Francisco Conference of the United Nations, the South African delegation told the Conference that South-West Africa had been administered for twenty-five years as an integral part of the Union, that there was no prospect of its ever becoming a separate state, and that the Mandate should be terminated and the territory incorporated as part of the Union. In November 1946 Smuts, then

Prime Minister, appeared before the Trusteeship Committee of the United Nations and asked for permission to incorporate South-West Africa. He maintained that the territory was already firmly integrated with the Union and that the uncertainty about incorporation was retarding its development, and he added that the wishes of the inhabitants had been consulted and were found to be overwhelmingly in favour of incorporation. During the long and bitter debate that followed this request, South Africa's Native policy was severely criticized and the deficiencies of her previous administration of South-West Africa were quoted as proof that she was unfit to have uncontrolled authority over the non-white inhabitants of the territory. South Africa's request was rejected and the General Assembly of the United Nations adopted a resolution inviting her to place the territory under the trusteeship system. This South Africa refused to do, though Smuts kept the door open for negotiation by continuing to send reports on the territory to the Trusteeship Committee.

In 1947 the General Assembly of the United Nations maintained its previous attitude and called upon the Union Government to propose a trusteeship agreement. The acrimonious debates at U.N., during which South Africa was bitterly attacked, did much to consolidate white opinion in the Union and in South-West Africa in favour of incorporation at all costs. The Nationalist Party blamed Smuts for having raised the question at U.N. and maintained that South Africa was no longer legally bound by the Mandate system since the League of Nations was defunct. The Nationalist Party under Malan came to power in 1948, and, in the next year, agreed to have the matter submitted to the International Court of Justice for an advisory opinion. This was given in 1950, to the effect that the obligations of the Mandatory Power under the League of Nations continued to be binding; that U.N. was entitled to exercise the supervisory functions formerly exercised by the League of Nations; and that the international status of South-West Africa could only be modified by the Union with the consent of U.N. Before the opinion was given Malan had decided to incorporate South-West Africa whatever international opinion might be, and in 1949 introduced a Bill to do this. The United Party did not oppose the Bill, except in a few details, because it knew that the white voters of South-West Africa were almost unanimously in favour of incorporation.

The South-West Africa Amendment Act, 1949, provided for the representation in the Union Parliament of the white inhabitants of the territory by six members in the House of Assembly and four senators, two chosen by an electoral college consisting of the six members of the South African House of Assembly and the eighteen members of the South-West Africa Legislative Assembly, and two nominated by the State President of the Republic; one of the nominated senators must be selected mainly on the ground of his acquaintance with the reasonable wants of the coloured races of South-West Africa. This representation was heavily weighted in favour of the territory, with its white population of only 69,000, and each elected member, therefore, represents a constituency about one-third the size of a South African constituency. The two major political parties in the Republic have branches in South-West Africa, and at the first election in 1950 the Nationalist Party gained all six seats, thus giving much-needed parliamentary support to Malan.

In local affairs an administrator and an elected Legislative Assembly of eighteen members govern South-West Africa in much the same way that administrators and provincial councils govern the four provinces of South Africa. Article 34 of the 1949 Act provided that any reference to a province in the Union shall be construed as including South-West Africa. To all intents and purposes, therefore, the territory became a fifth province of the Union, except for the important difference that, by agreement entered into before incorporation and embodied in the 1949 Act, South-West Africa was not subject to taxation by the Union Parliament. This provision, which has been dubbed representation without taxation, was introduced to allay the fears of the white inhabitants of the territory, which is economically weak and heavily in debt to South Africa.

South-West Africa is not of any great economic value to the Republic. It has never paid its way and is heavily indebted to the Republic, to whom it must look for further borrowing. The reasons, however, why South Africa was so determined to incorporate a territory that has been an economic drag rather than an asset are not far to seek. The first in point of time is the strategic one. After the 1914–18 War the South African Government of Botha and Smuts favoured outright annexation almost entirely on the grounds that South Africa could not afford to allow Germany to occupy a territory from which the Union might so easily be attacked, and whose harbours might prove a threat to the Cape route. The temper of the time, however, was opposed to outright annexation of ex-enemy colonies and the government had to be content with a mandate.

The second reason is that, once South Africa had begun to administer the territory, South African citizens settled in South-West Africa in sufficient numbers to warrant local self-government and to create ties of sentiment as well as of administration between what became, in effect, a mother-country and her colony. Both major political parties in South Africa came to regard the mandated territory as South African. The Nationalist Party was, for a time, slightly embarrassed by the situation because it had opposed the Treaty of Versailles as unjust and found it awkward to explain why Germany should have all her colonies back except South-West Africa. It resorted to the argument that the wishes of the inhabitants must be taken into account, and in 1938 Malan said that the Nationalist Party was not prepared to surrender the territory but wished to settle the matter in a friendly way with Germany.

Finally, there was considerable force in the arguments put before U.N. by Smuts and others that South-West Africa was firmly integrated with the Union, that it was improbable that the mandatory principle of developing the country to a state of independence could be carried out, and that, in the circumstances, it was reasonable to incorporate it.

None of these arguments for incorporation took account of the interests or the wishes of the non-white inhabitants, but it is improbable that they would be better off under a trusteeship agreement. Even a casual reading of the reports of the Permanent Mandates Commission up to 1938 shows that international supervision made little difference to the policy of the sovereign mandatory state. The obligation to submit an annual report to international scrutiny may have had a slight beneficial effect; but the economic backwardness of a territory and the pressure of its white inhabitants were far more potent policy-makers than distant international opinion unbacked by sanctions. Further evidence of this is to be found in the history of South-West Africa after its incorporation by the Union. Year after year there were attempts in the Trusteeship Council or in the General Assembly to bring South-West Africa within the cognizance of the United Nations, and these attempts were successfully countered by South Africa's contention that it was a matter of internal policy. In 1957 the General Assembly set up a Good Offices Committee to explore, with South Africa, the possibilities of giving South-West Africa an international status; and the Committee recommended the partition of the territory, the southern portion to be annexed by the Union and the northern portion (where most of the Africans live) to be administered by her under a trusteeship agreement. South Africa proposed, as an alternative, an agreement with France, Britain, and the United States of America; she was, in other words, not prepared to recognize the jurisdiction of the United Nations despite the advisory opinion of 1950. The Trusteeship Committee and the General Assembly turned down both these proposals and asked the Good Offices Committee to continue its efforts. Further attempts on the part of the Good Offices Committee all came to nothing in the face of South Africa's refusal to take part in any negotiations that seemed to cast doubt on her right to administer the territory as an integral part of the Union. Meanwhile, as more African states were admitted to U.N. and as international opinion against South Africa hardened, her position at U.N. deteriorated. In November 1960, Liberia and Ethiopia, both members of the former League of Nations, instituted an action against her in the International Court of Justice, asking the Court to adjudge and declare that South Africa was responsible to U.N. for the administration of South-West Africa and had violated her obligations in a number of ways.

The case dragged on until July 1966 when the Court, by the casting vote of the President, found that individual member-states of the former League of Nations—in this case, Liberia and Ethiopia— had no *locus standi* in the court except as parties in a dispute. They could not, therefore, institute action in regard to a mandate. This surprising decision begged the question and the General Assembly of U.N., where a majority had confidently expected that South Africa would be adjudged to be in the wrong, now found itself with the old problem once more in its midst: how to translate its majority decisions on South Africa into action. The South African government acknowledged that South-West Africa had a distinct status but denied that she was responsible to the United Nations for the administration of the territory. Moreover, the government had the support of a large majority of whites when it said it would resist, by force if necessary, any outside attempt to alter the situation. Even before the International Court had handed down its decision U.N. had tried other means of bringing South Africa to heel. The most effective of these was an embargo on arms in 1963; but even that, inconvenient as it was to South Africa, had little other effect. For the rest, the General Assembly took resolutions by overwhelming majorities which the government of the Republic did not ignore but had no intention of heeding.

The territory that has for so many years been a bone of contention between South Africa and the world has an area of 318,261 square miles, most of it desert or semi-desert. It had in 1966 an estimated total population of 610,000 people[2] of whom 96,000 are whites, 29,000 Coloured, and about 485,000 black, divided into ten groups that are distinct in regard to language and customs. The largest black group is the Ovambo who constitute almost half the black population. The gross domestic product of the territory is about R220 million, almost half of this being from mining, 17 per cent from agriculture, 3 per cent from fishing, and 33 per cent from all other sources. Diamonds account for two-thirds of mining production. Revenue and expenditure balance at about R40 millions. The greatest needs of the country are for water, power, and roads. The Odendaal Commission of 1962–63 made many recommendations for tackling these problems but, in 1968, it is too early to say to what extent and with what results these have been implemented.

The Odendaal Commission found that there were twelve 'different and divergent population groups'. For seven of these it recommended, along lines familiar in the Reserves of the Republic, the institution of legislative councils of chiefs and headmen and, to a maximum of 40 per cent of a council, elected members. Of the remaining five, the Rehoboth Baster already have a council dating back to German days; the Cape Coloured are to be settled near the three main urban centres and given local government; the Bushmen are nomadic and too primitive for self-government, and the Tswana are too few in number. The whites will retain their present political power but, if the recommendations of the report are carried out,

[2] Figures and facts in this section are taken from Muriel Horrell, *South-West Africa*, and the Odendaal Commission Report of 1964, R.P. No. 12/1964.

they may come under greater control from the government of the Republic. There is no suggestion that any non-whites will be given direct representation in the only bodies that have effective political power.

White men from Europe did not achieve control anywhere in Africa without, at some or other stage, provoking violence. The history of South-West Africa shows that the territory was no exception. In 1904 the Herero tribe rebelled against German rule because they believed they had been defrauded of land. In a four-years war the Germans suppressed the rebellion with ferocity and it is estimated that the Herero population was reduced from 80,000 to 15,000. Again, in 1922, a Hottentot tribe called the Bondelzwarts objected to a dog tax which, since they were hunters, bore hardly on them. The protests were badly mismanaged and the government decided to use force. After the Bondelzwarts had lost 115 men they were bombed from the air into submission. Since the territory was by then a South African mandate, the Bondelzwart 'rebellion' was noted by the Mandates Commission of the League of Nations though the Bondelzwarts gained nothing from the discussion.

After 1922 the history of South-West Africa was less disturbed until the fifties when, everywhere in Africa, there were nationalist stirrings. Strongly influenced by Africans in South Africa, organizations such as the Ovambo People's Organization, South-West Africa National Union, and the South-West Africa People's Organization arose, flourished, and then had their activities severely curtailed by legislation.

The early policy of African nationalists was to appeal to the United Nations. This still happens, but individuals and groups went over to violent methods when they found that the appeals had no effect. According to police reports, substantiated in court, some hundreds of young Africans were recruited and sent out of the country to learn how to conduct guerrilla warfare and it was hoped that they would apply their knowledge on their return. The South African government responded by increased police and military action and by the Terrorism Act of 1967 which provided that anyone found guilty of a rather widely defined act of terrorism could receive a sentence ranging from a minimum of five years to death. Moreover, a police officer of or above the rank of Lt.-Col. could detain persons indefinitely for interrogation. The first trial under the Act took place before the Supreme Court in Pretoria in 1967, and in 1968 those found guilty were sentenced, though the death penalty was not imposed. The defence, which was ably conducted by South African barristers, relied mainly on the point that the General Assembly of U.N. had, in 1966, terminated South Africa's mandate over South-West Africa and, therefore, that the Terrorism Act of a year later had no validity in the territory. In other words, the Supreme Court in Pretoria was incompetent to try the case. This same point was made at U.N. when it was demanded that the trial should be discontinued in Pretoria and moved to South-West Africa where the law in force in that territory should be applied. The Supreme Court dismissed this plea.

In May 1968 the Minister of Bantu Development and Administration introduced the Development of Self-government for Native Nations in South-West Africa Bill to implement the Odendaal Report. The Bill proposed to recognize 6 (not 7) separate 'nations' with their own homelands, destined for independence. In criticizing the Bill the Leader of the Opposition, Sir de Villiers Graaff, pointed out that 90 per cent of the 59,000 Damara were living outside Damaraland, the proposed homeland, and that the 24,000 Herero were scattered throughout the territory. 'Independence for such little groups', he said, 'could only be a mockery and a delusion'.[3]

The host of problems that arise in South Africa from the co-existence of a minority of white and a majority of non-white inhabitants exists in South-West Africa too, though not in such an acute form. There are poverty-stricken Reserves that cannot support themselves and whose chief export is their manpower, and urban areas where conditions of housing, health, and education are far behind those in the Republic, themselves admittedly inadequate. There are, too, the same dependence on untrained and inefficient African labour and the same policy of maintaining the position of the white population on the insecure foundation of colour-bar practice, and legislation that discriminates against non-whites. Finally, we find the same breakdown of tribalism in face of Western economy and the same tardiness on the part of whites and of non-whites to recognize this and to adjust themselves to these changing circumstances. South-West Africa has, in fact, become part of South Africa, and whatever virtues or vices there may be in the policies adopted in the Republic, these are likely to be found in her territorial acquisition.

LESOTHO, SWAZILAND, AND BOTSWANA

Lesotho, Swaziland, and Botswana were, until recently, known as the High Commission Territories of Basutoland, Swaziland, and Bechuanaland, and were administered by Her Majesty's High Commissioner in South Africa, whose post fell, not under the Colonial Office, but under the Commonwealth Relations Office. When South Africa became a republic and left the Commonwealth, Her Majesty's High Commissioner became Her Majesty's Ambassador, responsible to the Foreign Office, and in his capacity as High Commissioner for the territories, responsible to the Colonial Office. This latter change took effect on 1 December 1961.

This chapter is concerned with the relations between the Republic and her neighbouring states rather than with a detailed description of those states. A few general remarks must, therefore, suffice to illuminate the

[3] *Cape Times*, 10 May 1968

background to those relations and to explain why South Africa asked for, and Great Britain refused, the transfer of the High Commission territories.

Lesotho came under British control in 1868 when its chief, Moshesh, a man of great ability, fearing conquest by the Free State Republic, successfully applied to the British Government for protection which was accorded, albeit grudgingly because of the expense of administering yet another colony. In 1871 Britain persuaded the Cape Colony, on the eve of responsible government, to take over Basutoland but it was never a happy arrangement and when, in 1880, the Cape Government attempted to disarm the Basotho a so-called Gun War resulted. When that was over the major Basotho chiefs asked Britain to resume direct rule, and from 1884 till 1966 the country was under British rule. Basutoland was administered by a Resident Commissioner assisted by district commissioners and technical staff, and tribal institutions were recognized and played an active part in central and local government. By 1910 the Basutoland National Council, which had been in existence since 1903, was given statutory recognition. It consisted of the Paramount Chief and 99 members of whom 94 were appointed by the Paramount.

During the 1940's and 1950's various reforms were effected, both of the National Council and in local government, and in 1946 a National Treasury was instituted. These reforms were gradually leading up to self-government and independence, and the first constitution by which half the 80 members of the new National Council were elected, was granted in 1959. An executive council with equal official and unofficial membership was instituted. In 1961 the National Council took the next step in appointing a constitutional commission to make proposals for further constitutional advance, and this was in due course followed by a Basutoland Constitutional Conference in 1964 which led to an independence conference and to actual independence on 4 October 1966. Under the constitution the Paramount Chief, Moshoeshoe II, became King, and a parliament, consisting of a senate and an elected national assembly, was set up.

Though Lesotho has a climate suitable for agriculture and stock farming she is a poor country. For this there are several reasons. Four-fifths of the country consists of high mountains and steep hills that make soil conservation an expensive and difficult business. The soil is difficient in humus and minerals and has for generations been over-stocked and over-grazed. The land of Lesotho belongs by custom to the nation and is administered as a trust by the King and chiefs who allocate arable land to individual tribesmen, a practice open to corruption and petty discrimination. Grazing land is common and there are no fences in Lesotho. The constitution lays down that chiefs and headmen must exercise their function of allocating land in consultation with local advisory boards, and there is a final appeal to the King. Tentative efforts were being made in 1968 to reorganize the boards but the power of the chiefs was entrenched in the constitution and until that is changed bad farming methods that flow from it are likely to continue. Meanwhile, Lesotho's main export must remain her manpower.

In 1968 the population was just over one million of whom, it was estimated, 120,000 were in South Africa earning a living. There were close on 2,000 whites—chiefly officials, missionaries, and traders—and a negligible number of Asians and Coloured. Lesotho exports wool, mohair, cattle, beans, and wheat to an annual value of about R8 million and her import of consumer and capital goods usually exceeds that amount. Her national expenditure in 1966–7 was close on R10 million and her revenue only R4·3 million, the deficit being made up by grants from Britain. Lesotho has one great asset in the Orange River and by 1968 the governments of Lesotho and South Africa had reached substantial agreement on the building of the Oxbow Lake from which water and power can be supplied cheaply both to Lesotho and to the Republic. It will be some years before there are any results from the Oxbow Scheme but it promises to be one of the most practical and fruitful acts of co-operation between the two countries.

Swaziland is the smallest of the three territories and its control was for years a matter of dispute between Britain and the Transvaal Republic. In 1894 Britain recognized the Transvaal's right to protect Swaziland, and with the annexation of the Transvaal at the conclusion of the Boer War it was administered by the Governor of the Transvaal until, in 1906, it was transferred to the High Commissioner. In 1921 Sobhuza II was installed as King of the Swazi and at the same time an elected European Advisory Council was set up. In 1963 a new constitution came into force providing for a legislative council and a legislative assembly; and after further consultations Swaziland received self-government in 1967 and independence in 1968. There are two houses of parliament, an assembly and a senate. The assembly has 24 members elected by universal adult suffrage, and 6 members nominated by the King of Swaziland to represent special interests. The attorney-general is a member of the assembly but has no vote. The senate consists of 12 members, 6 elected by the assembly and 6 appointed by the King.

In 1968 there were about 390,000 Swazi, 8,000 white, and 4,000 Coloured inhabitants of Swaziland. Unlike Lesotho, nearly half the area is owned by whites and it is not a purely African state in which a small number of whites are living to serve the needs of the territory; they have established rights and property.

Swaziland is well watered and fertile but the eastern lowveld region is unhealthy because of the heat and malaria. The middle and highveld regions are good agricultural and stock-farming areas, but, like Lesotho and for similar reasons, Swaziland is not a wealthy country, though it is better off than Lesotho. In 1965 her exports amounted to R30 million—

sugar, forest products, iron ore, and asbestos; and she imported motor
vehicles, petrol, capital and consumer goods to the value of R26 million.
Her revenue and expenditure are in the neighbourhood of R7 million and
R9 million respectively, the deficit being made up by Britain. A railway
line of 137 miles, linking up with the Mozambique line and so gives access
to Lorenco Marques, was completed in 1964. Forestry, mining, manufacturing, and hydro-electric power all give promise of economic expansion. While numbers of adult Swazi find work in the Republic, the number
is not nearly as high as in the case of Lesotho.

The Bechuanaland Protectorate came under British control in 1896.
The eastern border of Botswana marches with the western borders of the
Transvaal, and a study of the map will show why the territory played such
an important part in Rhodes's plans. He called it the 'neck of the bottle',
the Suez Canal to the north, and it was vital to his schemes of expansion
northwards that it should be in British hands and not in those of Germany
or of the Transvaal. There had been continuous friction between the
Transvaal and the Bechauana tribes, and in 1885 Khama and two other
chiefs applied to Britain for protection, which, after some delay, was
granted. In 1895 southern Bechuanaland was annexed to the Cape Colony,
and, a year later, northern Bechuanaland came under direct Imperial
control as the Bechuanaland Protectorate. In exchange for British protection, the Bechuana chiefs had to surrender part of their tribal lands for
a railway to Rhodesia and for European settlement.

Botswana is about three times the size of Great Britain and had, in 1968,
a population of about 546,000 of whom 538,000 are African, 3,600 white,
3,400 Coloured; there are also some 25,000 nomadic Bushmen who
manage to exist in desert and semi-desert country in a never-ending
struggle against drought. The African people are the Botswana, related to
the Bosotho, and are divided into eight major tribes, unlike Lesotho and
Swaziland which each have a single nation or tribe. The largest of her
tribes is the Bamangwato which comprises 35 per cent of the total African
population and became prominent in the early fifties because of the dispute between Seretse Khama, his uncle Tshekedi Khama, and the British
government over Seretse's marriage to a white woman.

The administration of the Bechuanaland Protectorate was on the same
general lines as that in Lesotho and had the usual apparatus of indirect
rule—tribal authorities, councils, and treasuries. In 1920 separate African
and European advisory councils were instituted and in 1950 a Joint
Advisory Council was established. Ten years later the British government
accepted proposals from this body for a new constitution which provided
for a nominated advisory executive committee and a legislative council on
which nominated and elected whites, Africans, and one Asian sat. The
African council remained in being to advise the resident commissioner. In

1963-4 a number of constitutional discussions were held, as a result of which the British government accepted unanimous proposals for full responsible government based on adult suffrage. A pre-independence constitution came into force in 1965, and in the following year a conference in London agreed on full independence which became a fact on 30 September 1966. Under this constitution Botswana is a Republic with a parliamentary-type president, a national assembly, and a house of chiefs. The first President was Sir Seretse Khama, knighted on the occasion of independence, a man whom the British government had at one time forbidden to return to Bechuanaland.

Though much of Botswana is desert or semi-desert, the eastern portion, though subject like the rest of southern Africa to periodic droughts, is good ranching country with an average rainfall of 18 inches. Botswana is a poor country that depends on Oxfam, War on Want, the Red Cross, and other agencies to prevent many of its citizens from starving, and that needs the financial and technical aid that Britain and various international agencies supply. As in the case of Lesotho, revenue (in 1966) of about R5 million is not quite half of expenditure, and the balance is made up by British grants. Botswana exports cattle, other animal and agricultural products (including cotton) and minerals to the value of about R11 million, and imports general consumer goods, vehicles, maize and other foodstuffs and petroleum to the value of less than R9 million. The balance of trade is partially made up of remittances from migrant workers earning a living in South Africa.

There is, historically, much that the three former High Commission Territories have in common. In each case Britain and the two Boer republics contended for the control of well-defined African territories ruled by chiefs; and in each case Britain won. British rule followed much the same pattern in each territory as it did elsewhere in Africa; but it was necessarily modified by proximity to neighbouring states ruled by whites. When the Boer republics were themselves conquered by Britain, and when the four British colonies in South Africa decided to unite, it was generally accepted that the future of the three territories was incorporation in the Union of South Africa. Indeed, a schedule to the South Africa Act of 1909 provided in detail for such a transfer which might take place on addresses from both houses of the Union parliament to the Crown-in-Council. Such a request was never made, but the matter was from time to time publicly raised. Hertzog raised it in 1935 with J. H. Thomas, secretary of State for Colonies. At that time South Africa's race policy was hardening and British public opinion was sufficiently strong to enable M.P.s in the House of Commons to extract a promise that the government would not consent to transfer without consulting the wishes of the inhabitants. In 1938 the British government agreed to the establishment of a Standing Joint Advisory Conference of officials of the Union and of the territories.

There is no evidence that the Conference performed any notable function, least of all, as was freely suggested at the time, that of facilitating ultimate transfer.

The Second World War effectively put the question into cold storage, where it remained until the Nationalist Party came to power in 1948. Malan raised the question tentatively in 1949, and much more definitely at an official dinner in 1951 to Mr. Gordon Walker, Secretary of State for Commonwealth Relations. There were discussion between the United Kingdom and South Africa in 1952; and in 1956, at the Commonwealth Prime Ministers' Conference, Mr. Strydom and Mr. Louw reiterated South Africa's desire to have the territories transferred to her. By then, however, world criticism of apartheid had reached such a pitch that no British government would consider handing over three African territories to a country where that policy was so strongly entrenched. When South Africa became a republic and left the Commonwealth the possibility of transfer became even more remote.

It is not easy to establish with any degree of precision why South Africa wants the territories. They are not self-supporting, and require considerable investment of capital to make them so. What economic advantages she might expect to acquire by transfer are, in fact, already enjoyed by her in the shape of labour supply and markets, and Britain would hardly agree to terms which gave her additional advantages, such as making land in the territories available for white occupation. The territories are so closely bound to South Africa's economy that, from their point of view, there are good reasons for throwing in their lot with South Africa. But if the Africans are to be left in undisturbed possession of their tribal lands, there does not seem to be any immediate or long-term economic inducement for the Republic to take responsibility for what will be, in effect, three additional Native Reserves.

The close economic and administrative relation with, and dependence on, South Africa cannot be disputed. We have noted the constant flow of labour to the Republic. Most of the territories' import and export trade is either with the Republic or over her roads and railways and through her harbours. South Africa's banks and currency operate in the territories and their communication with the outside world depends largely—in the case of Lesotho, entirely—on South Africa. Most of the present (1968) officials, doctors, lawyers, and teachers in the three territories were trained in South African institutions and at her universities. This dependence of the three territories on the Republic has not decreased since independence.

Other reasons that have been advanced for South Africa's taking over the territories are extremely vague. It is said that 'geographical conditions' favour transfer, and there is talk of 'rounding off our territories'. In the speech referred to above, Malan spoke about the intolerable situation of having these territories 'in the heart of our country'. These topographical arguments come from a close study of the map and are part of the imperialism to which nationalism is always prone, but they are not in themselves a very convincing argument.

It is possible that the desire to change the map of southern Africa has an historical basis. Had Great Britain not taken Basutoland and Bechuanaland under her protection, it is highly probable that these two territories would have come, as Swaziland had done, under the control of the two Boer republics. The history of European settlement in Africa shows that, sooner or later, African tribal land was bound to pass into the control of the better-equipped whites, whether they were British, Afrikaans, German, or Portuguese, and it is a fair assumption that Moshesh and Khama would not have been able to maintain their independence. Great Britain, therefore, may be regarded as having prevented the Boers from acquiring the territories, and, just as the descendants of the Boers wanted to regain the republican independence which they lost in the Boer War, so they want to acquire what, but for Britain, would have been part of 'their' country. While most South Africans had vague desire to 'own' the High Commission territories, it is not without significance that the most ardent protagonist of transfer was the Nationalist Party, which regards itself as heir to the Boer republican tradition.

Another reason why the Nationalist Party took the lead in asking for the territories is that South African Native policy in general, and more particularly the Nationalist Party policy, is in strong contrast to British Native policy in the territories and in other colonial possessions. This contrast is seen in such matters as pass laws, industrial and political colour bars, and in the amount of attention given to education and social welfare. The rapid development of British colonial policy after 1948 soon made it evident that South Africa and Great Britain view Native policy from different angles. There is no room in the same country for both policies, and many South Africans regard British policy as a positive danger to white security in Africa. The natural conclusion is that the more areas there are under South African control, the more secure will the position of the white man be. The reactions of the Nationalist Press to the marriage of Seretse Khama to a European, and to constitutional developments on the West Coast, show how strong are the fears of those to whom the perpetual white control of Africa is a fundamental political tenet.

There is one further argument for transferring the territories that came into prominence after 1955. The Tomlinson Commission investigated the Native Reserves in the Union as a possible homeland for Africans and found that when all the land promised in 1936 had been added, the Reserves would constitute about 13 per cent of the area of the Union. If the High Commission territories were included in the term South Africa, however, and if they could be added to the existing Reserves, the percentage would amount to something like 45. Moreover, the addition of the territories would make it possible to reshuffle boundaries in such a way as to reduce the fragmentation of the existing Reserves. Some of the maps in the Tomlinson Report indicate clearly that the Commission did, in fact, rely on the transfer of the territories to enable South Africa to carry out the Bantustan policy. In speaking on the question in 1959, the Prime Minister, Dr. Verwoerd, tied up Bantustans and transfer more closely by saying that the Africans in the territories need not fear the transfer would involve a loss of their land because, he said, South Africa had just embarked on the Bantustan policy of giving the Bantu in her own areas increasing control.[4] This whole argument seemed to amount to saying two things at the same time: that South Africa could not establish Bantustans unless she had the territories; and, the inhabitants of the territories need not fear South Africa since she was following the enlightened policy of establishing Bantustans.

With the arrival of political independence a new phase in the relations between the Republic and her three neighbouring states set in. The South African government, no less than the governments of her neighbours, knows that political and economic independence are not synonymous. That Lesotho and Swaziland are kingdoms and Botswana is a republic does not make these states one whit less economically dependent on South Africa. Nor does it make the Republic less dependent on the labour that comes from her neighbours. White South Africans may have ceased to hanker after the High Commission Territories, but the farmers of the Orange Free State and the Transvaal, no less than the mining industry, know that unless they can continue to get labour they cannot continue to produce. Moreover, it is rapidly becoming clear that South Africa needs the water and power that could flow from the Orange River almost as much as she needs the labour that Lesotho supplies. Common sense and prudence, therefore, dictate a policy of friendly relations between Lesotho and South Africa. The same is true, not perhaps to the same extent, of relations with Swaziland and Botswana.

South Africa is by far the strongest economic and military state in southern Africa and could use her strength to secure her economic interests. To do so would however be to flout world opinion and to create greater internal opposition and risk of rebellion. She has, therefore, followed the policy of establishing sound diplomatic relations with her neighbours. She was officially present at their independence celebrations; she has entertained Cabinet ministers from Lesotho and Malawi with the same courtesy, and without any colour distinction, as she would accord any other foreign delegations; she has signed trade agreements with Malawi and Lesotho and has waived colour bar laws for an African representative from Malawi; and the Minister of Finance, Dr. N. Diedericks, told the *Handelsinstituut*[5] that economic contact with black Africa was essential

---

[4] *Hansard* (1959) Col. 5254.   [5] Afrikaans Chamber of Commerce.

for the country's economic, political, and military safety.[6] On a different occasion he issued an open invitation to all African states to enter into trade treaties with South Africa.

South Africa's relations with Lesotho, Swaziland, and Botswana, as well as with other African states, are important not only to the weaker states but to the stronger Republic whose own internal policies may have to be further modified in the interests of a wider peace.

[6] *Cape Argus*, 17 November 1967.

II

CONCLUSION

SOUTH AFRICA is a country of contrasts and contradictions. White and non-white, wealth and poverty, science and superstition, education and illiteracy, Christianity and heathendom live side by side in the same towns and villages and on the same farms. The country exports food while many of its people suffer from deficiency diseases. It lacks skilled workers, but limits immigration and legislates to prevent the majority of its population from acquiring skill. It is royalist and republican, and contains staunch supporters and bitter opponents of the Commonwealth which it left in 1961. It confines active citizenship to less than one-fifth of its population, and the programmes of its main political parties are compounded of fear of the remaining four-fifths and an assumption of perpetual superiority. In attempting to retain political control, the white inhabitants adopt policies that create the very forces that must, in the long run, overthrow their rule. South Africa is, in fact, a country of close on twenty million people who have not yet discovered a fundamental unity, a common South Africanism, a common purpose.

Perhaps the strangest contradiction, and the one that explains a good deal of what has happened in South Africa, is that this union of four former colonial possessions itself became a colonial power, with all the problems that face those European states that hold dominion over non-European people. This fact was obscured by the circumstance that colonial possessions are traditionally oversea possessions. Britain, France, Portugal, and Belgium became colonial powers with African possessions separated from the motherland by miles of ocean. South Africa is at once motherland and colony. No seas separate the governed from the governors, and the latter are unable to contemplate the former with that detachment which is such a valuable asset in administration. Until the dramatic events of the late 1950's the Belgian and the Briton, going about his daily occupations, was hardly aware of the millions of Africans who were subject to his government. The white South African is in daily contact with his colonial African subjects.

To the Briton and the Belgian of, say, 1950, an African colony was a romantically distant land from which raw materials came, in which his sons might serve until they retired to the homeland, and in which his country was, in the nineteenth century, involved in wars of conquest. When he thought about his country's colonies he reflected with pride on the work of civilization that followed on conquest. Both conquest and the work of civilizing took place at a comfortable distance from the homeland; it was something to read about in the papers, but it did not touch the daily life of more than an insignificant fraction of the inhabitants of the mother-land. South Africans who administer Africans and who bring Western civilization to Africa do not go home on periodic leave or retire to a distant country. The children of the conquerors live side by side with those of the conquered. Unlike South Africans, Belgians and Frenchmen did not regard African children as possible competitors with their own. African students from British colonies who study at a British university normally return to their homes when they have acquired professional qualifications; they do not remain to practise in Britain.

All African colonial powers had to evolve colonial policies. After 1930 African political self-consciousness developed with increasing speed, and colonial policy no longer connoted sound administration only. From the 1940's colonial policy meant primarily a system of government designed to train Africans for self-government so that, as soon as practicable, they would elect their own parliaments. Not only was this the whole trend of modern European thought on the subject of colonies, but from the Africans themselves the demand for a fully responsible government became increasingly clamant. This is true of Britain's, as it is of South Africa's, colonial subjects. But there is a great difference in the demand. Britain's colonial subjects demanded self-government, not a share in the govern-ment at Westminster. South Africa's colonial subjects demand a share in the government at Cape Town. To the European whose home is in South Africa there is a world of difference between granting responsible govern-ment to an African territory and granting Africans a share in electing the South African Parliament. In these respects South Africa's problems differ radically from those of most other colonial powers.

The position of the African inhabitants of the Republic differs from that of Africans in other territories. British and Portuguese colonial policies differed in many respects, but both had similar ultimate objectives—the association of Africans who have assimilated Western culture in the government of the territory. In Britain all political parties, backed by public opinion, were committed to such a policy, and well-informed, alert, and influential groups were ever watchful that this objective was not lost sight of or that African interests were not sacrificed to those of the few whites who chose to remain in the territories. African colonial subjects of Britain were aware of this; they knew that the laws and administration of Kenya or Basutoland were subject to the ultimate control of the British Parliament. Beyond the Governor and the local legislature there was always Whitehall and the House of Commons where questions could be asked of responsible ministers.

In South Africa there is nothing beyond Parliament, in which neither of the two major political parties has a policy remotely resembling those of other colonial powers in Africa. In theory the policy of apartheid would, indeed, involve ultimate self-government for Africans in their own areas. But in practice the social and economic structure of South Africa makes this impossible, at any rate for the majority of Africans. In law they are citizens of the Republic, but by law they are deprived of many of the rights normally associated with citizenship. And against such laws they have no appeal except to the politically impotent liberal opinion in the Republic.

This vital difference between the Republic and all other colonial powers in Africa, the fact that her colonial subjects live in the homeland and not 'overseas', has far-reaching effects on the political thinking of whites and Africans. Britain's problem was how to assist her colonial subjects to self-government in a way that would not leave the newly created state a prey to anarchy. She dared not go too fast, and was under pressure from the Africans themselves not to go too slow. She might claim that her policy was an honourable one framed in the interests of the Africans, and she could reasonably hope that the self-governing states would wish to remain associated with her. The chances of success for such a policy are considerable. But even more important for the present argument, the consequences of failure for Britain would be, at worst, that she would lose her colonies, and for the Africans, that they might have to pass through a shorter or longer period of misgovernment before reaching political stability.

In South Africa the problem of the rulers is not how to assist Africans to self-government, but how to train them to be full citizens of a country in which black and white live side by side; and the political problem for Africans is not to urge an already willing home government to speed up the process of self-government, but to persuade an unwilling class to surrender a share of its political power. To white and black in the Republic the consequences of failure to grapple with these problems would be greater than for other colonial territories. Europeans in South Africa would not merely forfeit a colony; they might lose a home. It is this fear of the consequences of failure that has driven most whites to adopt policies by which they hope to side-step the real problem and retain perpetual political control, and it is a realization of the vital issues involved that has made them so sensitive to criticism from countries whose problem is less crucial.

Sixteen years have passed since the first edition of this book was published. In Africa, political independence and political rights for colonial subjects have been granted on a scale and at a rate that would have been difficult to envisage in 1952. In the Republic of South Africa political control still rests with the white minority; but it has not escaped the pressures and tensions that have produced such remarkable changes elsewhere in Africa. To all outward appearances the white population has successfully used its political power to entrench its privileged position against the demands of the non-whites; and previous chapters have shown that this process has involved the curtailment of personal liberty and the concentration of power in the executive to an extent that has undermined the Rule of Law as understood in Western democratic society. It might serve some purpose, in this concluding chapter, to state the problems that face some twenty million human beings living in South Africa and to assess the forces that promote or hinder peaceful and happy solutions.

For the vast majority of the population the major personal problem is poverty—sheer, grinding poverty that condemns them to live below the bread-line and to forgo most of the necessities of life. Economically South Africa is a poor country, and the burden of poverty falls most heavily on those least able to bear it, the non-whites. Gold-mining is a waning asset. Great distances and the absence of navigable rivers, lack of skilled workers, and a low-wage policy for non-white labour continue to keep industrial output per unit of labour low. The soil is, on the whole, poor; the rainfall is variable and over large areas alternates between droughts and floods; the soil is eroding rapidly and efforts to restore it lag far behind; agricultural labour is traditionally low-paid and inefficiently used; the systems of taxation and of subsidizing exports encourage uneconomic agricultural practices; and as a result of all this, agricultural production is low and South Africa is unable to feed her population adequately.

Nevertheless, scientific knowledge and technology have made it possible to counteract many of the natural disadvantages from which South Africa suffers and to use more effectively her considerable mineral resources; but these matters can only be tackled with any prospect of success when they have been seen clearly as economic problems and are not obscured by racial ideologies. There are hopeful signs that commerce and industry have woken to these facts and are coming to realize that their own prosperity depends on enlarging the internal market by increasing both the productivity and the purchasing power of the non-white population. Industrial colour bars are coming to be regarded for what they are: a brake on economic prosperity. Pressure from organized non-white labour and threats of economic boycotts are combining with enlightened self-interest to undermine short-sighted policies that stem from racial fears and greed. Those policies are still dominant, and their supporters will cling to them as long as possible because they have paid such good party-political dividends; but few people seriously believe that policies which so clearly retard economic progress can be maintained.

Many thoughtful South Africans of all races, while agreeing that poverty is the most pressing personal problem in South Africa, believe that her economic problems will have neither a peaceful nor a happy solution until the political problem has been squarely faced. That problem is in many ways more intractable that the economic problem because it involves a little-understood emotionalism that stems from racial fears and from nationalism. The problem may be stated in the form of a question: can the inhabitants of South Africa arrange matters so that they may live together in harmony, that white and non-white may enjoy a common citizenship, that no one group need fear that it will have to forfeit its cultural identity? If the answer to this is, 'No', as it has been thus far by the majority of those in political control, there can be only one outcome in South Africa. It matters little whether South Africa is a constitutional monarchy or a republic, in or out of the Commonwealth, or whether Afrikaner nationalism or a broader white South Africanism dominates parliament; so long as this question is answered in the negative the final result will be the same: a resort to violence that will impoverish the country, and the ruthless suppression of the conquered, whether it be white or black.

Previous chapters of this book have indicated that South Africa seemed, before 1948 and, with quickened pace, after 1948 to be moving along the road that leads to this violent end. Nevertheless, here too, the picture is not wholly dark. By 1968 it was acknowledged by all whites of any consequence, in all parties, that political rights to non-whites cannot be denied. The very theory of apartheid is an acknowledgement by the Nationalist Party of this fundamental fact—hence the attempt to evade its consequences by the desperate and forlorn expedient of independent Bantustans; and the official Opposition has acknowledged the fact by its rather halting proposals for the representation of Africans in parliament. The Progressive Party, which broke away from the United Party, advocates a common franchise; and the small Liberal Party stood uncompromisingly for a common citizenship. Perhaps the most hopeful sign of all is the moderation that the most important non-white organizations have shown, often in the face of great provocation; bodies such as the African National Congress consistently rejected would-be-leaders who hoped to climb to eminence by preaching racial war and domination—a black nationalism that would grow by feeding on ever more extreme and violent measures. This moderation of African leadership argues a political maturity that will be a priceless asset to South Africa when affairs become more critical, as they assuredly will.[1]

At the beginning of this discussion, South Africa's political problem was stated in the form of a question. There is a growing awareness among

---

[1] The most striking example of this moderation was ex-chief A. J. Luthuli. He was deprived of his chieftainship by the government when he refused to relinquish his post as President of the African National Congress, some years before it was banned as an illegal organization. He himself was banned, which meant that he was confined to his small farm in Groatville, Natal, and was prohibited from attending meetings. In 1956 he was arrested on a charge of high treason (see p. 119) and subsequently found not guilty. He was once more arrested during the emergency of 1960. Despite the treatment that he received he consistently maintained a policy of non-violence and of co-operation between white and black. In 1961 Chief Luthuli was awarded the Nobel Peace Prize. He was killed in a railway accident in 1967.

thoughtful people of all races that if the answer to that question is to be, 'Yes', South Africa will have to undergo a major constitutional reform. There are those who maintain that Union came too soon after the Boer War and that it prematurely forced under one central government the Afrikaner republics, the strongly British Natal, and the Cape, where British and Afrikaner had already begun to co-operate. Certainly, the hopes in 1909 that Union would heal the wounds of the past have not been justified by the events.

There is, moreover, a more important reason for constitutional reform. The National Convention of 1908 that drafted South Africa's constitution consisted of whites only, and except for the Cape, its members represented the white population only. The constitution that emerged from the Convention did not have the consent of the great bulk of the population; and while such a state of affairs was normal in 1908, it is abnormal in the Africa of half a century later. That half-century has shown, too, that a close union with a highly flexible constitution is not the most suitable arrangement for a multiracial country. A federation, not necessarily based on the existing and outmoded provincial boundaries but with a rigid constitution and a bill of rights that cannot be tampered with by a chance majority in parliament, would seem to be a much more practical arrangement for South Africa. The best way to achieve this would be a new national convention, representative of all South Africans, and it is a hopeful sign that proposals for such a course are no longer regarded as entirely impracticable but are seriously considered by political parties and by non-party groups of all races.

It is desirable that the world outside South Africa, as well as people of all races in South Africa, should understand the true nature of her political problem. It is not that of preparing Africans for self-government, but of integrating them into the political life of the Republic while leaving social relations to the good sense of all concerned. Most South Africans have so far evaded the real issue, either by advocating a total territorial separation which is not practicable, or by dreaming of an equally impracticable perpetual trusteeship of whites over non-whites. Both policies are born of the false hope of being able to retain absolute political control, and neither has any real value except to catch votes. To the African, the Coloured, and the Asian alike, both policies are totally unacceptable on a long-term view. Since neither these nor the whites have any other homeland, there is only one alternative to an increasing antagonism—that is co-operation.

When the Europeans in South Africa can at last bring themselves to realize this, they will be on the way to solving their major problem. It is obvious, however, that co-operation must be on the basis of Western civilization. Indeed, in so far as the colonial subjects of South Africa are politically conscious, they are unanimous on this. But Western civilization is not acquired in a day, nor will the fears and the self-interested policy of whites disappear overnight. Many Africans have for a long time been fit for political citizenship in a Western democratic society; but many of those who think they are qualified will have to learn that admission to the family of Western Europe entails the assumption of responsibilities that are different from those under tribalism. Europeans in South Africa, when they really face this problem, will realize that Western civilization is not a matter of colour, and that it is not preserved by 'protecting' it by hot-house methods, but that it flourishes only when it expands and seeks to attract to its ranks on terms of equality all, of whatever colour, who are imbued with the spirit of liberty, of culture, and of humanity that is characteristic of the greatest traditions.

By 1961 race relations in South Africa had ceased to be amenable to solution along the lines of party-political dog-fights or of parrot cries of apartheid or trusteeship; and events in 1960 and 1961 showed emphatically that they were no longer amenable to solution by the application of sterner methods or the proclamation of states of emergency. That way lies nothing but devastation and misery for all. To consult with non-whites is not, as many in political control think, to renounce Western civilization; it is to strengthen enormously the only sure foundation on which it rests. South Africa is the largest outpost of Europe on the continent of Africa; and Africa and the world are anxiously, and with growing impatience, watching to see whether she will overcome the political difficulties that beset her or whether she is going to wait in fear, bogged down in past grievances and sorrows, until overwhelmed by disaster. Is she going to rid herself of the traditional approaches that betray her into asking the wrong questions and getting the wrong answers? Instead of asking, 'How can we improve standards of living?' she is asking, 'How can we protect white wages?'; instead of asking, 'How can we spread European civilization?', she is asking, 'How can we save white supremacy?' Until South Africa has seen her own problem clearly and has begun to ask the right question, her policies will be rejected by the world and by Africa; and, within her own borders, white authority will extend only as far as physical force can operate. When once South Africans, descended from Europe, from Africa, and from Asia, have learnt to co-operate politically, South Africa's moral authority in Africa will be immense and her citizens will make her the leader of the African community of states.

INDEX